COMPLETING BERKELEY'S PROJECT

Classical vs. Modern Philosophy

Theodore A. Young

UNIVERSITY
PRESS OF
AMERICA

Copyright © 1985 by

University Press of America,® Inc.
4720 Boston Way
Lanham, MD 20706

All rights reserved

Printed in the United States of America

Library of Congress Cataloging in Publication Data

Young, Theodore A., 1926-
    Completing Berkeley's project.

    Bibliography: p.
    Includes index.
    1. Berkeley, George, 1685-1753.   I. Title.
B1348.Y68   1985   192   85-17762
ISBN 0-8191-4945-4 (alk. paper)
ISBN 0-8191-4946-2 (pbk. : alk. paper)

All University Press of America books are produced on acid-free
paper which exceeds the minimum standards set   by the
National Historical Publications and Records Commission.

To Rick and Becca

Acknowledgements

If this book is readable it is in large measure because of the relentless criticism by Professor Bertram Davis of an earlier version. Criticisms of that same earlier version by Irving and Loretta Wasserman have been helpful.

My thanks go also to members of the Berkeley preceptorial at the Graduate Institute in Liberal Education, St. Johns College, Santa Fe, especially to Terry Dilley, who was like a second tutor, and to whom I am indebted for the one pun in the text, which both Terry and I found irresistible.

Thanks to the librarians at Grand Valley State College and Michigan State University.

Thanks to Grand Valley State College for their financing the word processing, and to Debbie Vander Wal for processing the words.

Thanks to the following publishers and authors for granting permission to quote:

Thomas Nelson & Sons, Ltd., The Works of George Berkeley, Bishop of Cloyne (A.A. Luce and T.E. Jessop, eds), Nine Volumes.

The Bobbs-Merrill Co., Inc., Descartes, Discourse on Method and Meditations (Lawrence J. Lafleur, trans. & ed.); and Shaftesbury, Characteristics (Stanley Grean, ed.).

Macmillan Publishing Co., Inc., Alfred North Whitehead, Science and the Modern World. Copyright, 1925.

Martinus Nijhoff, Gavin Ardley, Berkeley's Renovation of Philosophy. Copyright, 1968.

Colin M. Turbayne, The Myth of Metaphor.

Richard J. Connell, Matter and Becoming.

Thanks to Gerald Witherell for providing study space.

Thanks to the members of the A-1 car pool for the many stimulating conversations.

Finally, I thank the hundreds of thousands of solid families and solid citizens, including the Hillses, the Kuipers, the Hamms, the Halls, the Warrens, to name but a very few of my acquaintance, who because they are uncorrupted by modern modes of thought, their common sense prevailing against the onslaught of their modern philosophical teachers, make communities like mine, despite the considerable inroads of minute philosophy, delightful places in which to live; places which, if classical realism does not revive, will be looked back on ere long as enchanted isles.

Those great men, Pythagoras, Plato, and Aristotle, the most consummate in politics, who founded States, or instructed princes, or wrote most accurately on public government, were at the same time most acute at all abstracted and sublime speculations; the clearest light being ever necessary to guide the most important actions. And, whatever the world thinks, he who hath not much meditated upon God, the human mind, and the summum bonum, may possibly make a thriving earthworm, but will most indubitably make a sorry patriot and a sorry statesman.

Berkeley, *Siris*

TABLE OF CONTENTS

Preface

This book has three aims: first, to inform about George Berkeley; second, to contrast classical and modern philosophy; and third, to argue the crucial importance of metaphysics (and epistemology) to morals and politics.

George Berkeley's philosophy has influenced many, and continues to be written about by many. The interpretation herein is a novel one, not so much in what it says about Berkeley as a modern philosopher as in what it adds about Berkeley as a classical philosopher. In his theories of reality and knowledge Berkeley is modern, following the leads of Descartes, Locke, Newton, and others. If one reads Berkeley's works concerned with morals, politics, education, and religion sympathetically, one discerns the influence of a philosophical tradition I label classical.

The classical tradition began in the West with Socrates, Plato, and Aristotle; thrived in later periods through the works of such as St. Augustine and St. Thomas Aquinas; and is experiencing considerable revival today, although no one person has the recognized stature of these greats of the past.[1]

Another label that could be given to this tradition is classical realism. Its proponents believe that philosophy, being a love of wisdom and pursuit of wisdom, aims to refine and develop our common, ordinary understanding of reality, to the end of leading a good and happy life. Its difference from modern philosophy can be indicated by a citing of what its practitioners take to be four self-evident truths, one or more of which modern philosophers deny, or take to be unwarranted presuppositions, or questionable controlling convictions. The four truths are that reality is what it is independently of what any human being thinks or knows about it; that reality can be thought about and to some extent known by human beings; that human beings have the capacity to know things as they really are; and that reality is not radically different from what appears to human knowers in their ordinary experience.[2] How George Berkeley could be, or try to be, classical and modern simultaneously makes an interesting story.

With respect to the third aim, Berkeley was distressed by the growth in Europe in his time of atheism, irreligion, and immorality. Against it he argued for the classical moral philosophy of virtue. In and since Berkeley's time that philosophy has been on the wane, replaced by moral theories stressing duty, or utility, or in our time, emotion or will. But virtue is making a comeback. In recent years, a plethora of articles and books has appeared urging a return to the classical notion of morality understood primarily as development in

1

individuals of virtues such as prudence, courage, temperance, and justice.

In the most renowned such work so far to appear, After Virtue,[3] Alastair MacIntyre argues and hopes for a return of virtue, but without the help of either religion or metaphysics, especially what he regards as the unacceptable metaphysical biology of Aristotle. In an even more recent work, The Theory and Practice of Virtue,[4] Gilbert C. Meilaender argues for religion as playing a, perhaps the, crucial role in development of virtue; but says nothing explicitly about any role metaphysics might play. Berkeley, by contrast to MacIntyre, and with Meilaender, stresses the importance of religion to the theory and practice of virtue. But by contrast to both MacIntyre and Meilaender he sees a metaphysics, materialism, at the root of misguided morality; and hence wrote his major metaphysical works to refute materialism and put in its place a theory of reality supportive of right religion and morality. This book sides with Berkeley on the importance of metaphysics. Hence, interspersed in the text are crucial insights of classical philosophy, or classical realism, that Berkeley either missed or rejected in his attempts to controvert materialism and skepticism; and which open the way to restore the metaphysical support withdrawn from morality and politics in our modern era.

The book is intended for undergraduate students being introduced to philosophy, for students of the history of philosophy, and for the general educated reader.

Teachers especially interested in making clear to students the contrast between classical (or ancient) philosophy and modern philosophy, or between materialism and "idealism," or between skepticism and realism, might find the book helpful as either a guiding or supplemental text. For example, the fairly frequent references to Socrates and Plato, to Descartes and Locke, could be supplemented by readings in Plato, et. al. The student would be instructed in some fundamental elements of classical as opposed to modern philosophy; and at the same time might be intrigued by the attempt of one philosopher to live in both worlds simultaneously. The student of the history of philosophy will get a new slant on Berkeley, who is so often presented simply as the empiricist bridge from Locke to Hume. Certainly he was that, we can say in retrospect; but he was much more than that. Some students might conclude that he was a tragic figure in the history of Western thought.

The general reader, particularly the one concerned with the spiritual malaise of our time, might find the study provocative; for our time is not so different from Berkeley's. Many of the moral, political, religious, and educational problems we confront

2

were addressed in thoughtful ways by Berkeley. He may have something important to teach us, not as specialized academic philosophers, but as human beings concerned about the plight of our families, our political communities, indeed the human race.

The structure of the book is as follows. The introductory chapter provides a biographical sketch of Berkeley. Part I concentrates on Berkeley, the classical philosopher. It includes a brief account of free-thinking, Berkeley's thoughts on the relationship between religion and politics, and finally Berkeley's defense of classical philosophy against free-thinking. Part II turns to Berkeley's modern philosophy. It explains his opposition to scientific philosophy, his refutation of materialism and his alternative idealism, and finally his thoughts on the importance of language. Part III sketches relevant developments in philosophy from Berkeley to the present day, preparatory to review of some current interpretations of Berkeley's work. Finally an argument for a return to classical realism as of fundamental importance for a revival of an ethics of virtue is given.

Introduction

A Life Against the Current

George Berkeley lived during that period of European culture now known to us as the Enlightenment. Religious and political freedom and equality, which in our part of the world we now take so much for granted, was then being sought with special fervor, as a result of many causes, extending back for many centuries, and including at least the Renaissance, the Reformation, and the scientific revolution. Berkeley did not oppose any of those movements, or wish they had never happened. But to the extent that Enlightenment spokesmen fought against established authority, either religious or civil, in the name of freedom and equality, and argued an atheistic materialism, Berkeley opposed them. Throughout his Christian-oriented life he warned against the danger of making freedom and equality the ends of life, and against taking scientific philosophy to be the guide in life.

Benedict XIV, Pope of the Roman Catholic Church from 1740-1758, wrote to his fellow churchmen, "We cannot deny that today there are people who are notable for capacity and learning but they waste too much of their time in irrelevant matters or in unpardonable disputes among themselves, when it should be their sole aim to resist and destroy atheism and materialism."[1] In subsequent chapters we will see that Berkeley wasted no such time. In each of the periods of Berkeley's adult life, his writings showed concern both with the moral, political, religious, and educational crises of his time and with what he took to be the mistaken scientific philosophy of materialism that had produced them.

I   The Formative Years (1685-1707)

As A.A. Luce noted in his authoritative biography, "Berkeley was an Irishman of English descent."[2]   George was born in Kilkenny, Ireland, on March 12, 1685, to William and Elizabeth Berkeley; and while it is not clear that William had been born in Ireland, it is certain that both he and his father before him had settled in Ireland. Furthermore, there is evidence that George's mother was of Irish descent. More importantly, George was reared and educated in Ireland, wrote his most famous books in Ireland, and held two appointments in the Anglo-Catholic Church in Ireland, the second as Bishop of Cloyne for the last nineteen years of his life.

At age eleven Berkeley was entered at Kilkenny College, "the Eton of Ireland," among whose illustrious students, not many years earlier, had been Jonathan Swift. His ability and accomplishments were then already made evident by his being placed in the next to highest class. Here Berkeley remained for four years.

In March, 1700, at age fifteen Berkeley entered Trinity College, Dublin, with which he was to be associated, as student and later as fellow, until 1724. The undergraduate curriculum consisted of mathematics, languages, logic, and philosophy. Berkeley received the Bachelor of Arts degree in 1704; and by 1707, when he was awarded the Master of Arts degree and a fellowship, he had learned Latin and Greek, studied French and Hebrew, was conversant with great classical literature, and was schooled in the revolutionary thought of the seventeenth century that had culminated in Newtonian physics and a new scientific philosophy, represented in Berkeley's studies by John Locke. Given this mix of the classical and the modern, it is perhaps not to be wondered at that the precocious genius of George Berkeley would at once set to work to blend the two.

II   The Precocious Years (1707-1713)

It is easy to ignore one crucially important influence in Berkeley's formative years simply because it was ubiquitous: Berkeley was reared in the Anglo-Catholic Protestant faith; his formal education was in Anglo-Catholic schools. There is no evidence of any religious crisis in his youth. Instead, it is evident from his earliest writings that he was a devotee of the Christian religion, and opposed to all those in his time who attacked religion generally, and Christianity specifically.

It is not surprising, then, that in 1710 these words appeared on the title page of what is still regarded as Berkeley's principal philosophical work, A Treatise Concerning the Principles of Human Knowledge: "Wherein the chief causes of error and difficulty in the Sciences, with the grounds of Scepticism, Atheism, and Irreligion, are inquired into." Berkeley's aim--and it remained so throughout his life--was to provide a philosophical foundation for right religion and a sound body politic, in place of the theorizing, then gaining wide acceptance in the intellectual world, that led to atheism, irreligion, and immorality. The method he proposed for so doing--and again, it remained the same throughout his life--was not pulpit-pounding diatribe, or religiously authoritative denouncing, but instead clear-headed thoughtful discourse. In other words, he never opposed religion to science; he always opposed his idealistic philosophy to materialistic philosophy. Berkeley stated it succinctly with the words appearing on the title page of the second of his great metaphysical works, Three Dialogues between Hylas and Philonous, published in 1713: "The design of which is plainly to demonstrate the reality and perfection of human

6

knowledge, the incorporeal nature of the soul, and the immediate providence of a Deity: in opposition to Sceptics and Atheists. Also to open a method for rendering the sciences more easy, useful, and compendious."

During this same period Berkeley wrote and published work directly addressing, in a more popular manner, some of the moral issues of the time. In 1712 three talks he gave at Trinity College were published as Passive Obedience, an essay on the political virtue of loyalty to the supreme power in the state. A year later, after he had moved to London, and gained the respect and admiration of such luminaries as Swift, Pope, and Addison, he wrote twelve essays on a variety of timely moral topics, for Steele's Guardian, a widely read journal published only during that year.

The other major work of this remarkable period was the Essay Towards a New Theory of Vision. Its publication in 1709 not only served as an anticipation of the complete philosophy expressed a year later, but also revealed Berkeley's substantial grasp of the physical and mathematical principles underlying the new science that had come into being in the seventeenth century. Moreover, the essay disclosed for the first time to the reading public the perspicacity of this young Irish genius.

III   The Travel Years (1713-1721)

For most of this period Berkeley was on the European continent. The first tour, begun in late 1713, lasted less than a year. The second was from 1716 to 1720. On the first tour he served as chaplain to the touring party of a British lord; on the second, as tutor and companion to the young son of an Anglo-Catholic bishop. Most of his time was spent in Italy and Sicily, but there were also extensive trips through France.

Although the major writing of this period, diaries of his travels, has no particular relevance to this study, there were other writings showing Berkeley's widespread interests. Sometime early in this period he wrote most of what was to be Part II of the Principles of Knowledge; but he lost the manuscript in Italy and never rewrote it. While living in London in the interval between continental tours, and at the time of the Jacobite rebellion, aimed at restoring the Stuarts to the throne of England in place of the Hanovers, whose George I had begun reigning in 1714, Berkeley wrote and published anonymously Advice to the Tories Who Have Taken the Oaths, another treatise aimed at political stability.

Toward the end of his travels, in 1720, Berkeley submitted an essay in Latin, De Motu (Of Motion), to the Royal Academy of Sciences in Paris; in it he shows how, given his idealism, motion is to be understood. Having returned to England, Berkeley, shocked by an economic and political scandal that had upset political stability, was moved to write and publish, in 1721, An Essay Towards Preventing the Ruin of Great Britain, addressed to the general decline of morals in that kingdom.

IV The Bermuda Project (1722-1731)

The college and church politics that enabled Berkeley to travel so extensively while a Fellow at Trinity College and an ordained priest in the Anglican Church need not be explored. Suffice it to say that the practice was common in that time. Also customary was the "politicking" for a position, or preferment, in the Church of England. It was that task that now confronted Berkeley at the completion of his travels. After a disappointment or two he secured, in early 1723, the position of Dean of Derry, a diocese near Dublin. He now had a "living"; that is, a handsome income out of which he was able to hire lesser clergy to perform the church duties of the Deanery, leaving him free to employ his time and energy for whatever he saw fit.

What Berkeley saw fit to do he states in a letter to his friend, Lord Percival, two months prior to his appointment as Dean of Derry.

> It is now about ten months since I have determined with myself to spend the residue of my days in the Island of Bermuda, where I trust in Providence I may be the mean instrument of doing good to mankind. ... the reformation of manners among the English in our western plantations, and the propagation of the Gospel among the American savages, are two points of high moment. The natural way of doing this is by founding a college ... where the English youth of our plantations may be educated in such sort as to supply the churches with pastors of good morals and good learning, a thing (God knows!) much wanted. ... a number of young American savages may be also educated. ... well instructed in Christian religion, practical mathematics, and other liberal arts and sciences, and early endued with public spirited principles and inclinations, they may become the fittest missionaries for spreading religion, morality, and civil

life, among their countrymen, who can entertain no suspicion or jealousy of men of their own blood and language, as they might do of English missionaries, who can never be so well qualified for that work.[3]

Five and one-half years later Berkeley had secured a prospective faculty for the college, and had gained the support of wealthy backers, of the King, and of Parliament. The one loose end, which was to prove the undoing of the project, was that no time limit was given for disbursement of the necessary funds. Despite this, and as an earnest of his resolution, Berkeley with his bride, Anne, set sail for America in September, 1728, and arrived in January, 1729. When, in 1731, it became clear to Berkeley that Robert Walpole, the Prime Minister, was too cool to the project to release funds in the foreseeable future, Berkeley gave up. He and his family (he had fathered two children in America: Henry, and Lucia, who died an infant just days prior to their sailing) returned to England.

Berkeley never set foot on Bermuda. But this period of waiting, mainly at his home near Newport, Rhode Island, was put to good use, most memorably by the composition of Alciphron, advertised by him as an apology for the Christian religion against free-thinkers. Meanwhile, his attention to the subtleties and difficulties of his now famous theory of reality, which underlay his attacks on free-thinking, was compelled by the astute criticism of his best friend in America, Samuel Johnson, who then was an Anglican priest in Stratford, Connecticut, and was later to become the first president of what is now Columbia University. Some of their exchanges have been preserved in their correspondence.

V The Settled Years (1732-1753)

For over two years Berkeley remained in London, seeking and awaiting appointment to a vacancy in the episcopacy of the Church of England. In 1733 his son, George, was born.

In 1734 the appointment came, as Bishop of Cloyne, in southern Ireland. In this small, poverty-stricken district, Berkeley remained until 1752, except for one season when he attended the House of Lords in Dublin. Throughout this period, although his health was poor, he not only performed his episcopal duties, but also engaged in relief work for the district. He contributed to Irish industrial development, encouraged the fine arts, and promoted a pharmaceutical treatment for many of the common maladies seriously affecting the health of the Irish. His treatment was tar-water, about which Berkeley and many since have written much. Although Berkeley doubtless overrated the curative powers of this medicine, his prescription helped many and perhaps harmed none. It is also noteworthy that a preparation of tar is still in the British Pharmacopeia.

During this period the Berkeleys had four more children. John was born in 1735 and died in infancy. William was born in 1736 and died in 1751. Julia was born in 1738 and, with her brothers George and Henry, outlived her father. Sarah was born in 1739 or 1740 and died in infancy. His wife, Anne, stated that Berkeley was a most tender and amiable father as well as a most patient and industrious one.

Throughout his tenure at Cloyne, Berkeley's home was open to all manner of people, from the exalted to the lowly. His wife testified that humility, tenderness, patience, generosity, and charity to men's souls and bodies was the sole end of all his projects and the business of his life.

During this period there were published new editions of the Principles and Three Dialogues, The Theory of Vision ... Vindicated and Explained, and the Analyst, a work in mathematics containing criticism of Newton's work on calculus. Along with these metaphysical and scientific works there were The Querist, a work in political economy, and A Discourse Addressed to Magistrates and Men in Authority, in which Berkeley for one last time spoke to the symptoms and causes of religious and moral decadence in Great Britain.

Berkeley's last major work, Siris, escapes easy classification. Its chain of thought, linking tar water's palliative powers with spiritual forces pervading and guiding natural bodies, inanimate and animate alike, has led more to ridicule of tar-water as a nostrum than to an appreciation of Berkeley's idealism.

In 1752, on the occasion of his son George's beginning his university studies at Oxford, Berkeley, while retaining his bishopric at Cloyne, moved his family to Oxford. How long Berkeley intended to reside there is not clear, for on January 14, 1753, he died, while at tea in the comfort of his home. At the time of his death, he had been listening to and commenting on the passage from Paul's first letter to the Corinthians climaxed with "O death, where is thy sting? O grave, where is thy victory?"

PART I

Berkeley, the Classical Philosopher

Chapter 1

Free-thinking

On the title page of <u>Alciphron</u>, first published in 1732, Berkeley writes, "An Apology for the Christian Religion, against those who are called Free-thinkers." Because Berkeley took free-thinking to be destructive of religion, morals, education, and good government, what follows will sketch the origin and meaning of free-thinking, its aims, its doctrines, and finally its practical consequences.

I The Origin and Meaning of Free-thinking

"Freethought may be defined as a conscious reaction against some phase or phases of conventional or traditional doctrine in religion--on the one hand, a claim to think freely,...; on the other hand, the actual practice of such thinking."[1] The historian of free-thinking is inclined to say that the phenomenon is as old as man, and that "Modern Freethought, specially so-called, is only one of the developments of the slight primary capacity of man to doubt, to reason, to improve on past thinking, to assert his personality as against even sacrosanct and menacing authority."[2]

Modern free-thinking, to which we confine our attention, came into being in the Western world with the growth of the Reformation and the rise of modern science. If the Reformation, in the first instance, was only a vociferous objection to abuses within the established orthodox religion, it nonetheless in its spread fostered resistance against religious oppression. Thus, in English history, for example, the establishment of Anglo-Catholicism in England was followed, in the seventeenth century, by Puritanism, Quakerism, and later, by Methodism. The Toleration Act of 1689 (four years after Berkeley's birth) granted the right of religious worship to Protestant non-conformists (i.e., to all non-Anglicans, such as the Puritans and Quakers), and to Roman Catholics.

The rise of modern science gave a different sort of impetus to free-thinking. While the growth of the Reformation fostered resistance against one established orthodoxy, and hence promoted religious freedom, new theories in astronomy and physics were leading educated men to suspect that religion was not only oppressive, but also mistaken. If the earth is not the center of the universe, if the material world is a mechanism, then the Biblical account of things is at least subject to serious doubt. Among the intelligentsia who could not yet let science simply replace religion there was nonetheless a tendency to rethink religious doctrine so as to render it less mysterious, and more in the spirit of scientific thinking. Hence, some of the central doctrines of Christianity would come under attack: creation of the world from nothing; God becoming man in Jesus; the three-person nature of God; the Resurrection.

II   The Aims of Free-thinking

To the extent that an established religion requires all under its rule to be believers, and threatens non-believers with punishment, free-thinkers have as their aim liberty. To the extent that a religious orthodoxy requires all to believe what is doubtful, to subordinate reason to faith, free-thinkers have as their aim truth. In the England of Berkeley's day there was no religious inquisition, or even persecution. After the Revolution settlement of 1689, "The Church of England ceased to be a persecuting body, but remained throughout the coming era [through and beyond Berkeley's lifetime] a body with exclusive political and educational privileges...."[3] That is to say, only members of the Church of England could hold public office or attend the Universities of Oxford or Cambridge. In addition, Roman Catholics were not allowed to be members of Parliament. These practices continued into the nineteenth century. Hence, from the standpoint of free-thinkers, liberty from some sort of religious oppression was a continuing battle; some victories had been won before Berkeley's lifetime, more remained to be won before the warfare could end.

As for truth, so long as the major institutions of higher learning remained closed to all but members of the Anglican Communion, the pursuit of truth, in the eyes of the free-thinkers, was in those institutions at least greatly hampered. And indeed the fact is that during this period Oxford and Cambridge languished, and witnessed the rise of academies and schools established by non-Anglicans more in the spirit of what has come to be labelled the age of enlightenment.

What seems most characteristic of this enlightenment is the growing reliance of thinking and educated men on reason; that is to say, on reason as opposed to revelation or faith. The faith of the free-thinkers, if we may so paradoxically put it, is that reason, freed of religious dogmatic control, can and will discover on its own the truth about man and the universe.

III   The Doctrines of Free-thinking

Given the aims of liberty and truth, and the reliance on reason, it seems that free-thinking would be characterized by lack of doctrine, certainly by anti-dogmatism. By comparison to a venerable religious tradition, Christian or otherwise, which is rich in creed, in doctrine and dogma that the adherents are to learn, that is the case. Nevertheless, among the free-thinkers of

Berkeley's time there is a variety of doctrine that Berkeley found himself opposed to. Given the freedom to speculate about religious matters, some theologians, even within the Church of England, were fashioning new and different beliefs about God, man, and the world. These new theologies get to be labelled deisms, by contrast to the orthodox, traditional theism. What the deists all seem to have in common, besides a continuing belief in God, is the motive to bring religious belief into harmony with the new account of reality, based on the new science, that was gaining wider acceptance in the intellectual world. What sets them apart from theists is their belief, based on acceptance of the new account of reality, that God is not providential.

There is another doctrine that all modern free-thinkers seem to share, and it is one that goes along with the reliance on reason. That doctrine is equality. We will see subsequently that with respect to philosophy Berkeley was an aristocrat. He believed, with classical philosophers like Plato, that philosophy is the pursuit of wisdom, and that those who can and do pursue it fruitfully are few and far between. The free-thinkers, by contrast, believe that we are all equally equipped, by virtue of reason, to seek the truth. The more profound and serious of the free-thinkers in the eighteenth century, and beyond, looked to science as the model, and to scientific method as the proper use of reason. The more shallow and frivolous free-thinkers took equality to mean that any one of us is, as rational, free to interpret and criticize any doctrine, religious, scientific, or whatever, in accordance with his own lights, with reverence to no other authority whatever. Berkeley, we will see, faced head-on this challenge to religious and scientific authority.

IV   The Practical Consequences of Free-thinking

Free-thinking is in intent or in effect anti-religious. We noted in the preceding section that some of Berkeley's fellow churchmen exhibited free-thinking by developing heterodox theologies. Such heterodoxy is likely to be but a stage on the way to total abolition of religion. An unorthodox theology gives rise to a new religious sect, which establishes its own orthodoxy. If free-thinking continues within the new sect, then again another new theology is likely to emerge. The proliferation of sects in post-Reformation Christianity is precisely that phenomenon. The logical end of it seems to be that the serious free-thinker, in his love for truth, will turn away from these competing faiths to the discipline and method of science. The frivolous free-thinker, in his love of liberty, will establish himself as his own authority on any and every issue that is worth man's worrying and wondering about. In either case, authoritative and institutionalized religion is rejected.

15

Given this, the consequences in education become at once evident. The serious free-thinker will promote education in the sciences. The frivolous sort will conclude that nobody, no discipline can teach man about the nature of reality, although he might well still support job-training of some sort, whether in the "professions," such as medicine, law, or even in education, or in the less demanding fields of endeavor.

More difficult to judge is the practical effect that free-thinking has in the moral and political world. Let us consider the frivolous free-thinker. What must be paramount in his moral perspective is freedom. For him morality must be the freedom to say and do whatever he thinks best, especially as concerns himself. No external authority has the right to prescribe his behavior. The only restriction he might see to this freedom is that there are other free men, whose rights he must respect. If he does, the only moral problem for him is to do what he thinks best for himself while minimizing conflicts with others.

The serious free-thinker, by contrast, might well suppose that the arena of morality is as much subject to scientific and methodic discipline as the arena of chemistry. If so, his concern will be to work up a scientific system of morality that will apply to him and to all other humans, and in accord with which all rational men will come to see that they should live. However, the astute serious free-thinker cannot have helped noticing, in his devotion to science, that he is learning what in fact is; and that his scientific method is not at all equipped to tell us what ought to be. Given that, the serious free-thinker is then apt to join the frivolous free-thinker in concluding that so far as morality is concerned with what ought to be, there are no authorities because there is no scientific truth about the "ought" to be attained and agreed upon.

If we suppose, for the moment, that there is a science of morality, a knowledge of how men ought to behave so as to achieve well-being and happiness, it would follow that the state--the political regime--should be so constructed as to take advantage of that science. Thus, we would want as leaders in that state those who are most expert in the moral science, the ones most likely to promote the well-being and happiness of us all.

If we suppose, on the contrary, that the modern free-thinker is right, and that there is no science of what ought to be, then the political realm becomes problematic. Although anarchy may be the free-thinking ideal, still there seems no avoiding the practical conclusion that since we are all in this boat together, somebody must take the helm. That is to say, in any political organization, be it township, city, state, nation, some one(s) must make laws and some one(s) must enforce the laws.

Given the free-thinking ideals of freedom and equality, and the free-thinker's conclusion that there is no science of morality, who in the state should rule? The answer seems clear: the free and equal citizens should rule. In short, we should have democracy, rule by the people. If the political organization (let us call it "polis," for short) is small enough, like the early New England township, the legislating and the major decision-making can then be done by all the people, by vote, with the majority ruling. If the polis is too large for that, perhaps we can have representative democracy, different locales selecting their representatives to assemble together for that same purpose of legislating and major decision-making.

The trick (and the history of democracies attests to the difficulty of bringing if off) is to have such a political organization as will not only permit pursuit of selfish or party or factional interest, but turn that pursuit to the general welfare. That the founding fathers of the United States of America designed the Constitution with such a concern in mind is made evident in Madison's promotion of the Constitution in Federalist Paper No. 10. Incidentally, at least one historian of free-thinking ranks such early American luminaries as Benjamin Franklin, George Washington, Thomas Jefferson, James Monroe, Abraham Lincoln, as well as James Madison, among the leading free-thinkers of the eighteenth and nineteenth centuries.[4]

From the literary world we might take Mark Twain as one of free-thinking's best spokesmen. His devotion to freedom and equality is most evident in his revelation of the devastating effects slavery has upon both slave and slave holder. Pudd'nhead Wilson is perhaps his most poignant expression. That tale also reveals his devotion to scientific reason; its hero, Pudd'nhead Wilson, whom we learn early in the story to be a free-thinker, brings out the truth and achieves justice by way of developing the science of finger printing, while conventional and established morality and religion stand idly by.

There is no denying the attractiveness of such characters as Mark Twain and Pudd'nhead Wilson. Still, one may be forgiven for wondering what in their nature or their environment has made them such stalwart defenders of freedom, equality, truth, and justice. What are the sources of these values?

Chapter 2

Religion and Politics

If Berkeley was an enemy of free-thinking, and if free-thinking is opposed to religious oppression, and champions liberty, truth, equality, reason, and science, then it appears that Berkeley must be for religious oppression, and against liberty, truth, equality, reason, and science. Such a conclusion would rest on the supposition that religion and science are always and inevitably opposed to one another. While many, if not most eighteenth century free-thinkers supposed that, Berkeley did not.

The supposed warfare between religion and science rests on the assumption, so commonplace since the eighteenth century, that scientific investigation into reality will disclose no supernatural agency in natural phenomena. Given that assumption, belief in God and religion itself will ultimately yield to scientific or naturalistic explanation. In the meantime, any religion which claims revelation or inspiration from the divine must conflict with science. This was and remains the position of most free-thinkers.

Berkeley saw the naturalistic assumption for what it was: a bias insufficiently warranted by the science of his time, and not at all warranted by the common experience of mankind. At the same time he saw that the bias could not be countered with Bible-waving or pulpit-pounding. We will see in Part II his metaphysical rejoinder to materialism and skepticism. In his writing on morals and politics, Berkeley's response to free-thinking rests on classical philosophy.

Throughout his life Berkeley displayed a persistent and deep concern about moral and political questions. He was convinced that classical philosophy promotes moral and political stability, and that free-thinking undermines it. From a number of occasional pieces, directed to such questions as liberty, truth, equality, and loyalty, two main points emerge: the supposed warfare between religion and science is really between classical philosophy and minute philosophy (Berkeley's preferred term for free-thinking); religion is the principal source and support of moral and political stability.

I Liberty and Truth

"Freedom is either a blessing or a curse as men use it,"[1] Berkeley wrote in his forties. In his twenties he had already explicated that notion. In two essays in the Guardian,[2] entitled "Shortsightedness" and "Happiness," he had criticized the free-thinking ideals of liberty and truth. The point of his criticism is that liberty and truth may be instrumental to happiness, but do not in themselves constitute happiness.

His argument is that there are two sorts of goods; the one kind is desirable in itself, the other only as instrumental to obtain some other thing. The one is called end, the other means. The one is prompted by nature, the other is the result of choice and deliberation. For example, my desiring relief from a toothache is dictated by my animal nature; my visit to the dentist is deliberately chosen. I might, instead, choose to deaden the pain with aspirin or alcohol; or I might venture to pull the offending tooth myself. Only a fool, says Berkeley, would confuse the two kinds of goods.

This foolishness appears pre-eminently, Berkeley's analysis continues, in three human types: the critic (or pedant), the miser, and the free-thinker. The pedant masters Greek and Latin not for the sake of learning from Plato, et.al., but for the sake of criticizing. Where the pedant takes words for things, the miser takes money for things, and hence hoards it instead of using it.

His attack on the free-thinker rests on the classical notion that happiness, for oneself and one's fellow creatures, is prompted by human nature as the end of living. When happiness is construed to mean not evanescent, periodic or episodic joy, elation, or gladness, but instead a steady and persistent human well-being, then it is easier to grasp Berkeley's point that liberty and truth can be instrumental to happiness. Without the former we are limited in the good actions we can perform for others; lacking the latter we may not know what is appropriate in different circumstances to the end of happiness. But if liberty is taken as an end in itself we may, for example, defend adultery, by invoking liberty, against the unhappiness we bring to ourselves. If truth is taken as an end itself, we may defend our ridiculing of someone's blind faith, in the name of truth, without having anything better to put in its place. Moreover, Berkeley adds, the promotion of liberty as an end in itelf may encourage the rule in us of our appetites and inclinations, doing what we feel like doing, so that we become slaves to our passions, instead of free to achieve happiness under reason's guidance. Promoting truth as an end itself may encourage in us iconoclasm, so that we become skeptics if not cynics. Hence, while the pedant and miser are only ridiculous and contemptible, the free-thinker is also pernicious.

So much for the logic of the analysis and criticism. The foundation of the argument is classical. That is, Berkeley seems to agree with philosophers like Plato, Aristotle, and St. Thomas Aquinas, that there is a human nature, and that a man's happiness or well-being depends on the development or maturing of that nature. Man's happiness, on this view, depends in large part upon his developing the moral virtues of temperance, courage, justice, and the like. Liberty and truth may or may not be instrumental to that development.

It is evident that Berkeley is not preaching, not declaiming from the pulpit against the enemies of religion; he is philosophizing, countering one perspective, which he regards as shortsighted and pernicious, with another, which he regards as wise and useful.

These essays were written and published in 1713, when Berkeley was twenty-eight years old, the same year in which he published one of his two major works in philosophy, the Three Dialogues Between Hylas and Philonous. In the very early years of his career Berkeley already took philosophy and its task to be at least very close to what such ancients as Socrates, Plato, and Aristotle had taken it to be. Philosophy for them is not simply or only contemplation, meditation of or on eternal verities; but also has its practical side, aiming to bring insight and instruction on what happiness is and how to achieve it. In a 1709 letter to his friend, Percival, Berkeley wrote,

> Socrates spent his time in reasoning on the most noble and important subjects, the nature of the gods, the dignity and duration of the soul, and the duties of a rational creature. He was always exposing the vanity of the Sophists, painting vice and virtue in their proper colours, deliberating on the public good, enflaming the most noble and generous tempers with the love of great actions. In short, his whole employment was the turning men aside from vice, impertinence, and trifling speculations to the study of solid wisdom, temperance, justice, and piety, which is the true business of a philosopher.[3]

Berkeley was vividly aware of the practical consequences, for good or ill, of philosophy. As one of my teachers succinctly put it, there is nothing more real than ideals; for there is nothing else that a person ever lives by. Inevitably we all live in accordance with one philosophy or another, whether or not we can articulate it even to ourselves. According to Berkeley, the trouble with minute philosophy, by contrast with classical, is that it is shallow, inconsistent, incoherent. This is what happens in philosophy, Berkeley fears, when it is supposed that any one can philosophize as well as the next.

II Equality

In the very last paragraph of his last major composition, Siris, Berkeley writes, "Truth is the cry of all, but the game of a few."[4] There will be occasion subsequently to note the tendency in modern philosophy, in contrast to classical philosophy, to skepticism; i.e., to doubt that we can come to know things, or to know them as they really are. It has already been noted that free-thinking, whether frivolous or serious, tends to doubt that we can know what ought to be, i.e., that we can achieve moral knowledge. Throughout his life Berkeley was an enemy to skepticism, and hence resisted a prominent trend in modern thought. But like Plato and Aristotle, while Berkeley was sanguine about the intellect's power to know what really is and ought to be, he believed that genuine philosophers are rare. Truth is the game of a few, of the best, of the aristoi. When it comes to an intellectual, rational apprehension of what is and ought to be, not all men are equal.

Although philosophically Berkeley was an aristocrat, religiously he was an egalitarian. He believed that the New Testament revealed a covenant between God and men that promised a new life for all men, not for just an intellectual elite. Hence, as Berkeley saw it, the equality which free-thinkers supposed was grounded in reason was grounded instead in God's love for His creatures. However different we may be with respect to this or that capacity, bodily or mentally, before God we are all equally humbled and, through faith, hope, and love, equally uplifted.

The equality urged by free-thinking, Berkeley believed, undermines Christianity. According to the free-thinking notion, what makes us all equal is not a covenant between God and man, but reason. Nor did the free-thinkers of Berkeley's time hesitate to appeal to history to support this. That is, in surveying the history of men, we cannot help noticing the wide variety of religious beliefs and faiths, primitive or civilized, polytheistic or monotheistic, etc. But, it was argued, what all men in all times and places have in common is reason. As we have noted, to the serious free-thinker of the eighteenth century, the proper use of reason issues in scientific knowledge, about which there is growing agreement because it rests not on faith, but on rational evidence. Eighteenth century enlightenment, resting on faith in reason as against revelation, goes hand in hand with the rise of modern science. If there is any way to wisdom, scientific method must provide that way. We can all have a share in that, no matter what mysterious religious beliefs happen to prevail in our times and climes. While competing sects tend to set us against one another, agreed upon scientific knowledge tends to bring us together.

The flaw in all this, Berkeley believed, is that modern science is not philosophy, and the prevailing scientific method is not a way to wisdom. Even if science can tell us what is, it is not equipped to tell us what ought to be. The goal of philosophy, at least for its classical representatives, is not only knowing what reality is, but also, and following from that knowledge, living a good and happy life. But if science is dumb about what ought to be, than it seems that scientific reason can give us no guidance whatever about how we ought to live. Hence Berkeley concluded that scientific philosophy, deism, or minute philosophy lead to immorality as well as irreligion. For, while removing the religious motive to good behavior, the new philosophy has no substitute for it. As Dostoevsky succinctly put it in the nineteenth century, if God is dead, everything is permitted.

Still, one might object, if for Berkeley genuine philosophy is for the aristoi, then apparently that philosophy, no more than the new scientific philosophy, can guide most of us to moral living and happiness. With that point Berkeley is in full agreement. And with it comes the practical conclusion that religion, specifically Christianity, must be promulgated for the sake of the moral welfare of the many.

In review of this brief discussion of equality, let us note the dilemma. Berkeley believes that human reason can come to know not only what is but also what ought to be, and hence can provide guidance to happiness, to moral well-being. But only a very few men are blessed with the nature and nurture that are requisite for the task. The free-thinker, on the other hand, believes that truth is not the province of the few, but of all of us, that we are all equally rational. What this means in practical moral living, Berkeley believes, is that all we like sheep go astray and turn everyone to his own way. In neither case do we find moral authority and guidance for the many.

For Berkeley, the solution to the dilemma is religion. Moral and political stability depend upon strong religious institutions. Free-thinking, the enemy of religion, undermines both morals and civil society.

III Wicked on Principle

"...the freedom pleaded for is not so much freedom of thought against the doctrines of the Gospel as freedom of speech and action against the laws of the land,"[5] Berkeley wrote in 1738. Throughout his adult life Berkeley, although not unaware of the existence of religious bigotry, saw the opposite threat of libertinism as a much more live and present danger to the body politic. However true it might be that modern free-thinking in Great Britain began as opposition to religious oppression, by now

23

(1738), Berkeley is implying, it has led not only to freedom of thought in religious belief, but to freedom of speech and action in morals that bids well to destroy civil society.

His pessimism may be accounted for by his contention, in a number of writings, that "if men were wicked in former times, their wickedness was attended with remorse and shame. But now they are openly and courageously wicked, being so upon principle, and endeavoring to support themselves by argument, and by the general example of the age."[6] It is worth our paying close attention to Berkeley's explication of this notion.

> I know it is an old folly to make peevish complaints of the times, and charge the common failures of human nature on a particular age. One may nevertheless venture to affirm that the present hath brought forth new and portentous villainies, not to be paralleled in our own or other history. We have been long preparing for some great catastrophe. Vice and villainy have by degrees grown reputable among us; our infidels have passed for fine gentlemen, and our venal traitors for men of sense, who knew the world. We have made a jest of public spirit, and cancelled all respect for whatever our laws and religion repute sacred. The old English modesty is quite worn off, and instead of blushing for our crimes we are ashamed only of piety and virtue. In short, other nations have been wicked, but we are the first who have been wicked upon principle.[7]

Allowing that Berkeley was exaggerating for effect, we may nonetheless take this paragraph as Berkeley's portrait of a typical free-thinker of his, and perhaps of any, time. Indeed, it does seem to represent an understandable and perennial type, who laughs at public spirit, has lost respect for laws and religion, and has become worldly-wise, as we say. That is, he has experienced too much and too long the hypocrisy of his fellow men. The only remedy he can see for what he takes to be an almost universal ailment of mankind is to reject any and all notions of piety and virtue; and then to behave guiltlessly, shamelessly, in the name of liberty and honesty. The principle, in other words, that he is being wicked upon, is that acting on such principles as piety and justice leads only to hypocrisy.

Berkeley's contention is that to the extent this type becomes prominent in a polis, that polis is closer to destruction. He believes that irreligion encourages this type of man, and that proper religion promotes the opposite. He argues as follows: "Religion hath in former days been cherished and reverenced by wise patriots and lawgivers, as knowing it to be impossible that a nation should thrive and flourish without virtue, or that virtue should subsist without conscience, or conscience without religion;..."[8] What if the "wicked on principle" type comes to predominate in a society? "There is no magistrate," Berkeley writes, "so ignorant as not to know that power --physical power -- resides in the people: but authority is from opinion,..."[9] If the prevailing opinion is of the "wicked on principle" type, the obvious conclusion is dissolution of the state: anarchy. But Berkeley concludes the above statement as follows: "which authority is necessary to restrain and direct the people's power, and therefore religion is the great stay and support of a State.... Obedience to all civil power is rooted in the religious fear of God: it is propagated, preserved, and nourished by religion."[10]

Because such notions may sound strange to our ears, brought up as we are to believe not only that power resides in the people, but also that government (authority) is from the people, by the people, for the people, and that religion is to be tolerated, we need to examine Berkeley's position closely and carefully. Berkeley is not, so far as I can tell, opposed in principle to democracy, which, we noted, might be taken as a political consequence of free-thinking. It is true that he might be construed to be opposed, when he writes, "Too many in this age of free remarks and projects are delighted with republican schemes; and imagine they might remedy whatever was amiss, and render a people great and happy, merely by a new plan or form of government."[11] And perhaps he would be surprised by the formation of, before the eighteenth century was over, and the subsequent greatness and apparent happiness of a people for almost two hundred years in, a new political union of states on a republican scheme. But still, his opposition is not to republicanism as such, but is rather that "those men [who project new forms of government] do not seem to have touched either the true cause or cure of public evils."[12]

IV   The Polis is Natural and God-given

Berkeley does not care to argue the competing claims of monarchy vs. democracy, for example. His concern is deeper, with the roots of any government, whatever the form might be. Why are there organized political communities at all? What are the causes of men existing together in societies, with laws, civil authorities, civil powers?

During his twenties, while Berkeley was a tutor in Trinity

College, Dublin, he delivered three talks later published under the title Passive Obedience, on the Christian doctrine of not resisting the supreme power. The supreme power at the time in Great Britain was Queen Anne. Upon her death, which occurred two years later, in 1714, the crown was to go to the first of the Hanovers, George I, in accordance with the Act of Settlement, passed by Parliament in 1701, and aimed at establishing once for all Protestant rule in the British Isles. Given the disputes and wars since King Henry VIII about the monarchy, one might wonder who rightfully was the supreme power. In Berkeley's lifetime the last of the Stuarts, James II, was deposed (1688), but the Stuarts continued to claim the kingdom. Indeed, twice, in 1715 and 1745, Jacobite rebellions occurred and were put down. But again, that was not Berkeley's concern -- not with whether a Stuart, a Hanover, a Cromwell, should be the supreme power; but rather with the Christian position vis-a-vis that supreme power, supposing it is clear who or what it is.

To understand Berkeley's position, we will consider two theories about the nature and origin of societies that are at least as old as the writing of Plato in the fourth century, B.C. One theory is that people come to live together in a lawful civil society by way of a social contract. There are variants of this theory; the two prominent ones in Berkeley's time had been authored by two Englishmen: Thomas Hobbes (1588-1679) and John Locke (1632-1704). Both influenced the thinking of the founding fathers of the United States of America. All variations of the theory have in common the belief that civil society is entirely of human institution. In other words, on this theory, society is not natural to men, as it is apparently to bees; but rather is artificial, calculatingly and pragmatically entered into by men.

The opposed theory, and the one Berkeley held, contends that men are by nature social, or political, animals; and that only the variations in polities, or forms of government, are of deliberate human institution. In other words, on this classical theory, men naturally live together in a polis, a lawful community, although it is up to them to determine what the form of the polis will be. Man, like the bee, is a social animal; man, unlike the bee, decides the sort of political order he will have.

Berkeley's procedure, in Passive Obedience, is first to prove that there are absolute, universal moral laws, and then that "Thou shalt not resist the supreme power" is one of them. The proof rests upon there being a providential God. In the discourse Berkeley assumes that such a God exists; nonetheless, even though he is addressing a Christian audience, his appeal to support God's existence is not to faith or revelation, but to reason: "...it is a truth evident by the light of nature, that there is a sovereign omniscient Spirit, who alone can make us for ever happy, or for

26

ever miserable..."[13]   (For Berkeley, in all the fundamentals of morals and politics, right reason and true religion support one another.)

Given a providential God, we are bound by our rational nature, Berkeley argues, to discover those precepts which God has willed for the good of men. "Let any one who hath the use of reason take but an impartial survey of the general frame and circumstances of human nature, and it will appear plainly to him that the constant observation of truth, for instance, of justice, and chastity, hath a necessary connexion with their universal well-being; that, therefore, they are to be esteemed virtues or duties; and that 'Thou shalt not forswear thyself,' 'Thou shalt not commit adultery,' 'Thou shalt not steal,' are so many unalterable moral rules, which to violate in the least degree is vice or sin."[14]

Loyalty is one such virtue, and "'Thou shalt not resist the supreme power' a rule or law of nature, the least breach whereof hath the inherent stain of moral turpitude."[15]   But why? Because man is by nature a political animal. God has so made us that we cannot achieve happiness or well-being by each one of us being a law to himself, and living to himself; but instead can only achieve it by living together co-operatively, harmoniously, in a lawful community. And in any such community there is in fact a supreme ruling power. Hence, to resist that supreme power is to will what is unnatural and immoral for us, that each go his own willful way.

Berkeley is not being simpleminded. In the essay he displays vivid awareness of all the types of misrule that lead people to rebellion. He is subtle enough to distinguish passive from active obedience;[16] indeed, he defines loyalty as "the fulfilling of those laws [of the polis] , ... or, if that he inconsistent with reason or conscience, by a patient submission to whatever penalties the supreme power hath annexed to the neglect or transgression of them."[17] He is cognizant of all the objections that are commonly raised against his position, and responds to them. Finally, he emphasizes that his argument is not for or against specific rulers or types of rule, although along the way he shows antipathy to tyranny and suggests remedies for it.

For Berkeley, rebellion is inconsistent with right reason, moral duty, and Christian doctrine. Here is a solid foundation for the utility of religion, or at least of Christianity, for civil society. So committed is the right thinking, virtuous Christian to civil society, without which man can experience few, if any, of God's blessings, that rebellion against the supreme power is regarded as perverse. So far is the Christian from what appears to be the ideal of free-thinking, namely, anarchy.

With this as a base, none of what Berkeley wrote in addressing himself to particular moral-political problems is surprising.   Nor is there any wavering from his deepest convictions, from Advice to the Tories, penned in 1715, to Two Letters on the Occasion of the Jacobite Rebellion, addressed to his clergy (he was then Bishop of Cloyne, Ireland), and to the Roman Catholics in his diocese, in 1745, and A Word to the Wise, written for the Roman Catholic clergy of Ireland in 1749, four years before his death.

V   A "Supposed" Polis

So that we may the better understand and appreciate these writings of Berkeley, let us suppose that we live in a polis that is, like Berkeley's Great Britain, basically good; but in which there is growing disrespect for law; a disturbing rise in crime, among the rich and the poor; an increase in the practices of bribery and perjury among the people, as well as the "politicians," infecting even the highest rulers in the land, who not only practice it but exhibit no remorse or shame on being found out.   Let us also suppose that the pursuit of happiness seems to have come to mean pursuit of luxury, partying, conspicuous consumption of wealth, and lobbying for private interest; and that the public officials seem so little concerned with inculcating public spirit that not only do they not discourage private interest and luxury, but instead aid and abet it by rearranging holidays originally meant for the public celebration of great men and noble deeds, so that citizens can even more conspicuously consume wealth instead of honoring their dead heroes.   Finally, let us suppose that the public officials seem so little concerned with morals that they legalize and encourage gambling by way of state lotteries, while at the same time they make unlawful the teaching of religion in the public schools.

Supposing all this, might we not, to begin with, be inclined to observe that such a polis seems bent on being wicked on principle? What would we make of these disturbing symptoms? What would we recommend as the cure for the disease?   If these questions were put to Berkeley one could safely guess that he would at least entertain a strong suspicion that the cause is free-thinking, and that the cure is the learning and the practice of religion.   (More completely, as we will see later, he would identify the cause as materialism, and the cure as right philosophy buttressing religion.)

VI   How to Prevent Rebellion

In 1714 Queen Anne died. She was succeeded to the throne by the Hanoverian, George I, in accordance with the Act of Settlement of 1701. Although the Tories (the more conservative, the more right wing of the two British political parties) had supported that act, they were less than enthusiastic about King George I. (No wonder; the Whigs came into parliamentary power in 1714, and remained there for forty-seven years.) When, in 1715, there was suspicion of Tory support of an imminent Jacobite rebellion, Berkeley published the pamphlet, Advice to the Tories who have taken the Oaths. The first oath was of allegiance to King George; the second of abjuration of any pretence of James III, whose grandfather James II had been deposed in 1688, to the throne. It is noteworthy that the Whigs, more than the Tories, represented the spirit of free-thinking.

The gist of the pamphlet is that no matter how cloudy some political circumstances and issues might be (in this instance, how to determine the royal succession), there are religious and moral principles which are perfectly clear to any Christian and right thinking person: honesty, loyalty, truth. Denying the oaths would clearly violate those principles, and give the enemies of Christianity ammunition for their attacks on the Church.

It cannot be known what effect, if any, Berkeley's advice had on the Tories; but in fact the Jacobite rebellion that occurred later in the year of 1715 collapsed at least in part because of lack of support from the Tories.

VII   How to Prevent National Ruin

An Essay towards preventing the Ruin of Great Britain was written in 1721 on the occasion of a stock scandal, known as the South Sea Bubble. The South Sea Company had been established in 1711 to assist the government to pay the public debts left over from recent wars. By 1721, because of corruption in government officers as well as in directors of the South Sea Co., wild speculation in stocks produced new wealth for a few and ruined fortunes for many. Berkeley was moved by this national scandal to write on the moral and political decay of the nation: its symptoms, its causes, its remedies.

First of all, and with reference by Berkeley to the burst bubble of speculation, he notes the official support and encouragement of gambling ("gaming" is what Berkeley calls it).

> But surely there is no man of sense and
> honesty but must see and own, whether he
> understands the game or not, that it is an
> evident folly for any people, instead of
> prosecuting the old honest methods of industry
> and frugality, to sit down to a public gaming
> table and play off their money one to

29

another....

The more methods there are in a State for
acquiring riches without industry or merit, the
less there will be of either in that State:
this is as evident as the ruin that attends
it.[18]

Luxury. "Frugality of manners is the nourishment and
strength of bodies politic. It is that by which they grow and
subsist, until they are corrupted by luxury, the natural cause of
their decay and ruin....Men are apt to measure national prosperity
by riches. It would be righter to measure it by the use that is
made of them."[19] "This vice draweth after it a train of evils
which cruelly infest the public; faction, ambition, envy,
avarice,..."[20]

The masquerade. "This alone is sufficient to inflame and
satisfy the several appetites for gaming, dressing, intriguing,
luxurious eating and drinking. It is a most skilful abridgment,
the very quintessence, the abstract of all those senseless
vanities that have ever been the ruin of fools and detestation of
wise men. And all this, under the notion of an elegant
entertainment, hath been admitted among us; though it be in truth
a contagion of the worst kind."[21]

Bribery. "This corruption is become a national crime, having
infected the lowest as well as the highest among us, and is so
general and notorious that, as it cannot be matched in former
ages, so it is to be hoped it will not be imitated by
posterity."[22]

Perjury. "...there being no nation under the sun where
solemn perjury is so common, or where there are such temptations
to it. The making men swear so often in their own cases, and
where they have an interest to conceal the truth, hath gradually
wore off that awful respect which was once thought due to an
appeal to Almighty God; insomuch that men now-a-days break their
fast and a custom-house oath with the same peace of mind."[23]

Irreligion. "But in these wiser times, a cold indifference
for the national religion, and indeed for all matters of faith and
divine worship, is thought good sense. It is even become
fashionable to decry religion; and that little talent of ridicule
is applied to such wrong purposes that a good Christian can hardly
keep himself in countenance."[24]

At the end comes the passage concluding with, "In short,
other nations have been wicked, but we are the first who have been
wicked upon principle."

For each of the maladies Berkeley proposes remedies, sometimes quite specific. To replace gaming, he makes a number of concrete proposals to further the industry and resourcefulness of the British people. To combat excessive luxury he proposes sumptuary laws, appealing to history for evidence of the salutary effect such legislation might have. He is not so staid as to suppose that people should eschew all relaxation and entertainment. For this, though, he recommends such as will foster public spirit, and cites the success that ancient Athenians had to this end with their public sports and high-minded tragic drama, not forgetting that something like was accomplished by drama in England "above a century ago." He goes on to note to what noble ends architecture, sculpture, painting, history writing have been put by states in the past and could be again.

But the root cause of all the dis-ease, distemper, degeneracy in the body politic, Berkeley makes clear at the outset of the essay, is free-thinking; and the remedy religion, without which, as we quoted earlier, there is no conscience, no virtue, and no flourishing of the nation. It is worth quoting at some length to convey the radical nature of Berkeley's assessment of the corruption and its cure.

> Liberty is the greatest human blessing that a virtuous man can possess, and is very consistent with the duties of a good subject and a good Christian. But the present age aboundeth with injudicious patrons of liberty, who, not distinguishing between that and licentiousness, take the surest method to discredit what they would seem to propagate; for, in effect, can there be a greater affront offered to that just freedom of thought and action which is the prerogative of a rational creature, or can anything recommend it less to honest minds, than under colour thereof to obtrude scurrility and profaneness on the world? But it hath been always observed of weak men that they know not how to avoid one extreme without running into another.
>
> Too many of this sort pass upon vulgar readers for great authors, and men of profound thought; not on account of any superiority either in sense or style, both which they possess in a very moderate degree, nor of any discoveries they have made in arts or sciences, which they seem to be little acquainted with; but purely because they flatter the passions of corrupt men, who are pleased to have the

31

clamours of conscience silenced, and those great points of the Christian religion made suspected which withheld them from many vices of pleasure and interest, or made them uneasy in the commission of them.

In order to promote that laudable design of effacing all sense of religion from among us, they form themselves into assemblies, and proceed with united counsels and endeavours; with what success, and with what merit towards the public, the effect too plainly shews. I will not say these gentlemen have formed a direct design to ruin their country, or that they have the sense to see half the ill consequences which must necessarily flow from the spreading of their opinions; but the nation feels them, and it is high time the legislature put a stop to them.

I am not for placing an invidious power in the hands of the clergy, or complying with the narrowness of any mistaken zealots who should incline to persecute Dissenters. But, whatever conduct common sense, as well as Christian charity, obligeth us to use towards those who differ from us in some points of religion, yet the public safety requireth that the avowed contemners of all religion should be severely chastised; and perhaps it may be no easy matter to assign a good reason why blasphemy against God should not be inquired into, and punished with the same rigour as treason against the king.

For though we may attempt to patch up our affairs, yet it will be to no purpose; the finger of God will unravel all our vain projects, and make them snares to draw us into greater calamities, if we do not reform that scandalous libertinism which (whatever some shallow men may think) is our worst symptom, and the surest prognostic of our ruin.[25]

VIII   Advice to Public Officials

In the last of these occasional pieces to be considered, Berkeley is more expansive on the role of religion as essential to a healthy body politic. A Discourse Addressed to Magistrates and Men in Authority was written in 1738, in Ireland, and was occasioned by the disturbing influence of an impious society called The Blasters, evidently devoted to worshipping the devil.

The opening paragraph, given here in full, indicates that little had changed in the seventeen years since the publication of The Ruin of Great Britain, at least in Berkeley's assessment of the state of affairs in England and Ireland.

> The pretensions and discourse of men throughout these kingdoms would, at first view, lead one to think the inhabitants were all politicians; and yet, perhaps, political wisdom hath in no age or country been more talked of and less understood. Licence is taken for the end of government, and popular humour for its origin. No reverence for the laws, no attachment to the constitution, little attention to matters of consequence, and great altercation upon trifles, such idle projects about religion and government as if the public had both to choose, a general contempt of all authority, divine and human, an indifference about the prevailing opinions, whether they tend to produce order or disorder, to promote the empire of God or the devil -- these are the symptoms that strongly mark the present age; and this could never have been the case if a neglect of religion had not made way for it.[26]

The essay is an appeal to public officials to support religious institutions. Police force is not enough to restrain men; and even if it were, it is not the best or most human way of bridling the impetuous desires we all have. Far better is the way of education, aimed at instilling in all citizens the notions of order, virtue, duty, Providence. Religious institutions are the conveyers of these proper principles leading to right polity.

One of the most common stratagems of free-thinkers is to attack the religious or moral beliefs held by someone as being prejudices, mere opinions in which the someone has been catechised or indoctrinated. Berkeley counters this by in a sense granting the point. Young minds, he says, will not remain empty; if right opinions (call them prejudices, if you will) are not put into their minds, they will receive bad prejudices. It is a point perhaps obvious to men of good common sense; and is expressed poignantly albeit negatively by the lyricist, Oscar Hammerstein, in South Pacific, when an adult observing race relations notes that "you have to be taught to hate, before you're six, or seven, or eight." Earlier we noted that philosophically Berkeley is an aristocrat, although religiously he is egalitarian. To the extent that we sympathize and agree with Berkeley's answer to this stratagem of the free-thinker, we perhaps agree with him that while there are few, if any, wise enough to know, not merely believe, what is best and right for individuals and the community; still common sense is sufficient to recognize that whatever institutions instill attitudes and opinions that lead to behavior supportive of a good polis are to be encouraged.

In other words, Berkeley does not argue that Christianity is obviously true, or that this is the one true way for men to live; and that therefore the state should, without further question, support the Church. Instead, his argument here is common sensically practical: if we are agreed that the general good of its citizens is the raison d'etre for the polis, then the religious institutions that teach and inculcate virtue, order, a sense of duty, a sense of Providence, ought to be supported and encouraged, as ensuring the prosperity of the polis and thus the general good of mankind. Religion is the great stay of civil society. So concludes Berkeley; and so have concluded many wise men in the past, heathen and Christian alike.[27]

Berkeley ends this part of his essay by apologizing for proving by arguments and appeal to authority of wise men what perhaps ought to be obvious to magistrates: namely, the necessity of religion for the state.[28] But "the spirit of the times hath rendered this unavoidable."[28] Berkeley goes on to infer a causal connection between the spirit of the times (cause) and increased disorder, vice, crime (effect). He notes the high rate of highway robbery, murder and other violent crimes, of burglary, arson, sacrilege, public fraud, and of organized crime -- the effect. He reminds his readers of the spirit of the times by reviewing some major points made in two prominent eighteenth century writers: whether there is a future state (heaven or hell) should not be of concern to moral men; morals are no more certain than fashions in dress; what counts is the outward appearance of virtue. Then he concludes, "And yet the people among whom such books are published wonder how it comes to pass that the civil magistrate daily loseth his authority, that the laws are trampled upon, and the subject in constant fear of being robbed, or murdered, or having his house burnt over his head."[29]

Berkeley concludes the essay by wrestling with the thorny problem in free states of the limit(s) of free speech. Seventeen years earlier Berkeley had written, "Liberty is the greatest human blessing that a virtuous man can possess, and is very consistent with the duties of a good subject and a good Christian."[30] That states neatly and succinctly Berkeley's position, early and late, that liberty is indeed instrumental to well-being in the individual and the state, but that it can be and is abused. Free-thinking, in opposing and undermining religious and moral principles, abuses liberty, and in so doing tends to destroy the well-being of the individual and the state. But, says Berkeley, "I am sensible, that whatever looks like a restraint on freedom of inquiry must be very disagreeable to all reasoning and inquisitive men."[31] And then once again, this time in addressing magistrates, Berkeley insists that because there are but few qualified to engage in the noble, judicious, and impartial search after truth, the solution is religion: "where there is a sincere love of truth and virtue, the grace of God can easily supply the defect of human means."[32]

In summary, Berkeley's contention throughout his entire adult life was that religion is the principal stay and support of the polis; and that free-thinking tends to undermine both religion and the polis. But so far we have paid little attention to the diversity in free-thinking. It is to that we will now turn our attention. Can all free-thinking be as bad as Berkeley portrays it? We will find Berkeley answering in the affirmative.

Chapter 3

Classical Philosophy vs. Minute Philosophy

In his longest work, Alciphron, Berkeley counters free-thinking with a philosophical discourse which both presents and exemplifies classical philosophy. It is from the perspective of classical philosophy that Berkeley criticizes each form of free-thinking as being destructive of the moral-political realm. From the same perspective Berkeley argues for theism against deism, and finally argues for both the utility and truth of Christianity.

Once again, it will become apparent that, although Alciphron is a work in religious apologetics, Berkeley did not oppose religion to science, but did oppose classical to minute philosophy. We might put his point as follows: given classical philosophy, we can harmonize religion and science, and thus human living; given minute philosophy, we set religion and science at odds, and thus make human living discordant.

I   Making Good Use of an Untoward Event

"Convinced of the decadence of European culture and ethics, he fixed his hopes on America."[1] So wrote A.A. Luce as prefatory to his account of Berkeley's Bermuda project. Although Berkeley did not receive the funds to establish a college in the new country, he found many ways to spend fruitfully his nearly three years in Rhode Island.[2] One of them was to write on the decadence of European culture. The result was the Alciphron. "Events are not in our power," wrote Berkeley, in the first page of the book, "but it always is, to make a good use even of the worst."[3] Shortly after his return to England the book was published, in 1732. It is written in dialogue form, and as literature has received high praise from, among others, one of its editors, T.E. Jessop: "From the literary point of view this longest of his works is his best. Indeed, as a work of art it stands supreme in the whole body of our English literature of philosophy, and perhaps supreme also in our literature of religious apologetics."[4]

II   The Characters and the Aim

Throughout the seven dialogues that comprise the book, free-thinking is represented by Lysicles and Alciphron (Greek for "strong head"). The frivolity of the former makes him immune to any serious criticism of whatever position he pretends to hold; the latter, although strong-headed, is serious, and is willing to learn. Berkeley's convictions are represented by Euphranor and Crito. The former is an educated farmer; a plain man, but alert and somewhat sophisticated. The latter is erudite, conversant with free-thinking, and sometimes sarcastic.

37

The aim of the dialogues is two-fold: to show that free-thinking, in all its forms, is destructive of the moral-political realm; and to offer religion (specifically Christianity) as useful to morals and politics, and as probably true. The forms of free-thinking that Berkeley attacks might be labelled as sophistry, cynicism, humanism, and deism. There are overlappings, particularly between the first two forms; but there is also a marked development in gravity as Berkeley moves from frivolous to serious free-thinking.

III Sophistry

"Sophistry" is a word borrowed from the Greek. "Sophia" is the Greek word for wisdom; hence, a sophist is literally a wise man. Plato's relentless and devastating criticism of those who passed for wise men in ancient Greece, and his exposure of the shallowness of much of the free-thinking of his time, has made it appropriate to translate "sophist," using a modern English idiom, as "wise guy." Early in Alciphron, Crito is describing to Euphranor the two free-thinkers he is to meet and converse with. "They are both men of fashion, and would be agreeable enough, if they did not fancy themselves free-thinkers. But this, to speak the truth, has given them a certain air and manner which a little too visibly declare they think themselves wiser than the rest of the world."[5] Berkeley, in the first two dialogues of Alciphron, is engaged in the same enterprise vis-a-vis the free-thinkers as was Plato, in some of his dialogues, vis-a-vis the sophists.

When Euphranor, in the first dialogue, presses for what is distinctive about free-thinking -- for he, too, is opposed to slavery, superstition, false doctrine -- he draws out of Alciphron the following assertions. Priests and clergymen are enemies to truth; priestcraft is inspired by a persecuting spirit, and is avaricious, ambitious, vengeful; magistrates typically aim only to stay in power, and use religion to that end; the notions of God, immortality, future rewards and punishments are promulgated for the sole purpose of keeping people subjugated; the source of false doctrines is customary and traditional education; children receiving education by the Church of England learn a set of prejudices that set them against members of other Christian sects, who have learned a different set of prejudices; members of other religions in other cultures learn yet other sets of prejudices.[6]

Finally, says Alciphron, belief in Providence is at the root of all this being bound to tradition and custom. But as soon as on the one hand we ponder the wide variety of religious beliefs, and are led to doubt the veracity of any of them; and on the other hand consider that there is no sensible evidence of God's existence (who has seen, felt, smelled, touched, or tasted God?), we are freed from that belief; and along with it freed from "all those whimsical notions of conscience, duty, principle, and the like, which fill a man's head with scruples, awe him with fears, and make him more a thorough slave than the horse he rides."[7]

Berkeley's first concern in response is to show that free-thinking is destructive of the polis. That is why Euphranor's next question to Alciphron is not whether all this is true, but instead is what, for the direction of human living, Alciphron will put in place of the notions of God, duty, conscience, etc. Alciphron's reply is that once we are freed from all the artifice of custom and tradition, we realize what all men have in common, what deep down directs and moves them; and that is their senses, appetites, and passions. The wise man, says Alciphron, has overcome the traditional education, is no longer encumbered with the guilt, remorse, and shame that accompany behavior not in keeping with the rules of an established religion; and instead looks to ways to keep his animal appetitive nature lively and flourishing. The good man, the happy man is one who is in the prime of life, with a lust for life, we might say, ready, able, and eager to satisfy each and every appetite and passion as he is so moved. The advantage man has over other animals is that his reason makes it possible for him to be more successful than other animals in this gratification of appetites; reason is in the service of the animal nature.[8]

At this point Berkeley introduces the term "minute philosophers." The term was coined, Berkeley tells us, by Cicero, to stand for the free-thinkers of his day. The name suits them, Berkeley thinks, "...they being a sort of sect which diminish all the most valuable things, the thoughts, views, and hopes of men; all the knowledge, notions, and theories of the mind they reduce to sense; human nature they contract and degrade to the narrow low standard of animal life, and assign us only a small pittance of time instead of immortality."[9] Alciphron "gravely" responds that if man "...be a little, short-lived, contemptible animal, it was not [free-thinkers] saying it made him so." But he is willing to accept the term, because he thinks "...this appellation might be derived from their considering things minutely,.... Besides, we all know the best eyes are necessary to discern the minutest objects; it seems, therefore, that minute philosophers might have been so called from their distinguished perspicacity."[10]

If Berkeley is in this latter passage alluding to materialism, the theory of reality which he believes underlies free-thinking, his point for now is that sophistic free-thinking is destructive of the polis. For if Alciphron has accurately portrayed human nature, then our true and only freedom lies in doing what we feel like doing; eating, drinking, sexing, with all the refinements therein that rational animals can concoct and arrange, whenever we feel like it; and with impunity, guiltlessness, and shamelessness. Any sort of authority that restricts that freedom may have to be put up with temporarily, but it cannot be approved or encouraged. Freedom means anarchy, no rule, no law; in short, no polis.

But Berkeley is not content with that. Like Plato dealing with his antagonists, he wants first to expose the sophistry, to show that the reasoning of Alciphron is unsound and invalid; and second to show that genuine philosophy, by contrast with sophistry, is constructive and supportive of the polis.

First, then, expose of the sophistry. The unsoundness of Alciphron's argument is revealed by the consideration that reason, even though not very active at birth, is as natural to man as the appetites. Hence, although it is natural for man, who is indeed an animal, to be moved by appetites, it is also natural for him to be directed by reason. Given that change in one of the premises of Alciphron's argument, we can go on to show that diversity in mores and customs can be accounted for by rational considerations in and about different environments and locales. Thus, universally among men justice is considered a virtue and injustice a vice, because men are rational animals; even though there may be differences in different societies about what is just, and again because we are rational animals. For example, usury is considered to be unjust; but what reasonable men take to be usurious varies with time, place, and circumstances. Therefore, the argument that appeals to variety of customs, laws, and mores as evidence that the customary and the traditional is not natural to man rests upon a false premise, and hence is unsound.[11]

The invalidity in Alciphron's argument that because no two moral or religious systems are in full agreement, therefore none of them is true, is evident on careful inspection. It is like arguing that because no two witnesses agree on the details of an accident, therefore none of them can be telling the full truth. However, because Berkeley is sensitive to the sentiment behind this invalid argument (if there is but one true moral or religious system, why is there such widespread disagreement among sincere men?), he adds at once his conviction that right thinking men will and do come to the same conclusions, even on controversial matters like morals and religion. As evidence, he cites the general, albeit not detailed, agreement between Socrates and some more recent philosophers on the existence and nature of God; and the general agreement between Confucius and the traditional and customary morality in Europe.[12]

Berkeley thus recognizes philosophy (represented here by Socrates and Confucius) as capable of reaching truth in moral and theological matters, independent of revelation. This is another way of saying that his quarrel with free-thinking is philosophical; he does not pit revelation or religion against supposed scientific fact; he does pit classical philosophy against sophistic minute philosophy.

Having exposed the sophistry, Berkeley presents his version of classical eudaemonistic (having to do with happiness) moral philosophy, against sophistic minute philosophy's claim that the happiness of other men is not to anyone a true natural good. The classical view rests upon the claim that man is by nature a political animal; and hence naturally desires not only his own happiness, but also the happiness of all at least who are his fellow citizens in a polis. A corollary of this is that the happiness of each of us in a polis is dependent on the well-being of the polis. Berkeley explicates the notion by analogies to vegetables and their parts, animals and their parts, and the system of nature as a whole; and argues that for happiness (well-being) in mankind there must be, in the moral-political world, the same sort of order and regularity. Hence, the conclusion is that classical philosophy (Berkeley claims the support of Plato, Aristotle, and the Stoics, as well as Christianity), seeing the necessary connection that belief in God, a future state, and moral duties have, as cause, to the happiness of men in general, as effect, tends to support the body politic. The sophistic, narrowly and shallowly egoistic minute philosophy, tends to destruction of the moral-political realm.[13]

We have to tread carefully here, for this classical political philosophy can be, indeed has been, interpreted as totalitarianism. For if my well-being as a member of a polis depends on the well-being of the polis, in a way analogous to a cell of my body's well-being depending on the well-being of the body, then we wonder what sense there is in talking any longer about my or your happiness. However true it is that the cell cannot function if the body is dead, still the cell exists not in its own right, for its own sake, but only as contributory to the well-being of the body. If we as members of a polis are like that, it seems that we exist only for the well-being of the polis, for the glory of some Reich or other.

The answer to such an interpretation is presented most clearly, perhaps, by Aristotle. However true it is, he says, that man is a political animal, still the polis is not a natural primary being, as individual men are. Hence, the polis exists for the sake of the happiness of men, not the other way around. While Berkeley's version of the classical position is more susceptible to misinterpretation because of the analogies he employs, it would be unfair to attribute that view to an orthodox Christian, who believes that salvation is for individual men, not the polis. What Berkeley intended was to argue that while sophistic free-thinking can provide no basis for an orderly, harmonious, and good

41

polis, classical philosophy can.

Let us suppose that Berkeley and the other classical philosophers are right in their view of man as a naturally political animal, seeking the well-being of all members of the polis. Then, such political and moral harmony as exists among us is caused at least in part by human nature, and not simply by some specially contrived political system. On the other hand, if sophistic minute philosophy is right, then whatever harmony exists is artificial, and is such that in the long run no "political" genius can overcome with a specially contrived system the tendency to anarchy and chaos. If sophistic minute philosophy is right, men are in desperate straits; if Berkeley is right, men can at least be hopeful.

Even if Berkeley is right, the whole discussion might give us pause. That is, human nature, precisely because it is rational, is somewhat plastic; moreover, its changeability seems to a large extent to be under human control. If we suppose that the view of sophistic minute philosophy comes to prevail among men, could it happen that they would turn themselves into egoistic beasts, or into avaricious machines? Berkeley, at any rate, devoted his life to making men more human.

IV   Cynicism

A brief exchange between Euphranor and Lysicles reveals what might be taken as the cynical minute philosopher's position on education.

> EUPHRANOR. Thus much is certain: if we look into all institutions of government, and the political writings of such as have heretofore passed for wise men, we shall find a great regard for virtue.

> LYSICLES. You shall find a strong tincture of prejudice; but, as I said before, consult the multitude if you would find nature and truth.

> EUPHRANOR. But among country gentlemen, and farmers, and the better sort of tradesmen, is not virtue a reputable thing?

> LYSICLES. You pick up authorities among men of low life and vile education.

> EUPHRANOR. Perhaps we ought to pay a decent respect to the authority of minute

42

philosophers.

LYSICLES. And I would fain know whose
authority should be more considered than
that of those gentlemen who are alone above
prejudice, and think for themselves.

EUPHRANOR. How doth it appear that you are the
only unprejudiced part of mankind? May not
a minute philosopher, as well as another
man, be prejudiced in favour of the leaders
of his sect? May not an atheistical
education prejudice towards atheism? What
should hinder a man's being prejudiced
against religion, as well as for it? Or can
you assign any reason why an attachment to
pleasure, interest, vice, or vanity, may not
be supposed to prejudice men against virtue?

LYSICLES. This is pleasant. What! Suppose
those very men influenced by prejudice who
are always disputing against it, whose
constant aim it is to detect and demolish
prejudices of all kinds! [14]

The educational principle, in a word, is iconoclasm. Nothing
is sacred. No political or moral or religious principle
("prejudice" of course for the cynic) is allowed to stand; all are
smashed by the free-thinker's relentless criticism.

When Euphranor wonders what will replace all the traditional
directives to human living, Lysicles' reply presents a slight
variation on the sophistic theme of living naturally; that is, by
sense, appetite, passion. Lysicles sums it up as sensual
pleasure. "Now of all private interests pleasure is that which
hath the strongest charms, and no pleasures like those which are
heightened and enlivened by licence." [15]

So far, then, there is nothing new in this version of free-
thinking to set it apart from sophistry. What is new is the claim
that private vices and private pursuit of pleasure are public
benefits, or lead to the public good. The editors of Berkeley's
work establish that the second dialogue in Alciphron was
occasioned by the popular success in Berkeley's lifetime of
Bernard Mandeville's Fable of the Bees, or Private Vices Public
Benefits. This work, as Berkeley represents it, is directly
opposed to the classical position that there is a necessary causal
connection between moral and religious virtue and the public
good. Instead it argues, as the alternative title suggests, that
private vices cause public benefits. Drunkenness, for example,

43

"increases the malt tax, a principal branch of his Majesty's revenue, and thereby promotes the safety, strength, and glory of the nation."[16] It also makes possible employment of all those in any way connected with the production of beer and ale. Consumption of wine encourages trade with foreign countries, England exchanging their goods for the imported wine.

And so it goes, Berkeley drawing other examples from Mandeville's book to show that not only do these vices extend employment, but that some of them also, like gambling, insure quick circulation of money, and thereby stimulate the economy. Free-thinkers have appropriately given vice a better name than prejudiced people have: "Thus, in our dialect, a vicious man is a man of pleasure, a sharper is one that plays the whole game, a lady is said to have an affair, a gentleman to be gallant, a rogue in business to be one that knows the world. By this means we have no such things as sots, debauchers, whores or rogues in the beau monde, who may enjoy their vices without incurring disagreeable appellations."[17]

Berkeley patiently responds. A healthy, long-lived, temperate drinker will do more for the economy than the sick, short-lived drunkard. And if there are some people whose employment depends entirely on the vice or vanity of men, they surely might be better employed without loss to the public good. In short, there is nothing in vice itself that makes it a public blessing; any thing it can do toward the public good virtue can do as well or better. The most that Lysicles will admit in the ensuing conversation is that a state might subsist, and maybe even be said to be good, following classical principles; but he insists that a nation can only become great and flourishing by encouraging luxury and vice.[18]

At length, when Euphranor asks Lysicles whether in all candor it is the public benefit of vice that makes him plead for it, Lysicles confesses that "private interest is the first and principal consideration with philosophers of our sect."[19] And Mandeville, Berkeley thought, was such an egoist, although not all free-thinkers were or are. But the point for now is that we are back at considering whether or not the cynical principle of private interest, stated here as the pursuit of pleasure, is destructive of the polis. And again, it seems that the position has only to be stated for us to see the answer. A group of egoists, each pursuing his own pleasure, could come together into a polis, regulated by law, only out of fear of one another, only for the sake of security. The natural tendency, if egoism is the correct account of man, is to anarchy.

However, as in his discussion of sophistry, Berkeley is not content with that; he offers a criticism of hedonism, based on the

44

classical theory of man. If men are indeed rational animals, then it is within their power to govern and direct their lives, and thus escape enslavement to the senses, appetites, and passions. All animals indeed seem to pursue pleasure and avoid pain. Rational animals pursue rational pleasures, as well as animal or sensual pleasures. Furthermore, these rational pleasures not only are more befitting a rational animal, but they are more lasting and gratifying than the evanescent pleasures of sense.

The only sort of concession that Lysicles will make to this position is to grant that "there is something gross and ill-bred in the vices of mean men, which the genteel philosopher abhors." To which Crito immediately responds, "But to cheat, whore, betray, get drunk, do all these things decently, this is true wisdom, and elegance of taste."[20] Lysicles' cynicism and frivolity make it impossible for him to even understand, much less concede to, the classical view of man.

V Morality Without Religion

In the third dialogue Alciphron has turned his back on frivolous free-thinking, and become serious.

The word free-thinker, as it comprehends men of very different sorts and sentiments, cannot, in a strict sense, be said to constitute one particular sect, holding a certain system of positive and distinct opinions. Though it must be owned we do all agree in certain points of unbelief, or negative principles, which agreement, in some sense, unites us under the common idea of one sect. But then, those negative principles, as they happen to take root in men of different age, temper, and education, do produce various tendencies, opinions, and characters, widely differing one from another. You are not to think that our greatest strength lies in our greatest number -- libertines, and mere men of honour. No: we have among us philosophers of a very different character, men of curious contemplation, not governed by such gross things as sense and custom, but of an abstracted virtue and sublime morals, and the less religious the more virtuous. For virtue of the high and disinterested kind no man is so well qualified as an infidel; it being a mean and selfish thing to be virtuous through fear or hope. The notion of Providence, and future state of rewards and punishments, may indeed tempt or

45

scare men of abject spirit into practices
contrary to the natural bent of their souls,
but will never produce a true and genuine
virtue.[21]

Not only do these words show Alciphron's serious turn, but
they also indicate Berkeley's awareness of the variety within
free-thinking, and introduce us to this new form that earlier we
called humanism: there can and should be morality without
religion. Exploration of this topic will be helped by our
becoming acquainted with the man whose position Berkeley is here
reviewing and criticizing. One paragraph from one of
Shaftesbury's recent editors tells precisely and succinctly who
the man was, and how widespread was his influence.

Anthony Ashley Cooper, the third Earl of
Shaftesbury, was one of the most influential
writers of the Enlightenment. His major opus,
Characteristics of Men, Manners, Opinions,
Times, which first appeared in 1711, went
through eleven editions by 1790. Near the end
of the century, Herder saw Shaftesbury as the
"beloved Plato of Europe," and wrote that "this
virtuoso of humanity...has had a marked
influence on the best minds of our century, on
those who have striven with determination and
sincerity for the true, the beautiful, and the
good." Leibniz, surprised to find that much of
his Theodicy (1710) had already been expressed
in Shaftesbury's Moralists (1705), wrote that
"if I had seen this work before my Theodicy was
published, I should have profited as I ought
and should have borrowed its great passages."
Hume, even while criticizing "the elegant Lord
Shaftesbury," praised him as "a great
genius." Shaftesbury's importance is affirmed
even by the attacks made upon him, as for
example, by Berkeley in Alciphron; or, The
Minute Philosopher (1732).[22]

Why Berkeley should attack him as a minute philosopher is not
clear. Berkeley's disagreement with Shaftesbury's moral theory
seems to rest on misinterpretation by Berkeley. However, there is
an apparent dispute between them; and that is the role, in morals,
of rewards and punishments. Still, although Shaftesbury was
neither an enemy of religion nor a minute philosopher, Berkeley
did dispute with him on the question of ridicule. Despite this,
Shaftesbury might agree with Berkeley that religion is the main
stay and support of the polis.

In _Alciphron_ Berkeley presents Shaftesbury as holding a moral theory in which the mind apprehends moral excellence, or the beauty of virtue, by a "certain interior sense," analogous to the eye's perception of natural sensible beauty. According to this theory, as Berkeley presents it, the mind cannot understand this beauty, but can only feel it. Our being moved to virtuous activity is dependent on this moral sense, or taste, that we all, more or less, possess.

Berkeley attacks this theory by first noting that the conclusion that we are moved to good actions by a _sense_ of their beauty belies our common experience of acting from a _judgment_ of what is right and dutiful. From that he argues that our awareness of both physical and moral beauty comes about through judgment, and not mere sensation or sentiment. Whether Shaftesbury would agree with this criticism we cannot be sure; but we can be fairly confident that what Berkeley was criticizing is not Shaftesbury's position. It is true that one can isolate sentences in Shaftesbury's writings that lend themselves to Berkeley's interpretation: e.g., "I am ready...to own there is in certain figures a natural beauty, which the eye finds as soon as the object is presented to it."[23] Further, Shaftesbury is not as clear as we could wish: e.g., on one page he seems to be arguing for an innate (in man) sense of beauty, and on another that the distinctions between beautiful and ugly, admirable and despicable, have their foundations in nature, not in the mind.[24] But overall the careful reader will discern that in these same pages what Shaftesbury is intent to argue is that there is such a thing as beauty, and that the human mind has the capacity to come to know it. It is Shaftesbury, the Platonist, who is speaking in these pages in "The Moralists": awareness of beauty and goodness requires rational, not merely sensory, cognition. In Berkeley's argumentation against Shaftesbury there is an appeal to classical notions of beauty against the Gothic and modern -- in dress, architecture, and painting. With all this criticism Shaftesbury agrees; beauty (and goodness) are dependent, both as to origin and human awareness, on intelligence. The proportion, the order, the fitness, the suitability of beautiful objects bespeak an intelligent designer, not the chance workings of atoms in motion. For both Berkeley and Shaftesbury man's intelligent awareness of beauty and goodness is argument for form and designer against a world supposed to be nothing but matter in motion. Hence, it is patent that Berkeley misinterpreted Shaftesbury's moral theory. Why he did so is perhaps impossible to judge.

However that may be, there is an apparent dispute between the two on the question of the role that should be played in morals by rewards and punishments. Reviewing a classical discussion of rewards and punishments in a philosopher who was obviously teacher to both Berkeley and Shaftesbury will enable us to show that their

dispute is more apparent than real. In Book II of The Republic
Plato introduces the issue about what kind of good thing justice
is. Socrates, in the dialogue, says that it is a thing valued
both in itself (for the effect on its possessor, that is) and for
the consequences (for rewards, both in this life and the next).
The common opinion, according to others in the dialogue, is that
justice is valued only for its consequences; in general, people
regard it as difficult and irksome, and practice it only for the
hope of rewards or the fear of punishments. Plato shows that the
notion that justice is of instrumental worth only (valued only for
its consequences) rests upon the theory that men are not naturally
political, but instead come to exist in lawful society out of fear
of one another. On this theory of human nature, justice is as
artificial and arbitrary as the rules of a card game or athletic
contest; law and order depend entirely on a system of rewards and
punishments. That is to say, on this theory none of us is
naturally inclined to benevolent or altruistic behavior (with the
exception, perhaps, of a few good-natured simpletons); but most of
us are constrained to orderly behavior by the awesome presence of
the law, which offers protection to "right" behavior and threatens
punishment to "wrong." Hence, on this theory, the only motives
for right, just, virtuous, and good behavior are the promise of
reward and the threat of punishment.

Adeimantus, one of the characters in the dialogue, adds that
religion supports this theory. That is, religious experts, like
the poets Homer and Hesiod, teach that the gods bestow their
favors on righteous people; and that rewards and punishments in
the next life are meted out in accordance with merit achieved in
this one.

Most of the remainder of The Republic is given over to
Socrates' presentation and defense of justice as intrinsically
good; i.e., to be valued for the effect it has on its possessor,
whether seen of gods or other men, regardless of external rewards
and punishments. The foundation for the argument is the
contention that man by his very nature is a moral and political
animal. Rational animals achieve happiness and well-being by
living together virtuously.

On this issue Shaftesbury clearly sides with Socrates.
Virtue moves (or should move) men by its inherent
attractiveness. Any moral position which regards rewards and
punishments as the motivating factors is mean and degrading to
men; it treats men as slavish and mercenary; it regards them as
naturally vicious (or at least non-moral), and needing external
sanctions to curb their natural beastly appetites. But men are
not really that way, insists Shaftesbury; instead, they are
naturally inclined to just, courageous, benevolent behavior, and
need only have that natural inclination tutored, refined, and

developed to become good and virtuous men.

With this Platonic or Socratic moral philosophy in mind Shaftesbury could not help noticing, as Adeimantus had with respect to the religious teaching of his day, that some Christian teachers, at least, pin their hopes for good behavior among men on a system of rewards and punishments, in this life as well as the next. Suppose a Christian serves God, not out of love and respect for His infinite glory and goodness, but out of fear of eternal damnation, or because of a promise of heavenly bliss. Is not such service slavish? Nor could such a person be said to be truly virtuous. Indeed, it seems accidental that he is serving God rather than the devil. For, with no sense of the glory and goodness of God, but only fear of His might, such a man might well be tempted by a devil. On the other hand, suppose a man who has developed and refined his natural inclinations to virtue, who is moved by the beauty of virtue. Having learned what is really good in man, he can then the more praise a really good God; and in short, be on his way to becoming a profoundly religious man. Such a service to God would be, instead of slavish, uplifting. Any religious teaching, Christian or otherwise, which relies on promises and threats to goad men into lawful behavior really degrades man and God; it rests on mistaken notions both of man and of the Deity.[25]

Although Berkeley, on this matter, did not write as explictly and eloquently as Shaftesbury, he does not disagree. We have earlier explicated Berkeley's conviction that man is by nature, not by artifice, a moral and political animal. He agrees with Socrates that justice (virtue) is intrinsically good, that the happiness of men depends on their becoming truly virtuous. Nor does Berkeley suppose that a Christian can look for happiness only to the next life. Quite the contrary, he has Crito exclaiming a kind of Christian enthusiasm: "...can any ecstasy be higher, any rapture more affecting, than that which springs from the love of God and man, from a conscience void of offence, and an inward discharge of duty, with the secret delight, trust, and hope that attend it?"[26]

Given this agreement, where is the disagreement? Neither Berkeley nor Shaftesbury regards virtue and law as artificial and arbitrary; both regard justice as grounded in the nature of man. Neither of them, then, supposes that rewards and punishments exist for the sake of order in what would otherwise be an anarchic and chaotic contest of men against men. In fact, the disagreement is more apparent than real, arising from Berkeley's supposing that Shaftesbury saw no need whatever for rewards and punishments. "His [Shaftesbury's] conduct seems just as wise as if a monarch should give out that there was neither jail nor executioner in his kingdom to enforce the laws, but that it would be beautiful to observe them, and that in so doing men would taste the pure delight which results from order and decorum."[27] Following this, Berkeley maintains, with Aristotle as his chief support, that while ideally men practice virtue because it has become with them second nature, practically all youths and most adults need the guidance and direction to virtue that can only be supplied by a system of laws, or of rewards and punishments. Rewards and punishments, then, exist for the sake of virtue and happiness among men, not for the sake of securing men from one another.

What Berkeley failed to see is that this classical view of rewards and punishments is shared by Shaftesbury. In a passage in "The Moralists" he expresses exactly what we have just now presented Berkeley as arguing. Surely it is preferable that men serve God out of love for His goodness rather than for the sake of reward and fear of punishment. Still, it is for the good of men and the world that there should be obedience to right rule; and if not in the better way, then in the imperfect way. Moreover, since religion is a discipline, there is hope that beginning in the meaner way, some men at least will progress to the higher way.[28]

Not only was Shaftesbury in agreement with Berkeley on rewards and punishments, but also he was neither an enemy of religion nor a minute philosopher. There is a passage in his "A Letter Concerning Enthusiasm" which is reminiscent of no one so much as the classical thirteenth century Christian philosopher, St. Thomas Aquinas, who begins his Summa Theologica, aimed at instructing ordinary people in the Christian religion, with rational demonstrations of the existence and nature of God. It is here that Shaftesbury argues, much as does Berkeley in Dialogue IV of Alciphron, although more expansively and eloquently, that the same rational power which shows us the existence of God will also demonstrate, by analogy, God's goodness. The argument to His superior goodness depends on our first discerning the goodness in ourselves, and hence on the classical notion that man is by nature at least inclined to goodness, to moral and political virtue.[29]

There is another passage in which Shaftesbury compares the opposite moral tendencies of theism and atheism. His argument is basically the same as Berkeley's, that the natural tendency of atheism is away from morality and virtue, understood as intrinsically good to the human soul. A man who supposes that there is neither goodness nor beauty in the whole scheme of things, and supposes that there is no providential God, will not be likely to have his own natural goodness properly nurtured. And even apart from speculation about the hereafter, a theist finds support in his faith for his natural inclination toward goodness.[30]

50

And finally there is a passage denouncing minute philosophers ("modern moralists," Shaftesbury calls them), who pronounce a morality meaner than that of pagans, and declare that there is nothing more to morality than fashion, law, and arbitrary decree.[31]

If Berkeley misinterpreted Shaftesbury's moral theory, if he failed to see their agreement on the purpose of rewards and punishments, if he mistook him as an enemy of religion and a minute philosopher, then is there any real dispute? Yes. Shaftesbury did not agree with Berkeley on the importance of institutionalized religion to the polis. The last pages of the last essay in Characteristics encourage a skepticism with respect to authority in religion.[32] Elsewhere he encourages what Berkeley takes to be a definitive characteristic of minute philosophy: raillery, wit, ridicule. From what we have discovered about Shaftesbury, we can guess that these tactics of skepticism and ridicule are not proposed for the sake of undermining true philosophy and religion, but are to be employed to some other end.

Berkeley believed that all right thinking philosophers would encourage, for the sake of the polis, respect for the church. To which the witty and skeptical Shaftesbury replies, in effect, and by quoting from some of his contemporary churchmen themselves: which church? Rome? the established Church of England? the dissenting churches? whether Puritan, Quaker, or whatever? And where shall we go for the last authoritative word? to scripture? But whose? the Romish? the Anglican? Or should we go to creed? or to episcopacy? But again, whose? And so on.

All this, as Berkeley interprets it in Alciphron, is calculated to laugh men out of their religion, thus doing both them and the polis a great disservice. So likewise with ridiculing the lack of perfection and downright hypocrisy among the clergy. But Shaftesbury does not see it that way. Instead, "...what rule or measure is there in the world, except in the considering of the real temper of things, to find which are truly serious and which ridiculous? And how can this be done, unless by applying the ridicule, to see whether it will bear? But if we fear to apply this rule in anything, what security can we have against the imposture of formality in all things?"[33]

Shaftesbury puts this in another way at the end of "The Moralists." There Theocles points out to the skeptic, Philocles, that "if philosophy be, as we take it, the study of happiness, must not every one, in some manner or other, either skilfully or unskilfully philosophise?"[34] Then follows of course an encomium for skillful philosophy -- or, as Berkeley would put it, for classical philosophy vs. minute philosophy. For Shaftesbury then, ridicule and skepticism, at least in the hands of skillful philosophers like himself, lead to discovery of what is really grave and serious, which leads in turn to sound moral philosophizing, in turn to virtuous living, and finally to proper religious worship and praise of a good God, i.e., to true religion.

Berkeley's evident response to this is that most of us are unskillful philosophers. Neither has there been, nor is there likely to be, a polis ruled by skillful philosophers. Thus Berkeley would iterate that the remedy lies in religion; specifically, in institutionalized Christianity. Apart from the question of salvation, the moral and political welfare of men here and now depends more upon institutionalized religion than upon skillful philosophizing.

In this dispute most of us probably tend to side with Shaftesbury, so used are we to political and religious liberty. Moreover, there are humanists who practice virtue perforce without hope of future rewards, "unseen of gods and men," as Plato put it. Such people, some of them at least, might well agree with Plato and Aristotle that man is a moral and political animal.[35] But still, might not some of these people agree with Berkeley that man's rational political nature needs nurturing, and that nurturing requires as much institutional support as can be mustered? In other words, not all atheists are militant; many tolerate, even welcome, the support to moral and political stability that comes from religious teaching.

Finally, on the issue of morality without religion, perhaps we may conclude that Shaftesbury -- the real one, not Berkeley's misrepresentation -- and Berkeley are both right. On the one hand, can we come to revere and praise a good God without our first discovering goodness in our fellow men? On the other hand, can virtue be promulgated and widespread without the offices of institutionalized religion? At the end of the first chapter we cited an historian of free-thinking, J.M. Robertson, as listing some of the founding fathers of the United States among free-thinkers. But both Washington and Jefferson seem to agree with Berkeley and Shaftesbury on this issue of morality, religion, and politics. Washington, in his Farewell Address, declared:

> Of all the dispositions and habits which lead to political prosperity, religion and morality are indispensable supports. In vain would that man claim the tribute of patriotism who should labor to subvert these great pillars of human happiness -- these firmest props of the duties of men and citizens.

And let us with caution indulge the
supposition that morality can be maintained
without religion. Whatever may be conceded to
the influence of refined education on minds of
peculiar structure, reason and experience both
forbid us to expect that national morality can
prevail in exclusion of religious principle.

And Jefferson asked rhetorically, "Can the liberties of a
nation be thought secure when we have removed this only firm
basis, a conviction in the minds of the people that their
liberties are the gift of God?"[36]

VI   Theism vs. Deism

At the end of the third dialogue Alciphron, even though he is
close to being convinced that religious education is important to
the polis, protests that we should not sacrifice truth to
convenience. And the truth is, he believes, that either there is
no God or that if there is a God he is not providential. In
either case, there is no basis in the nature of things for
religion, for worship of Providence. In the fourth dialogue
Alciphron comments that he, "like the rest of the world," was in
his youth catechised into belief of a providential God. But he
has never been shown any reason for believing such. Hence, the
challenge he puts to Euphranor is to prove that there is
Providence.

Once again we see that Berkeley is opposing philosophy to
philosophy, not religion to science. That is, he does not have
Euphranor sermonizing, or trying to inculcate in Alciphron a
religious experience that will convert him to Christianity. Not
that Berkeley would want to deny that there is such a thing as
religious, even mystical, experience; rather, his concern here is
to combat what he takes to be mistaken philosophy. Hence,
Euphranor responds to the challenge by presenting a rational,
philosophical demonstration of the existence of Providence. Such
a demonstration would show that not only is minute philosophy
destructive of morals and politics, but also that its prime
leading notion is false.

It is interesting to note the support Berkeley might have
gotten from Shaftesbury. We have already quoted Shaftesbury on
the contrary tendencies of theism and atheism. What follows is
about deism.

...When a sceptic questions "whether a real
theology can be raised out of philosophy alone,
without the help of revelation," he does no
more than pay a handsome compliment to

53

authority and the received religion. He can impose on no one who reasons deeply; since whoever does so, will easily conceive that at this rate theology must have no foundation at all. For revelation itself, we know, is founded on the acknowledgment of a divine existence; and 'tis the province of philosophy alone to prove what revelation only supposes.

I look on it therefore as a most unfair way for those who would be builders, and undertake this proving part, to lay such a foundation as is insufficient to bear the structure. Supplanting and undermining may in other cases be fair war, but in philosophical disputes 'tis not allowable to work underground, or as in sieges by the sap. Nothing can be more unbecoming than to talk magisterially and in venerable terms of "a supreme Nature, an infinite Being, and a Deity," when all the while a providence is never meant, nor anything like order or the government of a mind admitted. For when these are understood, and real divinity acknowledged, the notion is not dry and barren, but such consequences are necessarily drawn from it as must set us in action, and find employment for our strongest affections. All the duties of religion evidently follow hence, and no exception remains against any of those great maxims which revelation has established.[37]

What this argues of course is not that there is Providence, but rather that religion has its proper foundation in proof of Providence; and that deism does not provide that foundation. Some minute philosophers, particularly of the serious, "scientific" kind, were willing to grant, or even to argue, that there is a God; but typically the God so granted or proved is one who has brought the mechanical universe into being and set it in motion, but who thenceforth is as unconcerned about the workings of it, or the creatures in it, as a clockmaker is about his clocks.

Deism, both Shaftesbury and Berkeley maintain, is effectively atheism. Furthermore, both foresaw that an attempt, in our modern world, to establish religion by revelation alone, without reason's support, was bound to be detrimental to religion. For if one cannot reconcile what he is taught by revealed religion with what he is taught by scientific reason, then it is likely to be the revealed religion that, for consistency's and truth's sake, one gives up.

So it is that Berkeley is concerned to establish theism -- a philosophical position, not a religion -- against deism and atheism. In other words, Berkeley was convinced that science, properly understood, does not in any way contradict Christianity; and that, furthermore, rational arguments lead us, independent of revelation, to conclude that there is a providential God. Berkeley is here in good company; St. Thomas Aquinas is the most impressive and most effective of his predecessors in Christian philosophy who so argued. And although Aquinas' and Berkeley's ancient Greek teachers, Plato and Aristotle, argued for neither a Creator nor Providence (or at least not as emphatically as did Aquinas), nonetheless Aristotle did argue convincingly that God's causal efficacy is always present and always drawing things in nature toward perfection. In short, theism is a venerable philosophical position; and has its origins among thinkers who had no religious axes to grind. Hence, if we can allow Alciphron, and his like, to abandon religious belief in the name of reason, we must allow other philosophers, even though they are religious and might be suspected of having a special interest, to try to show the rational foundation for religious belief.

The detail of Berkeley's argument for Providence will be given in Part II. Here we will give the gist of it, and consider what, if we suppose the argument sound, the consequences are.

Under the influence of the science of physics coming into being in the seventeenth century, many of Berkeley's immediate predecessors and contemporaries in philosophy had concluded that nature, the material universe, is a mechanism. Berkeley thought that mistaken, and believed instead, because of his work in theory of vision and theory of knowledge, that nature is a language, spoken to us by God, its author. Imbedded in that of course is an argument for God's existence; however, in Alciphron he presents a modified version of the argument, probably because he thought it would be more immediately accessible to the audience he was addressing. Instead of arguing that all nature is a language, he argues, more simply, that visual objects are a language; and from that to the conclusion that there is a supernatural spirit, or mind, who is the author of that language.

We commonly speak of seeing men, animals, plants, houses, etc. However, a moment's reflection might at least make us consider whether that common way of speaking is accurate. Would it not be more correct to say that strictly speaking the objects of sight are color and light? If we can grant that, then we will agree that objects of touch are different; we do not touch color, but instead textures such as smooth and rough, or shapes such as round or square. How is it that nonetheless we sensibly say that we see a spherically shaped fruit on the table? Berkeley's explanation is that from birth on we have been learning the

55

language of vision (where the color "orange" in this case signifies the orange on the table, much as the word "orange" on this page signifies to the reader that species of fruit), and have now so completely mastered it that we "see" right through the sign (the color) to the object signified by that sign. Hence, we do not speak falsely when we say that we see the orange, anymore than we would be speaking falsely if we were to say that in reading Tom Jones we see Squires Western and Allworthy, Tom himself, and so on. But very strictly speaking, as in the one case what we see are the words and letters on the pages of Fielding's book, so in the other what we see are various shades and degrees of light and colors. But just as there must be Fieldings to author the English language, so must there be an Author of the visual language. Therefore, God exists.

Let us conclude this brief resume of Berkeley's proof with these words from Crito.

> Some philosophers, being convinced of the wisdom and power of the Creator, from the make and contrivance of organized bodies and orderly system of the world, did nevertheless imagine that he left this system with all its parts and contents well adjusted and put in motion, as an artist leaves a clock, to go thence-forward of itself for a certain period. But this Visual Language proves, not a Creator merely, but a provident Governor, actually and intimately present, and attentive to all our interests and motions, who watches over our conduct, and takes care of our minutest actions and designs throughout the whole course of our lives, informing, admonishing, and directing incessantly, in a most evident and sensible manner. This is truly wonderful.[38]

There is every indication that Berkeley was greatly pleased with this proof, for the reason that it was unique. The "Alciphrons" of his day could not dismiss it out of hand, as Alciphron, early in this dialogue, had disallowed any of the old war horse arguments, originated among the ancient Greeks. Nonetheless, when later in the dialogue Berkeley faces the objection, brought by Lysicles, that this argument tells us nothing about the nature of God -- whether He is good, e.g., and also faces that dark, negative, mystical theology that proclaims we can know nothing of God's nature, Berkeley at once appeals to Thomas Aquinas and his successors for the doctrine that allows us to learn by analogy about God's attributes. His conclusion reminds us again of his kinship with Shaftesbury: "We may, therefore, consistently with what hath been premised, affirm that all sorts of perfection which we can conceive in a finite spirit are in God, but without any of the alloy which is found in the creatures."[39]

Given this brief review we are of course in no position to judge the soundness of Berkeley's arguments. But if we suppose that they are sound, then we agree that he has established theism, and driven the last nail into the coffin of minute philosophy. Furthermore, no free-thinker, no deist, is in a position to argue against Berkeley's proof for Providence; that is, if the proof is not sound, no modern contemporary of Berkeley could explain why it is not sound. The reasons for this will become clear when in Part II we review the coming into being of modern philosophy.

VII Christianity Useful

Take my word for it, priests of all religions are the same: wherever there are priests there will be priestcraft; and wherever there is priestcraft there will be a persecuting spirit, which they never fail to exert to the utmost of their power against all those who have the courage to think for themselves, and will not submit to be hoodwinked and manacled by their reverend leaders. Those great masters of pedantry and jargon have coined several systems, which are all equally true, and of equal importance to the world. The contending sects are each alike fond of their own, and alike prone to discharge their fury upon all who dissent from them. Cruelty and ambition being the darling vices of priests and churchmen all the world over, they endeavour in all countries to get an ascendant over the rest of mankind; and the magistrate, having a joint interest with the priest in subduing, amusing, and scaring the people, too often lends a hand to the hierarchy, who never think their authority and possessions secure so long as those who differ from them in opinion are allowed to partake even in the common rights belonging to their birth or species. To represent the matter in a true light, figure to yourselves a monster or spectre made up of superstition and enthusiasm, the joint issue of statecraft and priestcraft, rattling chains in one hand, and with the other brandishing a flaming sword over the land, and menacing destruction to all who shall dare to follow the dictates of reason and common sense. Do but consider this, and then say if there was not danger as well as difficulty in our undertaking. Yet, such is the generous ardour that truth inspires, our free-thinkers are neither overcome by the one nor daunted by the other. In spite of both we have already made so many proselytes among the better sort, and their numbers increase so fast, that we hope we shall be able to carry all before us, beat down the bulwarks of tyranny, secular or ecclesiastical, break the fetters and chains of our countrymen, and restore the original inherent rights, liberties, and prerogatives of mankind.[40]

This spirited declaration, from the mouth of the Alciphron of the first dialogue, reminds us that modern free-thinking's enmity to religion arose at least in part as opposition to abuses and corruptions within established churches. Nor has Berkeley forgotten it; nor is he unaware that the established Church of England fell more than a little short of the perfection a good Christian would wish for it. So, having done with his frontal attack against minute philosophy, he turns to defend Christianity and the established Church against the typical criticisms. In his metaphysical writings, Berkeley entertains every criticism of his position that he had heard of or could think of. So here. But to make what might be an unduly long story considerably shorter, we quote Berkeley's summary of the proceeding, toward the end of this dialogue, and then comment.

We allow that tyranny and slavery are bad things: but why should we apprehend them from the clergy at this time? Rites and ceremonies we own are not points of chief moment in religion: but why should we ridicule things in their own nature at least indifferent, and which bear the stamp of supreme authority? That men in divinity, as well as other subjects, are perplexed with useless disputes, and are like to be so long as the world lasts, I freely acknowledge: but why must all the human weakness and mistakes of clergymen be imputed to wicked designs? Why indiscriminately abuse their character and tenets? Is this like candour, love of truth, and free-thinking? It is granted there may be found, now and then, spleen and ill-breeding in the clergy: but are not the same faults incident to English laymen of a retired education and country life? I grant there is infinite futility in the Schoolmen: but I deny that a volume of that doth so much mischief as a page of minute philosophy. That weak or wicked men should, by favour of the world, creep into power and high stations in the church is nothing wonderful: and that in such stations they should behave like themselves is natural to suppose. But all the while it is evident that not the Gospel but the world, not the spirit but the flesh, not God but the devil, puts them upon their worthy achievements. We make no difficulty to grant that nothing is more infamous than vice and ignorance in a clergyman; nothing more base than a hypocrite, more frivolous than a pedant, more cruel than an Inquisitor. But it must be also granted by you, gentlemen, that nothing is more ridiculous and absurd than for pedantic, ignorant, and corrupt men to cast the first stone at every shadow of their own defects and vices in other men.[41]

A nice, balanced summary. But in the reading of the dialogue, even the person sympathetic to Berkeley is likely to get a bit exasperated at times, even though he knows that Berkeley is at least considering all the objections to Christianity. For example, early in the dialogue the characters are disputing who or what is responsible for the flourishing of vice in the nation, Alciphron and Lysicles blaming the clergy, Euphranor and Crito the free-thinkers. Crito had introduced the dispute by defining religion as a virtuous mean between incredulity and superstition, pleading for religion vs. profaneness, law vs. confusion, virtue vs. vice, and hope vs. despondency. At once he adds that he holds no brief for unchristian Christians; if a believer does evil, it is because of him, not his belief; and if an infidel does good, it is because of him, not his unbelief. In short, it seems that we are to judge men by what they do, not by what they say. But shortly thereafter we are told that we should judge the effects of religion by the religious, of Christianity by Christians. It seems that here is a quarrel that Berkeley cannot lose. Given Christian principles, a Christian is one who loves God and neighbor as himself, etc. And surely such a person is not inclined to wickedness. But then if a professed Christian disobeys the great commandment, or any of the Decalogue, we are told that he then is not so far really a Christian, even though he be a clergyman. That way Christianity gets all the credit, and can not possibly have any of the blame.

That Berkeley anticipates our exasperation is evident perhaps from Crito's statement that closes off this part of the conversation. "It is certainly right to judge of principles from their effects; but then we must know them to be effects of those principles. It is the very method I have observed with respect to religion and the minute philosophy. And I can honestly aver that I never knew any man or family grow worse in proportion as they grew religious: but I have often observed that minute philosophy is the worst thing which can get into a family, the readiest way to impoverish, divide, and disgrace it."[42] But still, some of us are going to object that if Crito observes the family growing worse, he will take that as evidence that they have become irreligious, no matter what they might say. Someone else might object that all this begs the question about better and worse; and the free-thinker insists that there could hardly be anything better than being freed from religious domination. Moreover, a behavioristic minute philosophy might object that people's becoming better or worse has nothing whatever to do with principles, but instead is wholly determined by environment, by whether they are well-fed, well-housed, can walk the streets safely, etc.

Let Berkeley clear the air for himself by responding first to this last objection. As old as philosophy and science themselves is the notion that men do not really have free will. Since the rise of modern science, and the accompanying mechanistic or deterministic accounts of change in nature, the perennial problem of free will vs. determinism has become more urgent. There are a number of contemporary thinkers who argue that man is mechanical;[43] that because we are not real agents in the world we must get beyond the sentimental notions of freedom and dignity, and instead of trying to improve men, improve the environment.[44] Berkeley was well aware of the problem and the dispute. Nor did it escape his attention that most, if not all, minute philosophers fall victim to an amusing contradiction. Declaring independence from religion (I will not have my beliefs and behavior dictated to me by a priest!), the typical free-thinker welcomes the support of a scientific philosophy that holds that because all actions are causally determined, none is free; and that therefore no one is really responsible for his behavior, there are no good and evil actions, no merits or demerits, and hence, no basis for feelings of guilt. Wonderful freedom! I can do just as I please with no fear of a supernatural being punishing me for breaking laws that priests have invented to keep themselves in power over the likes of me. And best of all, I need no longer feel any shame or guilt for whatever I do.

It seems very odd for a puppet, as Berkeley describes the man freed from religion,[45] to thumb his nose at the guardians of a faith that aspires to perfect love and justice, all the time declaiming that he now is free. Without our settling the free will problem, we can at least agree that it is pointless, because contradictory, to argue that men should be free from religion and religious principles because man is not free, but instead determined. We can at least assume, without contradiction, that we are free. And having done that, we can sensibly talk about competing principles for human living. In other words, Berkeley does not mean by freedom of the will sheer spontaneity, or uncaused action; for that is as contradictory as our freely asserting that we are not free. What Berkeley means is that because we are rational agents we are responsible and accountable for our behavior; and hence we can and do live in accordance with some principles or other.

As soon as we juxtapose the principles of Christianity to those of minute philosophy, we find on the one hand a system aimed at promoting in us that which is most godlike, which broadcasts the love of God and brotherhood of man, and promises true joy and happiness to those who join in this pursuit of perfection. On the other hand we find in sophistic or cynical minute philosophy a system apparently aimed at promoting that in us which is animal-like, which finds nothing for us to aspire to but the gratification of appetites, impulses, and inclinations; or in humanistic free-thinking a system that appeals to moral and political order, that in us which is most human. In either case, we cannot argue that minute philosophy is useful to mankind and Christianity not.

All that can remain of this dispute, then, is a quarrel -- and it seems a perennial one -- about the role of institutions in human life. There is no denying, by Berkeley or any other knowledgeable apologist for Christianity, that horrible things have been done by institutionalized, established representatives of Christianity. Berkeley's rejoinder is that those horrible things seem part of the human condition, were done before Christianity, and would have been done without Christianity. The question then becomes what positively might be said for institutionalized Christianity.

To begin with what is so obvious that Berkeley thought, perhaps, that it need not be discussed, there is the fact for anyone who has found real significance in life in the Christian faith, that but for the institution he would not have had that. Without established creed, canon, and episcopate Christianity probably would have disappeared at least 1700 years ago. No matter how inspired or enthused (filled with God, i.e.) the founder of a religion may be, his inspiration and enthusiasm is in vain for other men if it be not solidified and stabilized into institutional form. As Henri Bergson puts it,[46] the divine brilliance that fires a few privileged souls also lightens, via the institution, the great hosts of men who are not so privileged.

Beyond this, Berkeley argues that institutionalized Christianity shares responsibility for the preservation of ancient learning through the dark ages; that it (and certainly not minute philosophy) is responsible for the renaissance of classical learning in Europe. England is indebted to Christianity not only for exalted notions of humanity and divinity, but also for the arts and sciences. In comparing his contemporary Britishers with the ancient Greeks and Romans, whom he much admired, Berkeley concludes that despite all the political and climatic advantages those peoples had, Britishers are better. Under the sway of the Christian religion a phlegmatic people has become noble; northern boors have become gentle and humane. In short, for all its faults, and some of them no doubt attributable to weakness and corruption within the established church, eighteenth century England is better than ancient Rome or Greece, and that because of Christianity.[47]

Then Berkeley asks us to ponder what will become of a people ruled by the principles of minute philosophy. What in the long run can we expect if we base our national hopes on material and luxurious self-gratification? or on the conviction that we live in a mindless universe? or even on the conviction that there is nothing higher than man? At the end of the dialogue Alciphron acknowledges that Christianity is perhaps useful, and maybe should be tolerated. But still, Alciphron wonders, is it true?

VIII   Christianity True

What can be meant by saying that Christianity is true or false? Christianity claims historical foundation in the persons of Jesus Christ, his disciples, and the early apostles. The historical documents are the Scriptures, which are supposedly a divine revelation. In the sixth dialogue Berkeley entertains and responds to the criticisms current in his time with respect to the claim of divine revelation, first as to the form, second the contents, and third the external evidences of the Scriptures.

The doubts expressed are of the sort with which perhaps we today are all familiar: the canon (declaration of what is, and what is not, to be included as part of the revelation) was long in dispute, and still is in differing parts of Christendom; the style is unbecoming a divine author; there are nonsensical passages and absurd doctrines; God is reported as commanding or doing evil things; the earth is older than Genesis implies; the miracles are impossible. Berkeley replies to them all evenly and patiently. It is clear from his response that his orthodoxy does not require him to accept every word in the Old and New Testaments as literally true, or even literally inspired by God.

It is also clear that he regards the Old and New Testaments

as revelatory of what it is most important for man to know about God and man's relationship to Him; and that God Himself has revealed this, as no mere human wisdom could. Hence, in the second place, and in the seventh dialogue, he offers a philosophical consideration of the truth of Christianity. Because the tendency among the minute philosophers of his time was to pit scientific reason against religion, Berkeley's strategy is to show that there is in fact no contest between science and religion. His basic argument is suggestive. If either science or the Christian faith is taken as purely revelatory of truth about the world, then each is full of mysteries: e.g., in science, the idea of force; in faith, the notion of divine grace. If instead each is taken as it ought to be, as having practical import, then science can be properly regarded as promoting happiness, and faith properly regarded as directly affecting conduct. Hence, while no claim is made that Christianity has been "scientifically" established as true, a defense of the faith as rationally respectable has been made.

IX Education

Why is it that Christianity is under such attack in Berkeley's time? He, like Christian philosophers before him, has tried to show that Christianity is neither contradicted by, nor repugnant to, reason; that, quite the contrary, the rational proof of Providence and the other considerations we have reviewed lead a right thinking man to serious religious concern. Berkeley concludes that it is not reason, or science, that is attacking Christianity, but rather the pretence of reason, minute philosophy. The cure for it, he believes, is classical education.

Apart from religious training, education for Berkeley is moral and political. In other words, the aim of education is to bring into being in the citizens of a polis the moral and political virtues of prudence, courage, temperance, and justice. His sources for this are of course the teaching of such ancients as Plato and Aristotle. Berkeley appears to have no illusions that such education has ever been remarkably successful; he does not look back to some golden age. But he does claim that the great philosophers of the past, like Plato and Aristotle, have tried to raise and refine mankind; and that such moral and political stability as has existed among us can be attributed to this sort of teaching.

We can begin to see what formal education would be, given this moral and political aim, by noting Berkeley's education. We know (see introductory chapter) that the undergraduate curriculum at Trinity College, Dublin, consisted of mathematics, languages, logic, and philosophy. His pre-college schooling was preparatory for all that. By the time he had achieved the Master of Arts degree, he had learned Latin and Greek, studied French (some of his letters are in French) and Hebrew, was conversant with great classical literature, and was schooled in the revolutionary thought of the seventeenth century, including Newtonian physics and the new scientific philosophy.

Such education is hardly commonplace today. And yet there are colleges in America which have the same orientation and aim, and at least approach the scope of curriculum. St. John's College, in Annapolis, Maryland, and Santa Fe, New Mexico, is perhaps the best known. There are no majors, no departments, no professors. The tutors and students alike are responsible for the whole curriculum. The teachers are the great authors in Western civilization, from the time of the ancient Greeks to the present day. There are classes in areas that are included in the standard offerings of a typical liberal arts college today: in foreign language, mathematics, science, the arts, the humanities, philosophy. But there is no artificial separation into specialized areas. Moreover, in studies that can be categorized as in this or that area of specialization, the greats are read: Euclid, Newton, Descartes, Plato and Aristotle, Machiavelli, et. al. A number of other colleges, most with a religious orientation, have formed, emulating this pattern: Thomas Aquinas College, near Ojai, California; Magdalen College, in Bedford, New Hampshire, for example. Moreover, despite the growth in our time of the public school system, there is an abundance of private schools, most of them parochial, with something of the aim to prepare students for the higher learning.

What all such schools, in Berkeley's time and ours, have in common is the awareness that, as Plato expressed it in The Republic, education for moral and political leadership requires a long course of arduous, disciplined study. What such educators hope to achieve is expressed by Ronald McArthur, President of Thomas Aquinas College, writing in the newsletter of the college on the occasion of the college's moving to a permanent site. It is a statement that would be endorsed by Berkeley.

> [The College's] continued existence means that some of our young will be able to study from the great original texts, and that they will have the chance to begin the most laboring pursuit towards wisdom, towards a wisdom without which they, and we with them, will surely lose our way.
>
> The modern world provides us with more and better means to achieve our purposes as we become less able to define them; and modern education would have us become more and more

barbarous with respect to the ends for which we were made.

Our refinements, then, if they are separated from the genuine life of the mind, become our downfall, and our only hope lies with the traditional education which has formed our civilization.

The "more and better means" of course come about through the technology stemming from the rise of modern science. It is that rise, perhaps more than anything else, which has complicated and confused education in Berkeley's time and ours. We take it for granted that education must include, if not training in science for everybody, then at least an awareness of what science is, and how our modern technological world depends on it for sustenance and growth. Berkeley was so far from being an obscurantist that he learned enough about the science of his day to write a learned essay, De Motu, still read and respected, on the subject of motion in Newtonian science. He was not an enemy of science, and as we will see in the sequel, hoped to direct science in accord with sound philosophy. Perhaps he was too optimistic.

Jonathan Swift, one of Berkeley's eminent contemporaries -- who was also a fellow Irishman, a fellow churchman, and a friend of Berkeley -- satirically comments on man's laying waste of nature by modern scientific technology.[48] On the one hand, because of tremendous improvements since Swift's time in agriculture, transportation, communication, industry, and especially in medicine and hygiene, we are inclined to think that he was sourly mistaken in his assessment of the new world coming into being. On the other hand, given the variety of ecological disasters which, if not altogether imminent, are all now real possibilities, and unthought of before Swift's time, we might be inclined to look upon Swift as a prophet. Be that as it may, there is an obvious difference between conquering nature and knowing what to do with her after she is conquered. Moreover, it seems just as obvious that the expertise a person has achieved in science or technology does not in itself make him a moral or political leader.

Where then do we turn for moral and political leadership and guidance, as over against scientific and technological expertise? The astute, serious, scientific free-thinker is well aware that whatever knowledge and know-how he achieves by scientific method is not a knowledge of what ought to be. Ought the United States to have used atomic bombs in World War II? Among the scientists who cooperatively, and in scientific and technological questions about production of the weapons, agreed, there is of course disagreement about the morality of the use of the weapons. Clearly, neither the science nor the technology can answer the "ought" question.

If scientific education cannot provide moral and political leadership, perhaps our present day social and behavioral studies can. In these relatively young sciences we have already made great discoveries and advances: in psychology, sociology, anthropology, politics, maybe even history. And is not the future in these sciences even brighter? Have we not here perhaps some bridge between objective scientific fact and subjective value judgements? Berkeley presaged, albeit sarcastically, behavioral science, which by implication is to replace the meditations of the stodgy pedants of the old way. "...we have among us some contemplative spirits of a coarser education, who, from observing the behavior and proceedings of apprentices, watermen, porters, and the assemblies of rabble in the streets, have arrived at a profound knowledge of human nature, and made great discoveries about the principles, springs, and motives of moral actions. These have demolished the received systems, and done a world of good in the city."[49] We cannot help wondering what Lysicles, the maker of this speech, would think of our cities after two hundred years of such behavioral studies.

Such a wondering is of course unfair, both because our modern cities are not the creatures of behavioral science, and because of the great care and regard for scientific method that characterizes the burgeoning social sciences. Nonetheless, it is clear why Berkeley included social science in his criticism of minute philosophy. For it is inevitable that to the extent that behavioral studies emulate and imitate the "hard" sciences, they eschew any and all consideration of what ought to be, in order to concentrate on fact. Indeed, to that extent they proclaim themselves to be value-free. Hence, to suppose that such studies have anything to do with moral education would be to confuse minute philosophy with classical philosophy.

The point might be clearer, put another way. Berkeley sees that education, willy-nilly, has a moral end. That is, values, "prejudices," beliefs, about what is good and true and beautiful will be put into the minds of young people. The only question is, under the aegis of which philosophy, classical or minute? Science, as we have seen, is dumb on the question. Indeed, the very uses to which science is put depend upon its being under the aegis of one or another philosophy.

Every college and university, if not every high school, has its department of philosophy. And if teaching of values does not belong in the science departments, then perhaps it falls to philosophers, following in the wake of Berkeley and the like, to teach morality and politics.

Some professional and academic philsophers do still try to teach or inculcate what the good life is, and how to go about reaching it by development of moral and political virtue. But on the academic scene two established trends work against that endeavor. On the one hand, outside philosophy departments "scientific" study of morals and politics thrives. The scientific study of politics is done in a department with the name, usually, of political science; in such departments, classical political philosophy does not thrive. And while there is no one department labeled moral science, still there is no widespread hesitancy on the part of social and behavioral scientists to pretend expertise in moral values, and even to teach "enlightenment" to provincial students, even though, on their own principles only facts, and not values, are accessible to their professed scientific studies.

On the other hand, within professional and academic philosophy the established twentieth century trend, at least in English speaking countries, is to what is called analytic philosophy. Followers of this trend have tried to carve out a respectable specialty for themselves, in this age of specialization. Because the sciences have laid claim to knowledge of reality, human and non-human, there seemed nothing left over for philosophers to do. Thus, the analytic philosophers, instead of claiming to study (some part of) reality, now specialize in the logic and language of the varied inquiries into reality, including moral, political, and religious reality. "Philosophy" then is a misnomer, for as so practiced it is no longer a love of wisdom, or pursuit of wisdom; instead, it is but one specialty among others.

In our educational scheme today there is yet another area that thrives: the arts and humanities. It is here, it seems, that the student is encouraged to think about, discover, and appropriate aesthetic, moral, political, and religious values. Berkeley seemed to anticipate the humanities, understood as being cut off from a world of scientific fact. In _Alciphron_, Lysicles caricatures the capped and gowned academicians of the eighteenth century, pouring over dead authors who wrote in dead languages, cut off from the real world; and recommends the new philosophers, "...the best bred men of the age, men who know the world, men of pleasure, men of fashion, and fine gentlemen,"[50] who have no method but free and easy conversation. Alciphron, in his turn, caricatures the stuffy bookworms who meditate on "...obsolete notions, that are now quite exploded and out of use."[51]

The teachers and students of this new way of education are not found in the academies and universities, but instead "...in a drawing-room, a coffee-house, a chocolate-house, at the tavern, or groom-porter's. In these and the like fashionable places of resort, it is the custom for polite persons to speak freely on all subjects, religious, moral, or political; so that a young gentleman who frequents them is in the way of hearing many instructive lectures, seasoned with wit and raillery, and uttered with spirit. Three or four sentences from a man of quality, spoke with a good air, make more impression and convey more knowledge than a dozen dissertations in a dry academical way."[52] It cannot be scientific educators Berkeley has in mind when Alciphron adds that "...our chief strength and flower of the flock are those promising young men who have the advantage of a modern education. These are the growing hopes of our sect, by whose credit and influence in a few years we expect to see those great things accomplished that we have in view."[53] One noteworthy accomplishment of the minute philosophers in our time is moving from the coffee-houses and taverns into the academies and universities. Some might judge, Berkeley among them, I believe, that they pretty much have taken over; if classical education has not disappeared from the American educational scene, it seems to be fighting a rearguard battle.

Instead of a long, arduous course of methodical, disciplined, academic, and classical study, with its ultimate aim of moral and political insight and leadership, we now have either scientific training and/or "speaking freely" on all controversial subjects, like art, religion, morals, and politics. To be sure, scientific training is exact, methodic, disciplined, and often requiring long hard years of tedious study. However, its aim is the production of specialized experts, and thereby the advancement of scientific knowledge. It is in the arena of the humanities that the free-thinkers seem most clearly to have taken over. From grade school through college students are taught, not to ignore values, but instead to create their own systems of values. There certainly is authority in the realm of scientific fact; but with respect to values there is no science, no course of study and no method that will yield expertise. All that can be or is offered, it seems, is free and easy conversation; in short, one virtually endless bull session that the really serious and bright student quickly wearies of.

It seems far-fetched to attribute to Berkeley these petulant thoughts about present day education in the humanities. True, there is no firm authority, as there is in science; but far from encouraging free and easy conversation, today's practitioners in the arts and in the humanities -- in literature, history, and philosophy (so far as it is not a logico-linguistic discipline) -- do have artistic and scholarly standards that each generation passes to the next. And within this arena Berkeley's classical moral philosophy is not shut out, but is free to compete in the market place of ideas, along with other ideologies. Surely it is not moral to expose students to only one ideology, or to indoctrinate them in Plato, Aristotle, Christianity, or whatever.

68

A response to this in the spirit of Berkeley's classical education is bound to seem unacceptable to most of us, so imbued are we with free-thinking's ideal of moral liberty, extending that to include the students' right to freely choose their courses of studies, and the teachers' right to freely choose what will be read. Nonetheless, most of us having studied in the arts and humanities might acknowledge that there is little common ground for our conversation. Hardly any of us is required to read Plato, the Bible, Marx, or Shakespeare. Thus, when for example in the American Novel course we read a work on the theme of sexual permissiveness, we are more apt to react and converse with ideas taken from the faddish beliefs of our peers than with reasoned and reflective perspectives. Berkeley's point is not that Plato, for example, must be taken as authoritative, but instead that, as Ronald McArthur put it, "our refinements, if separated from the genuine life of the mind, become our downfall." If our conversation is not fed by the great thinkers in our civilization, it will not be truly thoughtful, but will be free and easy. And as we have seen Berkeley arguing, that tends to encourage in us iconoclasm or cynicism. Philosophy, understood as pursuit of wisdom, aims to lead us between the extremes of cynicism and fanaticism. If Berkeley's moral and political philosophy, instead, is taken as just one more ideology in competition with others, -- well, we have already reviewed his arguments for the classical perspective.

Nevertheless, there is no doubt that Berkeley would be grateful, as is any living advocate for Berkeley's moral position, that in our part of the world at least, the classical view is indeed free to compete with others for the students' minds. Berkeley, as we have noted, was sensitive to the issue of the limits of free speech. But again, he would emphasize that freedom is a means to, indeed a blessed means, but not the end of, the good life for man.

There is yet one more area in present day education that thrives more than all the rest. No one can be against professional and vocational training; but its prominence in the public schools and in most colleges and universities is a result of two factors. The first is that we have undertaken to educate everybody. Because there are very few idle rich, and most of us must work for a living, it is not surprising that most of us have come to regard education as most importantly training for a career. The second factor is that because we have lost the classical vision of education as moral and political growth, we tend to look upon the traditional education in the arts and sciences for those who will practice neither as a desirable but really unnecessary broadening of the mind. Given the great numbers now attending our colleges and universities, it could not be otherwise.

Given all this, who is it that guides our education? There can be little doubt that Berkeley's judgment would be that it is the minute philosophers. The potentially disastrous effects that Berkeley foresaw may be indicated by the following excerpt from an article by a contemporary minute philosopher.

Ever since the invention of the printing press, books have been published telling men and women how bad they are, giving advice on how to be a better person, and generally offering an alternative system or "way" which promises salvation or at least more friends and more influence over people. The Bible, of course, is the most obvious example of such a book. It fills us with lofty aspirations for personal salvation by loving more, stealing less, and avoiding the mere thought of fornicating with our neighbor's spouse.

More recently, however, beginning perhaps with Normal Vincent Peale's How to Win Friends and Influence People [sic] , there has been an avalanche of such books. Most of the recent books have come from one or more of the psychological fads that have been sweeping our country like hula hoops during the past ten years.

The article presents a list of such fads; and goes on to describe how each has its day, only to be replaced by another, with no apparent end in sight. The author laments that although none of these systems has worked, we continue to be suckers for them; and instead of achieving perfection or even improvement of personality, we add to our feelings of guilt and frustration. The author's proposed solution:

Somehow we must put an end to all this nonsense and come to appreciate our slob-selves for what we are. Because, like it or not, the chances are excellent that we will be basically the same slobs next year that we are today. So, ...what is needed is an attempt to develop a psychological system of slobism. Not a system offering personal salvation, or even a few handy guides to living; not a system of moral platitudes or rules to follow; but a system which simply describes and honors the human animal, that offers a modest amount of pride and self-respect to the individual as who he or she is, rather than what they can become,

70

that heretically suggests that <u>because</u> <u>of</u> our weaknesses, our foibles, our self-destructive, non-creative, stupid behavior we are still reasonably worthwhile people. In short, let us dump that salvation guilt and spend next Sunday afternoon in front of the boob-tube drinking beer, eating cold pizza and stale popcorn, watching Cartoon Carnival.[54]

Although Berkeley once wrote an essay in praise of public schools and universities,[55] he was not unaware of what happens to some men when they "come to riper years." "The grateful employment of admiring and raising themselves to an imitation of the polite stile, ... and noble sentiments of ancient authors, is abandoned for law-Latin, the lucubrations of our paltry newsmongers, and that swarm of vile pamphlets which corrupt our taste, and infest the publick. The ideas of virtue which the characters of heroes had imprinted on their minds insensibly wear out, and they come to be influenced by the nearer examples of a degenerate age."[56]

Vile pamphlets, then, existed in Berkeley's day; and presumably emanated from the coffee-houses or the taverns. The one quoted above comes from within the academy. Of course such discourse is not typical among today's academicians, and this piece might even be taken as an aberration. Still, that it should be authored, as in fact it was, by a dean of a college, is surprising and disturbing enough; but that after publication in the college newspaper of such a treatise he remained so, is enough to make us sensitive to what Berkeley feared. He predicted that "it is more than probable that, in case our Free-thinkers could once achieve their glorious design of sinking the credit of the Christian religion,...we who want that spirit and curiosity which distinguished the ancient Grecians would by degrees relapse into the same state of barbarism which overspread the northern nations before they were enlightened by Christianity."[57]

X   Religious vs. Classical Education

Early in Chapter 2, in the discussion of equality, we noted that Berkeley believed that very few men are endowed with the capacity to philosophize profoundly. In other words, very few can follow the long, arduous course of disciplined study. This seems inconsistent with his reliance on classical, and his criticism of modern, education.

The resolution depends on distinguishing moral, political, and religious leaders from the followers. Plato's program of education for a good polis, in <u>The</u> <u>Republic</u>, is two-fold. First, all citizens in the polis should receive an elementary education,

beginning in childhood and continuing to about age eighteen.
Beyond this, the prospective leaders continue a longer, harder
way, alternating cloistered study with apprentice work until about
age fifty, at which time the very best would take their turn at
ruling.

The aim of all education for Plato is to make it possible for
men to become as god-like as is humanly possible, or to acquire
the cardinal moral virtues of prudence, courage, temperance, and
justice. To that end Plato proposes that children should be
taught first what the gods are like: divinity is all-good,
responsible for all the good in the world, and none of the evil;
unchanging; dependable, not whimsical or capricious. Then
children should be presented with stories whose heroes exemplify
these god-like virtues. Plato implies that as the children grow
to maturity, what they had learned about divinity and heroes would
be amplified and sophisticated. Moreover, maturity for Plato
means that the most god-like part of the soul, reason, has gained
control over and directs the spirited and appetitive parts. The
crux of the elementary education is providing ways of developing
the intellectual virtues (the three R's, we call them) and the
moral habits of prudence, courage, temperance, and justice. True
freedom comes for the individual when he is no longer pulled by
impulse, inclination, and passion; but instead when sound reason
directs the person to the proper pleasures, to the most human way
of satisfying the appetites and desires.

With all this Berkeley agreed, but emphasized more strongly
perhaps than Plato the role of religious education. More
specifically, Berkeley believed that all citizens should learn of
the Christian God, as Creator, Covenanter, Redeemer, and
Paraclete; and should develop the Christian habits (virtues) of
faith, hope, and love. Just as Plato contended that his
elementary education is necessary for moral and political
stability, so Berkeley argued, as we have seen, that religion is
the main stay of the body politic.

But just as Plato believed that moral and political
leadership required a longer, harder way, so did Berkeley; and
that longer, harder way for Berkeley, as for Plato, is for a very
few. While for Berkeley leadership depends on a classical as well
as a religious education, it is the latter which will provide the
morale, the ethos, for the polis at large. Hence, the apparent
inconsistency is removed. Moreover, Plato and Berkeley seem to
present what is basically indisputable. For in every polis there
is leadership; and the morale of the polis in the long run is very
largely determined by the ideals and practices of the leadership.

Let Berkeley speak for himself. The second of these
quotations is the final passage in Alciphron.

72

The profound thinkers of [the free-thinking way] have taken a direct contrary course to all the philosophers of former ages, who made it their endeavour to raise and refine human-kind, and remove it as far as possible from the brute; to moderate and subdue men's appetites; to remind them of the dignity of their nature; to awaken and improve their superior faculties, and direct them to the noblest objects; to possess men's minds with a high sense of the Divinity, of the Supreme Good, and the immortality of the soul. They took great pains to strengthen the obligations to virtue; and upon all those subjects have wrought out noble theories, and treated with singular force of reason. But it seems our minute philosophers act the reverse of all other wise and thinking men; it being their end and aim to erase the principles of all that is great and good from the mind of man, to unhinge all order of civil life, to undermine the foundations of morality, and, instead of improving and ennobling our natures, to bring us down to the maxims and way of thinking of the most uneducated and barbarous nations, and even to degrade human-kind to a level with the brute beasts. And all the while they would pass upon the world for men of deep knowledge. But, in effect, what is all this negative knowledge better than downright savage ignorance? That there is no Providence, no spirit, no future state, no moral duty: truly a fine system for an honest man to own, or an ingenious man to value himself upon![58]

In good earnest, I imagine that thinking is the great desideratum of the present age; and that the real cause of whatever is amiss may justly be reckoned the general neglect of education in those who need it most -- the people of fashion. What can be expected where those who have the most influence have the least sense, and those who are sure to be followed set the worst example? where youth so uneducated are yet so forward? where modesty is esteemed pusillanimity, and a deference to years, knowledge, religion, laws, want of sense and spirit? Such untimely growth of genius would not have been valued or encouraged by the wise men of antiquity, whose sentiments on this

73

point are so ill suited to the genius of our
times that it is to be feared modern ears could
not bear them. But, however ridiculous such
maxims might seem to our ... youth, who are so
capable and so forward to try experiments, and
mend the constitution of their country, I
believe it will be admitted by men of sense
that, if the governing part of mankind would in
these days, for experiment's sake, consider
themselves in that old Homerical light as
pastors of the people, whose duty it was to
improve their flock, they would soon find that
this is to be done by an education very
different from the modern, and otherguess
maxims than those of the minute philosophy. If
our youth were really inured to thought and
reflexion, and an acquaintance with the
excellent writers of antiquity, we should see
that licentious humour, vulgarly called free-
thinking, banished from the presence of
gentlemen, together with ignorance and ill
taste; which as they are inseparable from vice,
so men follow vice for the sake of pleasure,
and fly from virtue through an abhorrence of
pain. Their minds, therefore, betimes should
be formed and accustomed to receive pleasure
and pain from proper objects, or, which is the
same thing, to have their inclinations and
aversions rightly placed.... This, according to
Plato and Aristotle, was the... right
education. And those who, in their own minds,
their health, or their fortunes, feel the
cursed effects of a wrong one, would do well to
consider they cannot better make amends for
what was amiss in themselves than by preventing
the same in their posterity.[59]

Berkeley's teaching on morals, politics, education, and the
necessity of religion for a healthy body politic was inspired by
classical philosophers. Socrates, Plato, and Aristotle not only
fought the minute philosophy of their time, but also developed
theories of reality and knowledge to oppose materialism, and to
provide metaphysical support for the moral philosophy of virtue.
Berkeley believed that materialism is at the root of any version
of minute philosophy, and hence is pernicious as well as being
false. Hence, like his classical predecessors, he undertook both
to destroy materialism and to provide a metaphysical foundation
for classical moral and political thought. It is to that work,
for which Berkeley has become famous, that we now turn our
attention. There we will find the modern, rather than the

74

classical, Berkeley.

PART II

Berkeley, the Modern Philosopher

Chapter 4

Scientific Philosophy

Understanding of Berkeley's metaphysics depends upon appreciating why Berkeley did not oppose science but did oppose scientific philosophy. Our word "science" is derived from the Latin "scientia," which is the equivalent of the Greek "episteme." For Greeks like Plato and Aristotle episteme was the best, the most certain, the most genuine knowledge. Philosophy, understood as love for and pursuit of wisdom, strove for episteme, whether in coming to know the natures and causes of things or in learning to live a good and happy life. However, in our time science has come to have a somewhat different meaning. For us it clearly denotes such disciplines as physics and chemistry, but not such as ethics and politics, let alone art and religion. Its meaning for our purposes can be expressed as follows: a systematic study of nature, insofar as it can be quantified, aiming at complete explanation of natural phenomena.

"Metaphysics" we will take to mean "theory of reality." If we hold that nothing exists but what can be sensed, that is a metaphysics; if we theorize that in addition to what can be sensed there is an intangible, but intelligible reality, that too is a metaphysics. Berkeley believed that one or another metaphysics underlies the moral theory and practice of individuals and political communities, and hence took metaphysics to be of crucial importance. Some philosophers, however, have been and are wary of theorizing about reality, and urge moral and political theorizing independent of metaphysics.

We have seen Berkeley's devotion to classical philosophy, understood as pursuit of wisdom, and read what, following Socrates, Berkeley takes to be the true business of a philosopher. At the same time, we have studied Berkeley's opposition to minute philosophy, which could hardly be described by him as a pursuit of wisdom; or if so, as a misguided pursuit. "Philosophy" is used by Berkeley, and by us, to denote ways of living. In what follows perhaps we can take "philosophy" to mean a complete account of reality; a metaphysics (or the eschewing of metaphysics), along with all that follows from it with respect to the nature of man, and hence including morals, politics, religion, art, and education. For example, if in metaphysics we claim that nothing exists but particles of matter moved by forces or laws over which human beings have no control, then we must conclude that man, too, is nothing but matter in motion, and that purposive or goal-directed behavior by man is illusory, not really real.

With these meanings in mind, the difference between science and philosophy can be indicated by the following. When we learn in a chemistry class about reactions of various elements and compounds, we take that, properly, as part of the science of chemistry. If we "learn" in the same class that our being in love is nothing but chemical reactions in the body, we can properly suspect that that is not part of the science of chemistry, but of a philosophy. In a handbook for physical science, prepared by a college instructor, there is a listing of various academic disciplines, according to relative abstractness or concreteness. Such a list is the work of a philosophy; no physical science studies other disciplines to discover their relative abstractness. If a sociologist tells us that because different societies have different customs, there are no natural moral laws, we know that he is philosophizing, and not presenting scientifically established fact. His reporting of the variety of customs, albeit trivial, may be regarded as scientific, but his conclusion rests upon a metaphysics, not upon scientific investigation.

"Scientific philosophy" can be said to be the theory that science is the only genuine study of the world; that other efforts (via the arts and humanities, for example) are pretenses. The way the world shapes up, then, for scientific philosophy depends on the state of science at different periods. Berkeley's opposition was to the predominant scientific philosophy of his time.

I   Berkeley's Opposition to Scientific Philosophy

That Berkeley was not opposed to science is evident from what he wrote in optics, issuing in a significant theory of vision;[1] in mathematics, where he suggested improvements in the calculus;[2] in the theory of motion, commenting helpfully on Newton's theory.[3] However, he was opposed to the predominant scientific philosophy of his time because it was unbelievable, and because it was materialistic, and hence, in his view, pernicious. He was also convinced that it was false, because it was materialistic. His showing of its falsity is reserved for Chapter 5.

He thought it unbelievable because seventeenth and eighteenth century scientific philosophy declared that the world is not really what it appears to be. To receive the full force of this, and to begin to sympathize with Berkeley, we must ask ourselves what the world does appear to be. The opening paragraph of Berkeley's introduction to his first major metaphysical work, where he delivers his first jab to scientific philosophy, provides an excellent starting point:

> Philosophy being nothing else but the study of wisdom and truth, it may with reason be expected, that those who have spent most time and pains in it should enjoy a greater calm and

serenity of mind, a greater clearness and evidence of knowledge, and be less disturbed with doubts and difficulties than other men. Yet so it is we see the illiterate bulk of mankind that walk the high-road of plain, common sense, and are governed by the dictates of Nature, for the most part easy and undisturbed. To them nothing that's familiar appears unaccountable or difficult to comprehend. They complain not of any want of evidence in their senses, and are out of all danger of becoming <u>sceptics</u>. But no sooner do we depart from sense and instinct to follow the light of a superior principle, to reason, meditate, and reflect on the nature of things, but a thousand scruples spring up in our minds, concerning those things which before we seemed fully to comprehend. Prejudices and errors of sense do from all parts discover themselves to our view; and endeavouring to correct these by reason we are insensibly drawn into uncouth paradoxes, difficulties, and inconsistencies, which multiply and grow upon us as we advance in speculation; till at length, having wander'd through many intricate mazes, we find our selves just where we were, or, which is worse, sit down in a forlorn scepticism.[4]

Assuming that we, even though literate, walk the "high-road of plain common sense," and that each of us is "out of all danger of becoming a sceptic," then how does the world appear to us? To put it in the simplest terms, we would say that our ordinary, everyday world appears to be made up of people, plants, animals, the sun, the planets, etc. These things, moreover, have a variety of attributes, or traits, or properties; that is, each has qualities, such as color, odor, and size, and each exists in a certain place and at a certain time. As I look out my window now it appears that there is a tree, a building, a flagpole, a flag; and that the leaves of the tree are green, the building is located behind the tree, the flagpole is very tall and slender, the flag is red, white, blue, and waving.

If the scientific philosophy of Berkeley's time is right, most of that is mere appearance. What really is the case, we are told, is that generally "out there" there is only matter in motion. Specifically, there is no real difference between the tree (a supposed living thing) and the building, but only different arrangements of material particles. Moreover, the colors we see and the sounds we hear, are not really there. All such experience is the result of matter in motion, light waves affecting the eye, sound waves the ear. There is of course matter out there; and the sensory receptacles are also material. But that is it; there are no <u>real</u> differences among things, and no colors, sounds, or odors.

It may be true; but at first glance, it is incredible. We will explore this more later, but for now it is enough to notice that Berkeley also found it incredible, and held out for common sense against it.

Second, Berkeley objected to scientific philosophy because it is materialistic. "Materialism" perhaps needs defining. In metaphysics, it is the theory that the only reality is matter; and that thought, will, feeling as well as all variety of change, is to be explained solely in terms of matter in motion. In the practical, moral version of materialism, such intangible ideals as honor, justice and love become problematic. It is not surprising, then, that Berkeley is opposed to materialism. But is it really true that scientific philosophy is, or needs to be, materialistic? After all, most of the great contributors to the new physics -- Copernicus, Kepler, Galileo, and even Newton himself -- believed that there is a God. None of them is noted for immorality; some of them were deeply religious. But perhaps that is because, although they were great scientists, they were not scientific philosophers. And even among the philosophers, not all were materialists. If Thomas Hobbes was, Rene Descartes not. At least, so it appears.

II Descartes' Metaphysics

Rene Descartes (1596-1650) plays a crucial role in any account of Berkeley. He can be taken as an enlightened representative of scientific free-thinking, and as the first great modern philosopher. While Berkeley rejected Descartes' proposed philosophical method, he nonetheless accepted significant parts of his metaphysics and his theory of knowledge.

The new science culminated toward the end of the seventeenth century in the magnificent system of Sir Isaac Newton, a system that seems to show that the physical, material world is a kind of mechanism, the behavior of which can be fully understood in accordance with a few simple laws of motion. While Descartes did not live to see this culmination, and while the detail of his own theory to explain the material world turned out to be mistaken, still he was convinced early in the century, in the light of work done up to that time in what we now know as physics, that the material world is a set of extended particles moving in accord with mechanical laws. His significance does not lie in that conviction, but rather in his clear awareness of the problem that mechanism posed for anyone who takes seriously the dignity of man.

82

The problem is simply put: if the world is a mechanism, if all changes in the world are to be explained in accordance with mechanical laws, then all events in the world are determined by causes and/or laws that are impervious or blind to what we take to be our wills, our aspirations, our plans, our activity. In short, if mechanism is true, then there is no such thing as free will; and if there is no free will, then man is a being of no greater worth or dignity than a rock or an earthworm. To be sure, this view of the world and of man had been advanced many centuries before the time of Descartes and Berkeley, and had had its defenders from the ancients to modern times. But since the seventeenth century it has assumed great urgency because of the rise of modern science. Indeed, because of the awe with which most of us behold "science," there is a great temptation to simply surrender to this mechanism and grant that all we have been taught to the contrary by philosophy, religion, and common sense is mistaken. Why not admit that each one of us is a complicated mechanism determined in behavior by a host of causes and laws biological, psychological, social, cultural -- all of which may reduce to the physical; and that our freedom is thus an illusion? Part of the great appeal of this mechanical world view is its simplicity; for if it is true, then there is only one kind of reality -- matter; one kind of motion -- locomotion of bits of matter; and only one science -- mathematical physics.

Descartes both yielded and did not yield to the temptation; he was attracted and repelled by the simplicity of mechanism. Mechanism, he argued, is true of the material world, where all changes, all events, are determined, and there is no freedom. However, there is another reality besides matter, to deny which is to deny part of human experience; namely, our day to day, moment to moment experience of our own causal efficacy, our own power, our own free will. He called this other reality mind, and defined it by differentiating it from material reality. Whatever we can say of matter we cannot say of mind, and vice versa. Mental reality, mind, escapes determinism, is not subject to mechanical laws, is free to initiate changes. Hence, each one of us is two beings in one -- a mind in a machine, with the mind in some measure directing the machine. Descartes espoused and defended this dualism, so it seems, because he was not willing to surrender man to mechanism, and because it seemed to him incontrovertible that the material world is a mechanism.

Descartes' presentation of this metaphysics is both fascinating and intriguing. Fascinating, because he first tears down in order to build. Discouraged by lack of growth in philosophical knowledge, Descartes decided on mathematics as a paradigm for coming to know. Given a starting point, by way of definitions and axioms in a geometry, for example, the mind can work its way through a system of theorems, building deductively on the starting point(s) and each theorem proved. To transform this into a universal or philosophical method of knowing, all we need do is discover the absolute presuppositions of our thinking. We can do it by doubting or calling into question everything possible that heretofore has been taken as knowledge, either by way of ordinary experience or tradition, or custom, or whatever. If then there is something we cannot doubt, we have arrived at the starting point for each one of us; and can proceed to build knowledge following the mathematical model.

Descartes performs the task for us, asking only that we follow along. We can doubt away the whole material world. Descartes reminds us that our senses sometimes fool us; what we took to be a hard object turns out to be soft; what looked at a distance to be round appears on closer inspection to be square. But if the senses sometimes fool us, perhaps they always fool us. At least, we can suppose not only that things are not what they appear to be, but also doubt whether there are any things out there at all. We cannot doubt, however, that we have ideas -- of soft, square, red, etc. What we are left with, at the extreme of our doubting, is the doubter with his ideas. Since we have doubted away the material world, the doubter must be mind.

Intriguing! For consider the impact of that conclusion in an intellectual world marvelling at new explanations of nature. All attention, it seems, is focused on matter and the laws governing its behavior; as for mind, perhaps it does not even exist. And so at least Hobbes had already concluded. Now suddenly Descartes proves that the reality we cannot possibly doubt away is mind, and perhaps it is matter that does not exist. At least, its existence will have to be proved.

Descartes found himself, in the Meditations, equal to that task. He points out, however, that the demonstration rests on our first proving the existence of a providential God. Nor was he unequal to that task; he provides more than one argument, each one following from his new found method.

So far, surely, a Christian philosopher like Berkeley could not be worried about this new philosophy, even though it be dubbed "scientific." If there be any uneasiness, it might appear when Descartes describes material objects, immediately after he has proved their existence. "Nevertheless, they [the material objects] are not perhaps entirely what our senses perceive them to be, for there are many ways in which this sense perception is very obscure and confused; but we must at least admit that everything which I conceive clearly and distinctly as occurring in them -- that is to say, everything, generally speaking, which is discussed in pure mathematics or geometry -- does occur in them."[5] To simplify the language slightly, the only features we can be sure of about material objects are those we can study and verify quantitatively. Thus, although Descartes gives us back the corporeal world, it is one we no longer recognize, since it has been stripped of most of its ordinary sensible qualities -- sound, color, odor, texture, taste. Indeed, so far as nature goes, Descartes has concluded a materialism; and thus one possible objection to his metaphysics is that it destroys our common sense understanding of the world.

Such an objection is hardly conclusive. But there is another one which, in the eyes of most of Descartes' philosophical successors, is decisive. Grant that the two kinds of reality -- mind and body -- are postulated so as to do justice to man's moral experience and man's scientific experience. In solving that problem the theory creates a greater one: the supposed interaction between mind and body. The insistence that these two kinds of reality are utterly distinct, having no characteristics in common, is made to guarantee on the one hand that as bodies we are indeed part of this mechanical world, and on the other hand that as minds we are free from the mechanical determinism, and able to act. But what a divorce! What Descartes has rendered asunder, let no man put together again. When we conclude that mind and body are utterly distinct, there is no way that we can explain or understand how either one can affect the other.

One story of modern philosophy is that of the ingenious speculative attempts of Descartes' successors to resolve the insoluble problem of interaction. The obvious "solution" is to avoid the problem by denying one or the other of the two kinds of reality. Should we affirm that only mind is really real, we would be theorizing what in English has come to be called idealism. If our sympathies lie that way we are so far following Berkeley. If we affirm that only matter is really real, then we are taking the path of most modern philosophy, a path that curiously enough is marked out clearly by none other than Descartes himself.

III   Descartes' Method

The _Meditations_ gives a picture of Descartes as the first great modern philosopher, and the one who set the stage for much of philosophy from then to the present day. The _Discourse on the Method of Rightly Conducting the Reason and Seeking Truth in the Field of Science_ (_Discourse on Method_, for short) reveals him as an enlightened representative of scientific free-thinking.

As prelude to this, and for the sake of intensifying the shock of the _Discourse_, it is important to note still a bit more about Descartes' metaphysics, as presented in the _Meditations_ and other works. Not only is there a God, Descartes tells us, but also God is infinite mind so providential that no particle of matter can move without His causal power. In other words, the material, natural world owes not only its origin, but also its preservation from one moment to the next, to God. Moreover, each finite human mind is a special creation of God, and being incorruptible, unlike bodies, is destined for immortality; its destruction could only come about through God's willing and effecting it.

Given all this we would expect Descartes to concentrate on the mental, the moral, the religious; on what is at stake for us as special creations of God, destined for immortality. We would not be surprised to find him interpreting and explaining this temporary bodily existence of ours by reference constantly to the spiritual, the divine, the hereafter. The mind after all is destined for immortality; the body will soon dissipate and return to dust. However, in the Discourse we find Descartes leaving religious and moral matters to revealed theology, thereby declaring his philosophical independence from religion. Moreover, he rejects rather scornfully the classical philosophy and education which intend to promote that in us which is most godlike. In their place he puts what we today know as science.

In Part One of the Discourse, Descartes tells us he had gone to one of the most celebrated schools in Europe, but did not find wisdom, either among his professors or the great authors. With subtle sarcasm he goes on to assure us that such classical education need not be wasted. At the worst, it will make us dilettantes; at the best, it will inoculate us against its pretensions.[6]

He saves his most biting remarks for the studies he had pursued in morals, theology, and philosophy. The ethical writings of the ancient pagans, for all their magnificence, are built on sand; revealed theology, he learned, is beyond the weakness of his reasoning, and discloses the way to heaven as easily to the most ignorant as to the most learned; philosophy, having been studied for many centuries by the greatest minds, has produced nothing but disputatious doubt and uncertainty; and since all other branches of learning depend on philosophy, nothing solid can be found in them. That is why, he tells us, "I gave up my studies entirely as soon as...I was no longer under the control of my teachers."[7]

In Part Six of the Discourse we come to the new scientific philosophy. In case we have forgotten his disparagement of the traditional way, Descartes prefaces his account of the new physics with the assertion that in speculative questions and morals he pretends no authority. He feels obliged, however, out of concern for the general good of mankind, to disclose the notions and principles of the new physics which gives promise of making us masters and possessors of nature. He foresees the technology that will be useful in agriculture, industry, and in the conservation of health, "the principal good and the basis of all other goods in this life. For the mind is so dependent on the humors and the conditions of the organs of the body that if it is possible to find some way to make men in general wiser and more clever than they have been so far,...it is in medicine that it should be sought."[8]

That Descartes should foresee so clearly modern science and technology is testimony to his genius. But it is surprising that despite all his reassurances about God, and the soul's immortality, he foresees the only possibility of men's becoming wiser to be in medicine. Indeed, from the sentences immediately following, one might get the impression that the only "immortality" Descartes was really concerned with was whatever longevity of healthy life an improving science of medicine might bring about.[9] There is no appeal here for instruction in morals and religion; no encomium on the virtue of piety. Instead, we are told that if we have our health, we have just about everything. The way to heaven is prescribed by the theologians; but the way to a good, and maybe even wise life here and now will be prescribed by the science of medicine, developing under the aegis of the new scientific philosophy.

A bit further on Descartes expresses the spirit of modern scientific research. Having discovered the general principles and first causes of all that exists in the world, for which Descartes is indebted to "certain indications of the truth...in our own minds," he deduces from them the commonest effects. So far we have the picture of nature moving mechanically under the power and laws of God. It is when we descend to particulars that induction and experimentation are necessary.

It thus appeared impossible to proceed further deductively, and if we were to understand and make use of things, we would have to discover causes by their effects, and make use of many experiments. In consequence, reviewing in my mind all the objects which had ever been presented to my senses, I believe I can say that I have never noticed anything which I could not explain easily enough by the principles I had found. But I must also admit that the powers of nature are so ample and vast, and that these principles are so simple and so general, that I hardly ever observed a particular effect without immediately recognizing several ways in which it could be deduced. My greatest difficulty usually is to find which of these is the true explanation,

and to do this I know no other way than to seek
several experiments such that their outcomes
would be different according to the choice of
hypothesis.[10]

It appears that for Descartes this is _the_ method; knowledge
pursued in any other way must be suspect. Moreover, Descartes'
idealism seems to have disappeared; despite his talk about God and
finite minds being the only powers and causes in reality, when he
gets down to the particulars in the material world, the ample and
vast powers of nature are admitted, and the discovery of causes
through experimentation is urged.

Here indeed is a testament for scientific free-thinking. A
little more than one hundred years after publication of the
Discourse on Method (1637), Berkeley lamented the influence of
this "corpuscularian and mechanical philosophy." Such a study, he
says,

> ...might usefully enough have employed some
> share of the leisure and curiosity of
> inquisitive persons. But when it entered the
> seminaries of learning as a necessary
> accomplishment, and most important part of
> education, by engrossing men's thoughts, and
> fixing their minds so much on corporeal objects
> and the laws of motion, it hath, however
> undesignedly, indirectly and by accident, yet
> not a little indisposed them for spiritual,
> moral, and intellectual matters. Certainly had
> the philosophy of Socrates and Pythagoras
> prevailed in this age among those who think
> themselves too wise to receive the dictates of
> the Gospel, we should not have seen interest
> take so general and fast hold on the minds of
> men, nor public spirit reputed to be...a
> generous folly, among those who are reckoned to
> be the most knowing as well as the most getting
> part of mankind.[11]

IV   The Ultimate Solution

It is ironic that Berkeley gives no indication of
understanding Descartes to be representative of scientific free-
thinking, and as responsible as anyone for the educational ethos
that in Berkeley's time was coming into being; even though there
is some evidence (albeit inconclusive) that he did read the
Discourse. But there is no doubt that he read the Meditations,
and was profoundly influenced by it.[12] In fact, he took the
idealism much more seriously than Descartes appears to have

done. How then undo that "general passion for the corpuscularian and mechanical philosophy"?

One possible way to counter the growth of materialism is to show that "matter" has been misunderstood. Perhaps the natural world is not to be identified with matter, pure and simple. This is the way that Aristotle took in the fourth century, B.C., in answering the materialists of his day. But despite Berkeley's evident devotion to Aristotle, among other ancient writers, it is a way that Berkeley either overlooked or rejected. Instead, he resolved to try the ultimate solution: to destroy matter; i.e., to prove that it does not exist. More precisely, he convinced himself, and tried to convince others, that what the philosophers call matter (stuff that occupies space and moves in accordance with mechanical law) does not exist; and that what the plain man calls bodies are totally dependent upon mind for their existence.

V The Theory of Representative Perception

Berkeley's refutation of the philosophers' matter also relied upon the theory of knowledge he inherited from Descartes and Locke. Descartes' version of that theory will be clearer if we emphasize how far removed Descartes' metaphysics is from that of Berkeley's plain man. Descartes radically differentiates man from the rest of nature. Classical philosophy by contrast defines man as the rational animal; a species that has in common with other animals powers of sensation, feeling, and locomotion, but different in that in this species there is also a power to know what and why things are. Nor, presumably, would the plain man care to take issue with that definition. But Descartes does; in his second Meditation he considers it and rejects it.[13] For Descartes, the only thing that man has in common with other animals, or anything else in nature, is that he occupies space and is as a whole, or parts of him, either moving or at rest. Hence, that man feels and is passionate and emotional is due to his being a mental substance, not a bodily substance. All so-called living bodies are machines, automata. Not only do animals not know, but also they do not feel.[14]

By contrast, the plain man recognizes a distinction between living and non-living things; and among the living he distinguishes plants from animals from men. Beyond that he recognizes a wide variety of kinds of things, both among the non-living and among plants and animals. And still beyond that he recognizes, for example, the difference between cats (as things) and the shades they come in, black, white, red, and calico. Descartes' natural world is much simpler, dispensing with all such distinctions. There is no life; there are no kinds; there are no colors. There are only particles of matter moving mechanically. There is no generation (birth) or destruction (death); there is only matter in motion. No growth; only matter in motion. Indeed, regarding man in the midst of this world, we must conclude that he is, if not supernatural, then at least extra-natural. In short, considered as mind, he does not fit into nature.

Now if we look at the theory of representative perception and note how it differs from the plain man's view, we can then consider why Descartes and others nonetheless hold to it. The theory is that the immediate objects of our knowledge are ideas in our minds; that these ideas are representative of realities external to the mind; and that by the mediation of these representative ideas, we come to be aware of an external world. How this differs from common sense may be shown by our citing here the main difficulty in this theory: it opens the door to skepticism. If the immediate objects of awareness are ideas in our minds, how can we ever know whether they, regarded as representations of external realities, adequately or properly or accurately represent those external realities? For we can never get outside our own minds to compare the external realities with the representative ideas. Indeed, we may even begin to wonder what evidence there is for an external world, given this representative theory of perception. Just stating the difficulty is enough to show the difference from common sense, for surely the plain man never for an instant supposes that there is no world external to his own ideas. Nor does he ever suppose that the immediate objects of awareness are ideas; instead he takes for granted that we are immediately aware of the world external to us, and of that world as it really is.

Descartes and others theorized otherwise because some of the discoveries of seventeenth century science demanded, so they thought, some such theory; and also because some of the ordinary experience of men could be better explained with this theory. With regard to the latter reason, we have already followed Descartes in noting that sometimes our senses fool us: what we saw as a bent stick was really straight, what we felt as lukewarm was really cold, etc. When we add to this hallucinations, it is easy to see how we might conlude that the immediate objects of awareness are not things in themselves, but rather ideas, some of which are taken to be representations of these things.

The other reason is an appeal to scientific experience. Seventeenth century scientists developed transmission theories of light and sound, with which we are all more or less familiar. There are competing theories about the nature of light; but whether it is regarded as composed of particles or of waves or of wavicles, all the theories agree that light is transmitted from natural and artificial bodies, like the sun and the lamp; and that our seeing colors is accounted for by the reflection of those particles, waves, or wavicles off the surfaces of things into our

90

eyes. So it is with sound, although now we speak of sound waves being transmitted and affecting the sensory receptor we call the ear. Hence it seems clear, and beyond dispute, that we see colors, hear sounds, etc., because of the physical influence of subtle material beings on our sensory apparatus. The reflection of light off a surface into the eye gives rise to the perception of a color; the impression of sound waves on the tympanum of the ear gives rise to the perception of a sound; etc. But can we then say that the colors we see, the sounds we hear, are really there? It is true, the colors, sounds, etc., are really in the mind -- that is, we really experience them -- but would it not be better now, in the light of this scientific knowledge, to regard those ideas (colors, sounds, etc.) as at best representative of something external, but not necessarily revelatory of the external as it really is? And if all this opens the door to skepticism of our knowledge of reality, so be it; for we can not be intellectually dishonest simply to escape being skeptical.

As a matter of fact, Descartes was not a skeptic; indeed, there perhaps has been no philosopher more confident than Descartes that man can achieve certain, indubitable knowledge. What saved him from skepticism was the conviction that whatever ideas are indubitable, whatever are clear and distinct, are revelatory of reality. Ordinary sense experience may not be trustworthy, but reason is. Relying on reason, Descartes thought through, he tells us, to the starting points of knowledge, which turn out also to be kinds and principles of reality: mind, God, extended (material) nature, principles of causality, logic. Hence, as we have seen, when we come to the detailed study of nature, we already know what it is -- matter moving mechanically; and hence we know what to look for in our experimentation. Now we are no longer relying on ordinary sense experience, but instead on rationally controlled and directed sense experience.

Those of us who have a layman's simple faith in science might be inclined to accept this Cartesian view. After all, most of us are taught to believe that if one wants real objective knowledge, it is to science one must go, not to ordinary experience. Thus, we all know now that the movement of the planets around the sun is explained in basically the same way as the movement of falling objects, or of projectiles. We know now that fire, earth, air, water are not elements, and that oxygen, hydrogen, silver, nitrogen, et.al., are.

However, despite the confidence most of us have in scientific knowledge generally, many philosophers wonder whether the scientific enterprise is directed to knowledge of the natures and causes of things, or whether instead it simply enables us to exploit nature in more and more sophisticated ways. This is not to say that Descartes' modern philosophical successors have completely rejected his epistemology or his account of scientific knowledge, and returned to the ordinary experience of the plain man. But it is to say that from the moment Descartes published his epistemology his fellow philosophers have noticed the roots of skepticism in it, and have worried about how to overcome the skepticism. Nor should this be surprising when we remember the radical divorce of mind from body. It is the mind, not the body, that is the knower; hence the knower is cut off from the material world it tries to know. As we have seen, the knower does not even seem to fit, or to belong, in that material world.

Furthermore, even ideas that seem to be born with the mind, says Descartes, are representative of something external to the mind.[15] Thus with the theory of representative perception (or knowledge) we commit ourselves to beginning to philosophize in the mind. At once, the existence and nature of anything external to the mind -- matter, nature, God, even the body itself, and other minds, becomes problematic and must be proved. Descartes thought he had proved all that needed proving; and that he and others could proceed to a complete detailed experimental knowledge of nature, including man. Other philosophers, however, have wondered whether we are required to suppose, as does Descartes, that external reality must correspond to the mind's "clear and distinct" ideas about it. Late in the eighteenth century, Immanuel Kant established modern skepticism by proclaiming that henceforth "knowledge" must be regarded as reality's conforming to mind, and not mind's conforming to reality. But as Kant himself clearly saw, such a position means that we forever give up the claim that our knowledge is of things as they really are, independent of what we think or experience about them.

By contrast, the plain man is a realist; i.e., he believes that he knows, or at least can come to know, things as they really are. His realism is doubtless naive, but it has found support in classical philosophy (in Aristotle, for example, and on the contemporary scene in Edward Pols,[16] for example) where an attempt is made to refine the realism; and it found support, albeit of an extremely unusual sort, in Berkeley.

Before we come to Berkeley's realism, we must consider one more of his influential philosophical predecessors. John Locke (1632-1704) was wary of theorizing about reality but so far as he does he seems to follow Descartes' dualism; i.e., he takes man to be a compound of material and mental substances.[17] But given that, his preoccupation was with theory of knowledge, as the title of his major philosophical work, <u>An Essay Concerning Human Understanding</u>, indicates. Berkeley's frequent references to this work, both in the notebooks he compiled in preparation for his major metaphysical works, and in the works themselves, provide the evidence of Locke's influence. One of the crucial questions Locke was wrestling with was about the idea of material substance. For Descartes, the clear and distinct idea we have of matter is, so to say, a mathematical idea. Matter is extension, or that which occupies space. Hence, of any particular material thing -- planet, rock, plant -- we can say that it has dimensions and that it is either moving or at rest. Those are fit objects for mathematical study. The size, shape, and motion of bodies, then, can be said to be primary qualities, i.e., qualities really belonging to, or characteristic of, bodies. But the colors, odors, textures, etc., in short, most of what we perceive in ordinary sense experience as characteristic of bodies, are secondary qualities; they are ideas produced in the mind by matter in motion, and in ordinary experience are projected by us onto the external, material things.

Locke accepts the distinction between primary and secondary qualities; but wonders how we come by the idea of material substance. It is clear how we have ideas of the secondary qualities -- through sense experience: of color, by sight; of sound, by hearing; of odors, by smelling; etc. But none of the senses discloses the substance. Descartes seems to suggest that we are born with the idea, or that God Himself has planted the idea in our minds. But that is at least highly suspect. Would any of us claim to have an idea of material reality prior to our experience, through the senses, of an external world? Surely all our knowledge of, all our ideas of, an external reality, come through sense experience. But then again, what about the idea of material substance? Strictly speaking, what we see is color; hear, sound; smell, odors; taste, tastes; touch, textures. The immediately experienced ideas of external reality seem to exclude material substance. Rather than to give up the distinction between primary and secondary qualities, Locke tried to avoid skepticism by concluding that material substance is the "supposed but unknown support of those qualities which we find existing, which we imagine cannot subsist sine re substante ... which ... is, in plain English, <u>standing under or upholding</u>."[18] In other famous words of his, substance is a something-I-know-not-what which I must conceive as underlying the primary qualities and causing the secondary qualities.[19]

However true it may be that the unsuspecting layman, and perhaps even the typical scientist, trust the "objective knowledge" of modern science, philosophers have been aware right along that the typical epistemology of modern scientific philosophy is subjectivist. Far from guaranteeing "objective knowledge" of the way things really are, it puts us into our subjective minds, and makes us wonder in a variety of ways whether and how we can get out and into the real world external to us as knowers. If Locke is right, it seems that we can not even be sure that the subject matter of science exists.

93

VI Setting the Stage

Berkeley resolved at an early age to make war against materialism, which he saw to be at the root of minute philosophy. At the same time he accepted the subjectivist epistemology of the burgeoning modern philosophy. Locke's version seemed to show Berkeley the way. For if matter is a something-I-know-not-what, philosophers ought not to go on supposing that it exists. With Descartes Berkeley agreed that there is ample evidence for minds, finite and infinite. But it seemed to Berkeley that we can and should do without matter. If he could prove that it exists only as a figment of some philosophers' imagination, then he would have undermined materialism. Once men generally are convinced that there is no reality radically distinct from mind, they will be ready to give proper attention to their immortal souls.

Chapter 5

Immaterialism

In Science and the Modern World Alfred North Whitehead sums up how the world appears to scientific philosophy early in the eighteenth century, when Berkeley was studying such as Descartes, Locke, and Newton. Whitehead reviews the subjectivist analysis of both ordinary and scientific experience, which fosters the commonly accepted distinction between primary qualities of material bodies (extension, shape, location, mass) and the secondary qualities (color, sound, odor, etc.) which we perceivers project "so as to clothe appropriate bodies in external nature." He then concludes,

> ...Thus the bodies are perceived as with qualities which in reality do not belong to them, qualities which in fact are purely the offspring of the mind. Thus nature gets credit which should in truth be reserved for ourselves: the rose for its scent: the nightingale for his song: and the sun for his radiance. The poets are entirely mistaken. They should address their lyrics to themselves, and should turn them into odes of self-congratulation on the excellency of the human mind. Nature is a dull affair, soundless, scentless, colourless; merely the hurrying of material, endlessly, meaninglessly.
>
> However you disguise it, this is the practical outcome of the characteristic scientific philosophy which closed the seventeenth century.
>
> In the first place, we must note its astounding efficiency as a system of concepts for the organisation of scientific research. In this respect, it is fully worthy of the genius of the century which produced it. It has held its own as the guiding principle of scientific studies ever since. It is still reigning. Every university in the world organises itself in accordance with it. No alternative system of organising the pursuit of scientific truth has been suggested. It is not only reigning, but it is without a rival.
>
> And yet -- it is quite unbelievable.[1]

95

That Berkeley found it unbelievable, and meant to defend common sense against the "characteristic scientific philosophy" of his time (which, if Whitehead is right, is still the predominant if not the only scientific philosophy) there can be no doubt. That he had trouble convincing his reading public of that there can also be no doubt. For after all, if a man tells you that matter does not exist and in the same breath says he only means to defend common sense, you might begin to wonder about his honesty or his sanity. Hence, it is imperative to try to resolve this perennial paradox or puzzle of Berkeley the realistic defender of the plain man vs. Berkeley the eccentric advocate for a world void of matter. In other words, we must try to understand how Berkeley could simultaneously argue against material substance and for a philosophical realism.

Having done that, we can consider two conflicting philosophical accounts of matter. After that we will turn to Berkeley's attack on the predominant scientific philosophy; to the presentation of his own metaphysics; and to the entertainment of objections to the immaterialism, and Berkeley's replies to them.

I The Paradox

Berkeley first presented his metaphysics in The Principles of Human Knowledge, published in 1710. Three years later he published Three Dialogues Between Hylas and Philonous, the theme and argument of which are basically the same as in the former work. The Three Dialogues was written after it became evident to Berkeley that he was being misunderstood and was being taken as an enemy of common sense rather than as an enemy of the characteristic scientific philosophy of the modern world. Hence he strives in the Three Dialogues to correct the misunderstanding. At the outset of the first dialogue, Philonous (friend of mind), who throughout the dialogues is the spokesman for Berkeley, speaks to his companion, Hylas (from the Greek word for matter): "Can there be a pleasanter time of the day, or a more delightful season of the year? That purple sky, these wild but sweet notes of birds, the fragrant bloom upon the trees and flowers, the gentle influence of the rising sun, these and a thousand nameless beauties of nature inspire the soul with secret transports..."[2] This is not idle chit chat Philonous is engaging in. Quite the contrary, Berkeley deliberately wants the reader to understand that he is far from concluding that in reality there is no color in the sky, that birds do not produce pleasing (or for that matter, unpleasant) sounds, etc. The world is as we perceive it. Common sense is so far right.

In the first dialogue, and early in the second, Berkeley tries to show that it is belief in material substance that leads to the skepticism characteristic of modern scientific

96

philosophy. Then immediately he has Philonous say the following words:

> Look! are not the fields covered with a delightful verdure? Is there not something in the woods and groves, in the rivers and clear springs that soothes, that delights, that transports the soul? At the prospect of the wide and deep ocean, or some huge mountain whose top is lost in the clouds, or of an old gloomy forest, are not our minds filled with a pleasing horror? Even in rocks and deserts, is there not an agreeable wildness? How sincere a pleasure is it to behold the natural beauties of the earth! To preserve and renew our relish for them, is not the veil of night alternately drawn over her face, and doth she not change her dress with the seasons? How aptly are the elements disposed? What variety and use in the meanest productions of Nature? What delicacy, what beauty, what contrivance in animal and vegetable bodies? How exquisitely are all things suited, as well to their particular ends, as to constitute apposite parts of the whole! And while they mutually aid and support, do they not also set off and illustrate each other? Raise now your thoughts from this ball of earth, to all those glorious luminaries that adorn the high arch of heaven....Is not the whole system immense, beautiful, glorious beyond expression and beyond thought! What treatment then do those philosophers deserve, who would deprive these noble and delightful scenes of all reality? How should those principles be entertained, that lead us to think all the visible beauty of the creation a false imaginary glare? To be plain, can you expect this scepticism of yours will not be thought extravagantly absurd by all men of sense?[3]

Given those last three rhetorical questions, there can certainly be no doubt about Berkeley's conviction regarding the world of common sense vs. the world of scientific philosophy.

Berkeley is saying (and convincingly arguing, too, as we shall see) that the distinction between primary and secondary qualities is spurious; that the world is as we perceive it, full of colors, sounds, odors, etc.; that whatever be the merits of seventeenth century science, the characteristic philosophy emerging from that science is fundamentally mistaken, and that common sense is a better guide philosophically than the typical modern philosophers.

Toward the end of the third dialogue there is an exchange between Hylas and Philonous that makes clear again that Berkeley does not mean to upset what the plain man means by "matter," but rather what philosophers have come to mean. He is willing to keep the term, except that other terms, like "body" or "stuff" could do as well in ordinary parlance. "And in philosophical discourses," he concludes, "it seems the best way to leave it quite out; since there is not perhaps any one thing that hath more favoured and strengthened the depraved bent of the mind toward <u>atheism</u>, than the use of that general confused term."⁴

II Conflicting Accounts of Matter

The philosophers' "matter," which Berkeley seems intent to deny, is the "matter" found in scientific philosophy. Let Descartes be its spokesman. Descartes' definition of matter is extension, or that which occupies space. Descartes also believed that the material universe is a plenum; that is, there is no empty space. We also need to note that for Descartes matter is a substance; that is, it is a kind of reality. It is important to stress this latter point, because as soon as we take matter to be a <u>kind</u> of reality, we have committed ourselves to the position that it is matter itself that essentially characterizes every thing in nature. If we ask ourselves what kinds of things exist around and about us, we typically would reply that there are books, chairs, tables, animals, plants. Descartes would not want to say that we are speaking falsely, but he would try to convince us that each of these apparently different things is essentially matter.

If we then add that human beings are material things we come to the conclusion that so far as our bodies are concerned we are not fundamentally different from earthworms or rocks. If the world <u>appears</u> otherwise, if it seems that there is a variety of kinds of things, that is because (in Descartes' version of nature) God has decreed laws in accordance with which particles of matter move; and God's forming or creating the world can be understood as His decreeing that there shall be matter and that matter shall move in accordance with laws. That nature, including our own bodies, appears to us as it does is the result of God's infinite wisdom and God's causal power. Nature itself is utterly powerless. God, in the beginning, set it in motion in accordance with His laws. Matter itself is inert, passive, incapable of any change or motion. What we call "change" in our ordinary experience is the result of particles of matter in motion. Thus, when an animal "grows," what really happens is that food (conglomerate of material particles) enters the mouth, is chewed (broken up into smaller pieces of matter), swallowed (matter in motion), digested (matter in motion), moved, some of it, to different parts of the remarkably sophisticated machine called animal body, and bit by bit added to the extent of that body. But in principle nothing different occurs in such "growth" from what happens in the motion of the planets around the sun. It is all matter moving in accordance with law, with God supplying the power. What is really real is disclosed when the animal dies and decays. The stuff out of which the machine was organized remains, unchanged. The stuff is what is really real, and it never changes; it is only moved about, rearranged.

One might wonder why Berkeley would suppose that such a notion of matter should strengthen "the depraved bent of the mind toward atheism,..." We have noted Descartes insisting that God is the creator and preserver of this matter and moreover that God has also created finite minds or souls that are altogether distinct from the (human) bodies they are (temporarily) conjoined with, and that the moral and religious experiences of men seem thereby warranted.

Before we try to answer that question, we will take a look at another sense of "matter," introduced by other philosophers. The spokesman for the one notion of matter was Descartes; for this different philosophic notion it will be Aristotle.[5] And quite appropriately, for Descartes reckoned Aristotle to be his enemy when it came to theorizing about nature, matter, and change.

Where Descartes speaks of matter as a substance (or kind of reality) Aristotle says that natural substances are material things, matter being one of the sources or principles of changing substances, but not itself a substance; where Descartes suggests that matter signifies the essential sameness of all natural things, Aristotle says it signifies the changeability of all natural things; where Descartes asserts that matter does not change, but only is moved about, Aristotle says that matter is the source of changeability; where Descartes says that change is only locomotion of matter, Aristotle says that change is the forming of matter. In sum, it would be hard to imagine two notions of "matter" more different from one another; Berkeley's criticism of the one is not likely to be a criticism of the other.

As to the definition of matter, Aristotle does not want to deny that all material things occupy space, or have three dimensions. But yet, he suggests, that is not the most fundamental feature of material things. Instead, to say of something that it is material is to say of it most essentially that it is a changing thing. By way of analogy, we might consider man defined as a clothed primate. In a way, that seems an adequate definition, for it does put the species "man" in a genus (primate), and differentiates (clothed) that species from every other species in the genus. In other words we all would agree that that is characteristic of all (normal) men; each does wear clothes and each is a primate. Something, however, is missing in this definition: however much it serves to differentiate men from other kinds of things, still it does not bring out what is fundamental, or essential, in man. By contrast, definitions of man as the rational animal, or the moral animal, or the political animal strike us (whether or not we agree that they are adequate definitions) as trying to disclose what is essential in man.

To return from the analogy, while it seems to be characteristic of all material things that they occupy space, that is not what is most essential or significant in designating them material; what is most significant is that they are changing or changeable. To emphasize this point Aristotle came to use, as synonymous with "matter," the term "potentiality." Material things are changeable things; whatever at the moment any one of them is, it is potentially other than that, or different in some way from that.

Aristotle came to this understanding of matter out of a concern to give a plausible account of change. In our ordinary experience every change is a case of something changing from something to something else. As Aristotle refines this, in part by introducing technical terms, he concludes that there are three principles of change: privation, form, and matter. The "from something" is the privation, the "to something" is the form, and the "something changing" is the matter. Thus, e.g., water being heated in the kettle is changing from cold to hot. It becomes apparent that matter is not a substance; rather, it is a principle or source of change. Hence, with respect to the water heating, Aristotle does not mean that water is matter pure and simple; instead, it is that in the change which is changing. To say of water that it is a material thing is to say that it is changeable, in this example from being cold to being hot.[6] But then it becomes clear that we do not understand changing things (natural substances, Aristotle calls them) by reference to matter alone, but also by reference to form. Our world is not one of sheer flux; it is instead one of changing things acting and being acted on. Each changing thing is best understood, not as matter in motion, but as a composite of matter (potentiality) and form (actuality). And thus change is understood as the forming of matter, or the actualizing of potential. The water was actually cold, but potentially hot. The change in it was the actualizing of the water's potential (water as material) to be hot water.

Now when we say of water and of a man that they are both material things, we mean to say primarily that they are both changeable. But the water is still water, for all that, and the man man; i.e., cold water cannot become hot man, for water is what it is, not simply by virtue of its matter, its potentiality, but also by virtue of its form, its actuality. And that form is radically different from the form humanity. Form, in other words, is as much a principle or source of changing things, as indispensable to a plausible account of change, as is matter.

With matter so understood as a source, concomitant with form, of change and changing things, we have not only an intelligible and plausible account of nature, but also one which is harmonious with our ordinary everyday experience, that indeed seems a refinement of the experience of the plain man. Man himself, on this scheme, can be fitted into nature; and not as a mere machine. We all, common sensically anyhow, and before we become learned in scientific philosophy, take ourselves to be changing things, but for all that, substantially the same from beginning to end. At the beginning, at conception,[7] a substantial change occurred; i.e.. a human being came into existence. At death, another substantial change will occur; that human being will cease to exist. All the change in between, the growing, maturing, and decaying, is presided over, so to say, by the substantial form, man. What we are, substantially, essentially, it seems, is man, not matter in motion. Hence, without our claiming that this account of matter and natural changing things resolves all the perennial puzzles in the mind-body relationship, still we can see that it does seem to escape the difficulties attending the absolute split between mind and body, where each is taken to be an altogether different kind of substance. And with that, this account seems to replace us in nature, as perhaps belonging there with other animals, other living things, which like us come into being, grow, develop, decay, and die.

With this notion of matter, we have a nature rich with form, with power, energy, vitality, agency, and even intelligence. Descartes' nature, by contrast is stupid, lifeless, inert, passive, powerless, formless; as Whitehead put it, "merely the hurrying of material, endlessly, meaninglessly."

If we accept Aristotle's account of matter, does it not seem that when we are concerned to explain things, to give the causes of change, our attention will naturally be focussed upwards and forwards, so to speak? That is, since we would not then be inclined to speak of change as matter in motion, but rather as the forming of matter, we would naturally look more to what things are becoming, tending toward, rather than merely to what they have come from. The really real, the substantial, is more form than matter. If we want to understand the oak tree, we look to the fully developed and mature specimen, and not merely to the acorn. When we ponder ourselves, as rational animals, we find

101

ourselves naturally aspiring to ideals, striving for the well-being or happiness appropriate to rational animals. We might even suppose that there is such a thing as wisdom for men to achieve. In short, given this account of matter, the natural bent of the mind is toward theism, toward the belief that there is God, theos, or as Aristotle put it, pure Form, the ultimate explanation of changing nature.

By contrast, if we accept the other (Cartesian) account of matter, where change is nothing but matter in motion, then when we are concerned to explain things, our attention will be focussed downwards and backwards: "down" to the stuff out of which we suppose everything is made, and which everything substantially is; "back" to where it was, and not forward to what it might become. The really real is the "stuff," not the apparent forms and varieties of it. Is it any wonder, given this account of matter, that Descartes sends us for wisdom, to medicine? Tinker with the machine; grease it; make adjustments. Therein lies well-being and happiness. In short, given this account of matter, the bent of the mind is toward atheism. At least, given belief in a nature that is itself powerless, lifeless, and inert, it is no wonder that we would not be naturally inclined to theism.

At any rate, it is historical fact that any philosophy that reads matter as Descartes does, tends toward atheism, and that any philosophy that reads it as Aristotle does tends toward theism. Clearly, then, there lies in this other account of matter another alternative, besides the idealism that Berkeley concludes, to materialism. Another, succinct, way to put it is that all materialisms seem to take "matter" as a term that stands for the ultimate identity or essential sameness of things in nature, rather than as a term signifying the changeability of everything in nature.

Now our question becomes: why did Berkeley not take this alternative? If we could find a text in his writings that reads, "I did not take that alternative for the following reasons:...", our interpretive task of course would be finished as soon as it begins. However, that there is no such text does not excuse us from trying to answer the question. Indeed, we must try to answer it; for interpretation of Berkeley depends on the answer. Chapters 2 and 3 have shown how profoundly indebted Berkeley was to classical philosophers like Plato and Aristotle for his deepest convictions about morality, politics, education, and even religion. Furthermore, Berkeley knew that "the philosophers' matter" was not Aristotle's: "Neither Plato nor Aristotle by matter, <u>hyle</u>, understood corporeal substance, whatever the moderns may understand by that word. To them certainly it signified no positive actual being....That matter is actually nothing, but potentially all things, is the doctrine of Aristotle,...and all the ancient Peripatetics."[8] True, that was written late in his life; but nothing surrounding it in Siris indicates that Berkeley thought that he should exchange his immaterialism and idealism for Aristotle's hylomorphism (matter-form-ism).

Did Berkeley not realize that the classical moral philosophy of virtue depends upon the metaphysics and theory of man that he seems to be rejecting? The answer must await Part III. For now we must be content to see that he did not so much miss this alternative as reject it. Moreover, despite his devotion to classical thought, he accepted the subjectivist bias of modern philosophy.

III Subjectivism

What subjectivism is should be evident from the previous chapter's review of the epistemological theory of representative perception, where (for Descartes and Locke, among others) the immediate objects of knowledge are ideas. It is called "subjectivism" because the theory starts with the subject, the knower and his ideas, and tries to work its way outward to the objects supposedly represented by the ideas.

To understand more fully both subjectivism and Berkeley's metaphysics we must once again contrast classical philosophy and modern philosophy, and this can be done most effectively by returning to the opening paragraph of Berkeley's Introduction to the Principles of Human Knowledge.[9] "Philosophy being nothing else but the study of wisdom and truth," Berkeley wrote, "it may with reason be expected that those who have spent most time and pains in it should enjoy a greater calm and serenity of mind, a greater clearness and evidence of knowledge, and be less disturbed with doubts and difficulties than other men." This thought could have been written by Plato or Aristotle; classical philosophy is the pursuit of wisdom. It is by and large presupposed in classical philosophy that common sense is the starting point, and that a philosophic or scientific or exact account of reality would be a refinement of common sense. Presupposing that wisdom lies in coming to understand what and why things are as they are, and then in living accordingly -- in other words, in appropriating that knowledge into one's very being -- classical philosophy is preoccupied with theorizing about reality, and only in afterthought does it theorize how we know reality. In short, it is objectivist in its stance, rather than subjectivist.[10]

From what we have so far discovered about Berkeley, we cannot but conclude that he, too, regards philosophy as pursuit of wisdom. It is somewhat surprising, then, to turn to the opening lines of the Principles of Human Knowledge, appearing of course after the Introduction. "It is evident to anyone who takes a survey of the objects of human knowledge that they are either ideas actually imprinted on the senses, or else such as are perceived by attending to the passions and operations of the mind, or lastly, ideas formed by help of memory and imagination -- either compounding, dividing, or barely representing those originally perceived in the aforesaid ways."[11]

What has happened to common sense? Surely it would never occur to the untutored plain man to say that the objects of his knowledge are anything but those things he takes to make up this world we live in: men, other animals, plants, dirt, planets, stars, etc.; as well as the colors, sounds, odors, etc., of those things. And whatever those objects are, they are surely not ideas imprinted on the senses, or passions or operations of the mind, or compoundings, dividings, representations of other ideas. And yet here is Berkeley, so classical in other respects, in the very first statement in the <u>Principles</u> expressing the subjectivist bias and sharing it with Descartes and Locke.

If we go back for a moment to the first paragraph of the Introduction to the <u>Principles</u>, we note that after the first sentence, in which Berkeley shows his classical leanings, he goes on to contrast, contrary to what we would expect from what he writes in the first sentence, the lack of skepticism among plain folk with the "uncouth paradoxes, difficulties, and inconsistencies, which multiply and grow" upon those who advance in speculation and end up in "a forlorn scepticism." We are not likely to find comparable passages in ancient classical philosophers like Plato or Aristotle, for the reason that science and philosophy had not yet parted company.

Among the ancients science <u>was</u> philosophy. Part of the explanation of why the two have parted company in modern times is evident in what we have already reviewed in the chapter on scientific philosophy. The apparent conclusion coming out of the new scientific philosophy that marks our modern world is that reality is far different from appearance. So far as nature is concerned the real is matter, stuff occupying space, that moves about regularly, i.e., in accordance, it seems, with laws. The apparent world, by contrast, is the world of common sense. While science ever since has been preoccupied with its exact mathematical study of the "reality," philosophy has been preoccupied with all the problems attending the difference between reality and appearance.

Berkeley hoped to forestall that turn. It is worth quoting once more from a 1709 letter to a friend: "Socrates spent his time in reasoning on the most noble and important subjects, the nature of the gods, the dignity and direction of the soul, and the duties of a rational creature.... In short his whole employment was the turning men aside from vice, impertinence, and trifling speculations to the study of solid wisdom, temperance, justice, and piety, which is the true business of a philosopher."[12] To make it possible for philosophers to turn to their true business, Berkeley hoped to mend the split between science and philosophy by overcoming the reality/appearance dichotomy.[13] He tried to do it from the subjective side. In his immaterialism he tried to defend common sense by denying the existence of matter.

IV The Subjectivist Attack on Matter

It was Berkeley's opinion that the restatement of his position in the Three Dialogues Between Hylas and Philonous would lead to better understanding than his earlier Principles of Human Knowledge. Hence, we will follow the strategy of the Three Dialogues, which is to show first of all (first dialogue) how the predominant philosophy of his day leads to extreme skepticism; then to show (second dialogue) how his own philosophy of immaterialism both escapes that skepticism and answers the demands of common sense and of religion; and then finally (third dialogue) to respond to all imaginable objections to this unusual and novel philosophy of immaterialism.

At the outset of the first dialogue the reader is reminded that Philonous (Berkeley) is a defender of common sense and an opponent of the sophisticated skeptical philosophy issuing from seventeenth century speculation. But then Hylas reminds the reader that Philonous seems to be the one who is skeptical, the one who holds the most fantastic position; for he is the one who denies the existence of matter. Philonous acknowledges that he does indeed deny the existence of what philosophers call material substance, but suggests that it is precisely the idea of material substance that leads to skepticism. The two participants in the dialogue readily agree that a skeptic is one who either denies the existence of, or professes ignorance of, sensible things.

What are sensible things? The plain man would answer that at least some of them are precisely those material things that make up the world -- rivers, mountains, plains, plants, animals, etc.; and so far Berkeley will agree, because he presupposes, with common sense, that we are at home in this world, that things in the world present themselves to us as they really are. But Berkeley also holds the subjectivist bias of modern philosophy, and more importantly the typical epistemology of his time. In accordance with that epistemology the mind is, with respect to sense perception, a passive receptacle, upon which are impressed colors, sounds, odors, etc. What mind does with the ideas once received is the work of reason. In other words, Berkeley shares a common presupposition of modern philosophy that the mind of man, as we might say in late twentieth century, is something like a computer, into which information is fed, via the senses and the passions, and which then ratiocinates, or computes, with that information. On this view, the mind has no more to do with what is fed into it than does the computer. Berkeley argues for this view by asking us to consider what role our will can play in sense perception. Suppose, for example, that one wants to smell a flower in the garden. It is within one's power to pluck it, bring it to the nose, and inhale; but then, willy-nilly, the fragrance is impressed upon the passive mind.[14]

It is a compelling argument, and the passage is rich for commentary. The point for now, however, is that Berkeley believed that in sensory perception the mind is inactive. Further, the name that Berkeley gives to these data of sense experience is, following Descartes and Locke, ideas. It is this presupposition that underlies the statement at the beginning of Part I of the Principles of Human Knowledge, quoted earlier, which seemed quite contrary to common sense. But given this presupposition, it makes sense to say that the immediate objects of knowledge are ideas, and that in the reception of these ideas the mind is passive.

To return to "sensible things," Hylas and Philonous come easily to agree that they "are those only which are immediately perceived by sense."[15] Philonous runs through the catalog of the immediate objects of sense -- color, sound, odor, etc. -- and the perceptive reader is at once aware that material substance is conspicuously missing from the list.

However, most of us, like Hylas, would at this point still contend that to exist is one thing, and to be perceived is another. But given the presuppositions noted above, and given that matter is, as scientific philosophy holds, a passive, inert, unthinking substance, defined by its occupying space, it is easy for Berkeley to show that to separate "to be" from "to be perceived" (or "to be a perceiver") is an untenable position. Berkeley's strategy at this point is to show that none of these sensible qualities can exist without the mind. But so far he is only demonstrating what was commonplace in the scientific philosophy of the time, that the so called secondary qualities do not exist independent of perceivers. In the dialogue Hylas readily agrees to this, acknowledging that there is such an opinion current among philosophers. However, he makes clear, this does not yet show that material objects are not real.[16]

Berkeley's next step is to show that what holds for the "secondary qualities" also holds for the "primary qualities," that they cannot be said to exist without the mind. Here Berkeley is being consistent in applying the subjectivist principle as his modern predecessors had not been.[17] A careful analysis of these "primary qualities" -- extension, figure, solidity, gravity, motion, rest -- will show that they too are to be understood fundamentally as elements in the experience of a subject, and not as attributes of a supposed material, inert, passive, unthinking substance. Berkeley's argument with respect to these qualities is as follows:

Extension, e.g., is a sensible quality, immediately perceived by us,

and hence is an idea.

But no idea can exist in an unperceiving substance (matter).

Therefore, no mode of extension can really exist in matter; and hence

must exist in mind.

Therefore, to be a sensible quality is to be an idea is to be perceived. There is nothing else in our experience of an external world but these qualities, henceforth not to be distinguished as primary and secondary, but all to be regarded as ideas having no existence without the mind, or the perceiver.

We might reply that there are ways of measuring objectively -- determining "scientifically" -- what the primary qualities are in reality independent of my perception of them. For example, I can use a yardstick to determine the dimensions of the desk on which I am writing. And will that not show a quality belonging to the desk without the mind, independent of my perception? Berkeley's reply is in effect this. What do you experience of the yardstick? Color, sound, shape, extension! What that extension is, is as dependent upon you as perceiver as is its color or as is the extension of the desk. As you use it to measure the desk it appears a certain length. As you withdraw from it, and view it from a distance, it appears a different length. And so on with each of the "primary qualities"; given this analysis of experience, they can no more be said to exist without the mind than can the "secondary qualities." Any instrument that is used to measure is just as much an object of perception as are the things it is measuring. Hence while we can assert that the measurement is objective in the sense that we can agree about it because it is open to public inspection, we cannot grant to the extension an existence without the mind.[18]

Berkeley's critique so far shows that neither "secondary qualities" nor "primary qualities" can be said to exist without the mind, that is, without being perceived. But does that prove that material substance does not exist? Have not philosophers, including Descartes and Locke, always meant by "matter" that

107

substratum or substance that bears or possesses or underlies the attributes that our senses do perceive? Or have they not meant that matter underlies some of the qualities we perceive, and gives rise to, or causes, the others? The answer to these questions is not a simple "yes." That most assuredly is Descartes' matter, and so is it of any philosopher in the history of thought who considers matter to be a substance, a kind of reality. We have seen that in the history of philosophy there is a tradition going back at least as far as Aristotle that, while not denying the existence of material substances, does insist that matter is itself not a substance, not a kind of reality; and that according to this tradition "matter" is another word for "potentiality" or for "changeability." For those like Descartes who take matter to be a substance, matter is itself permanent, unchanging, the stable substratum underlying, persisting, abiding amidst all the change we are aware of. Clearly it is the "Cartesian" matter that Berkeley means by the "philosophers' matter." We suggested earlier that Berkeley accepted parts of Descartes' metaphysics; a part he could not accept was of course matter. In showing that matter does not exist Berkeley is denying the matter of the mind-matter dualism. Again, he does not mean to deny the existence of the world of nature as we perceive it, and that certainly seems to common sense to be a world of changing things.

In demonstrating that the qualities we perceive cannot exist unperceived, or without the mind, Berkeley has not yet completed the denial of material substance. In the representative theory both Descartes and Locke (among many others) contend that the immediate objects of knowledge are ideas in the mind. Berkeley has so far argued, following Descartes and Locke, that these immediate objects of knowledge cannot exist without the mind, that their "to be" is "to be perceived." But now Berkeley points out that there is no advantage and no sense in contending that these ideas are representative of a material reality beyond. Admittedly -- by Descartes and Locke -- the material reality is not perceived, is not sensed. Further, can there be any meaning, Berkeley asks, in substance as substratum, as that underlying, which is not already there in our perception of extension; which, it has been granted, does not exist without the mind?

Berkeley's refutation of the representative theory rests on the following assumptions: 1. matter, if it exists, is a substance altogether different from mind; 2. the immediate objects of our awareness are ideas; 3. the mind, in the reception of ideas (in perceiving), is altogether passive. Descartes, Locke, and Berkeley are all agreed on the presuppositions.

In the first part of the refutation Philonous reminds Hylas of their agreement that only ideas are immediately perceived, and that no idea can exist without the mind. However, to make sense of our ordinary experience Philonous claims that there is <u>mediated</u> perception of sensible things, made possible by the mind, through memory of past experience, connecting ideas. Thus, e.g., when I "hear" a coach driving along the street, I immediately hear only sound; but from past experience, I connect that idea with other ideas I have come to associate with the word "coach," and hence can be said to hear the coach. But how does that argue for what Hylas calls real things or material objects? Sarcastically Philonous wonders whether Hylas remembers having sensed them formerly as they are in themselves.[19]

The second part of the refutation leads to the conclusion that Hylas, the believer in material objects, is the skeptic. The argument is as follows. According to Hylas ideas are copies or likenesses of real things; and real things have fixed, stable natures. But how can our ideas, which are perpetually fleeting and variable, be said to be like what is fixed and stable? Or if it is claimed that some one idea among the many variable ideas is like the real thing, how could we possibly know which one? Moreover, for Hylas the real things are insensible, and ideas sensible. But how can the sensible be like the insensible? an invisible thing be like a color? an inaudible thing be like a sound? No, only an idea can be like another idea.[20] The conclusion, voiced by Philonous, is inescapable. "You are therefore by your principles forced to deny the reality of sensible things, since you made it to consist in an absolute existence exterior to the mind. That is to say, you are a downright <u>sceptic</u>. So I have gained my point, which was to shew your principles led to scepticism."[21]

After all this, it is probably no accident that a few lines later Berkeley ends the dialogue by having Philonous say, "Hark; is not this the college-bell"; and Hylas respond, very common sensically, thank goodness, "It rings for prayers."

V Immaterialism and Theism

According to the representative theory of knowledge that Berkeley learned from Descartes and Locke, the immediate objects of our intellectual, human awareness are ideas; and these ideas are themselves representative (some in better ways than others) of a material reality external to our minds which are the passive recipients of the ideas. Berkeley's epistemology disposes of the material reality that supposedly is represented by the ideas. Apparently it is good riddance. Given that representative theory, we seem doomed to skepticism and to a denial of common sense.

But the issue is not so simple. Although we might have agreed that matter is not perceived by us, that it is not among sensible things, still our being aware of sensible qualities (ideas, i.e.) requires explanation; and why not theorize material things as the causes of ideas? After all, we have a strong inclination to believe there are material things, as Descartes pointed out; and how can we protect God from a charge of deceit if indeed there are no material things? Berkeley's response to this we can perhaps anticipate. God's veracity, so far, is not the issue. As for matter being the cause of anything, the notion is absurd. According to the scientific philosophers, Descartes among them, matter is an inert, inactive, passive substance. In Descartes' metaphysics, matter is so impotent that it can not get from one moment to the next without God re-creating it.

Hylas, however, does not quite yet give up, but instead suggests "...that, subordinate to the Supreme Agent, there is a cause of a limited and inferior nature which concurs in the production of our ideas, not by any act of will or spiritual efficiency, but by that kind of action which belongs to matter, viz., motion."[22] Berkeley was not unaware of the transmission theory of light. The light waves (or particles) move, bounce off of objects, move into the eye, put other matter in motion, etc., and cause my perception of color. In fact, this sort of scientific theory was rather decisive in moving modern philosophers to subjectivism, and hence to the theory that the world is not as it appears to be; that what the world really is, is matter in motion.

Berkeley's response to this seems conclusive. Your motion does not move, he says. "I ask whether all your ideas are not perfectly passive and inert, including nothing of action in them?" Hylas agrees they are. "And are sensible qualities anything else but ideas?" Hylas acknowledges that they are not. "But is not motion a sensible quality?" It is, says Hylas. "Consequently it is no action."[23] Hence, however impressive scientifically a transmission theory of light may be, it shows with respect to our knowledge and experience of nature anything but what the scientific philosopher makes out that it does.[24]

With this showing that material substance is not only not perceived, but also that it serves no theoretical purpose, we can reject it as without foundation in our experience, without significance, and hence restore the view that the world is as we perceive it. There is now no screen between our minds and an external reality; instead, the external reality is made up of the ideas we immediately perceive. The ideas are not representative of an external reality; they are the external reality.

Imagine how excited Berkeley must have been by this discovery. For in addition to restoring the world of common sense, it seemed to provide a direct and convincing proof of the existence of a mind that is infinite and omnipresent. We have seen how the sensible world (ideas) cannot exist without the mind; and how material substance is neither experienced nor explains anything. To account for the sensible world, the world of ideas, we cannot say that we are the cause of them. We have already noted the passage in which Berkeley shows how far the mind is active in perceiving: in the smelling, the seeing, etc., the mind is passive. We can will to open or close our eyes. But we cannot will to see or not see what is there when the eyes are open. So the finite individual mind is not the cause of the sensible world. But if the sensible world cannot exist without the mind, the only explanation for it is that there is an infinite mind in which it exists. A neat theory. The sensible world, the world of nature, cannot exist without the mind; but obviously it does not depend for its existence on our finite minds; therefore, it depends for its existence on infinite mind, or on God. In one fell swoop we have refuted skepticism and atheism.

So far, so good. But what about common sense? What has happened, in this theorizing, to the "material" things of the plain man? For Berkeley, they are congeries, or combinations, or clusters of ideas. Do apples exist? Of course. What then, are they? Berkeley responds to the plain man: what exactly are you aware of, and hence what can you mean by apple? Are you not aware of red, round, tart, smooth, etc.; and can we not say, then, that the apple is that bundle of sensible qualities? We need only to add, for Berkeley, that there are no abstract natures that material things can be said to share in -- appleness, for example. Each thing is what we perceive. If there is more to any concrete real thing than what we perceive, then at least that something more is in the mind of Superperceiver, God.

To be, says Berkeley, in his famous formula, is to be perceived or to be a perceiver. There are two kinds of reality: minds and ideas. The former, both infinite and finite, are active; the latter are wholly passive, depending for their existence on the former. The world of nature, then, is a system of ideas utterly dependent for its being and activity on God, the Infinite Mind.

Such is Berkeley's metaphysics. The remainder of the second dialogue is given over to Berkeley's making clear how his theory of reality differs from those of other modern philosophies, particularly Malebranche's, with which Berkeley's position had been confused. Malebranche was a Cartesian philosopher, convinced, as was Descartes, that there are the two substances, mind and matter, which somehow interact in man, who is composed of both. Malebranche "solved" the problem of interaction between two altogether different kinds of reality by a theory which has come to be known as occasionalism. Matter, it seems, cannot affect mind, nor can mind affect matter. But God certainly can and does

111

affect both. Hence let us say that on the occasion of my finger touching the red hot stove, God causes the idea of pain in my mind; and then on the occasion of my willing to remove the finger from the red hot stove God moves the finger. With this theory Malebranche is able to maintain the dualism (able to resist the temptation we noted earlier to reduce reality to matter in motion) and to avoid the insoluble problem of the interaction between mind and matter. And given this view, as we perceive pain, so we perceive anything else of that external world. That is, the immaterial mind perceives by virtue of its union with God; or it sees all things in God.

It is no wonder that Berkeley wanted to make his position clear. To him Malebranche's philosophy must have seemed a futile effort to maintain the existence of material substance. The difference between the views of these two very concerned religious thinkers is amusingly set forth by Etienne Gilson, who tries to imagine the conversation that might have passed between them when they were supposed to have met. Malebranche was aged and also seriously ill. After reviewing the dispute between them, Gilson repeats the story that Malebranche was so upset that he took a turn for the worse and died within a few days. Gilson concludes: "If the story is true, it is a good one; if it is not true, it is better than true, for it should have happened. No wonder then, that De Quincey inserted it in his famous Essay on Murder as One of the Fine Arts. What a murder case, indeed: 'Murder by Metaphysics!'"[25]

Whether or not Berkeley can be charged with murdering Malebranche, there is no doubt that he would gladly take the responsibility for destroying matter -- the philosophers' matter, i.e., and more specifically, the scientific philosophers' matter. Whatever might be said in criticism of Berkeley's own theory -- and there is plenty, and said even by Berkeley himself -- it should be clear by now that any philosopher who undertakes to explain reality with the subjectivist bias, and who supposes that he can conclude a materialism, had better read his Berkeley first. That there are many minute philosophers who suppose it not only possible, but also accomplished,[26] reminds us of Berkeley's epigram, "Truth is the cry of all, but the game of a few." Perhaps also Berkeley would be pleased were we to interpret this as testimony for the sort of classical education Berkeley advocated; and now Berkeley would be included among the greats.

VI Objections and Replies

By the end of the second dialogue Berkeley believed he had destroyed matter and had established idealism. At the outset of the third dialogue, as a reminder to us that he is the champion of the plain man against the sophisticated scientific philosopher,

Philonous speaks the following.

> I assure you, Hylas, I do not pretend to frame
> any hypothesis at all. I am of a vulgar cast,
> simple enough to believe my senses, and leave
> things as I find them. To be plain, it is my
> opinion, that the real things are those very
> things I see and feel, and perceive by my
> senses. These I know, and finding they answer
> all the necessities and purposes of life, have
> no reason to be solicitous about any other
> unknown beings.... Wood, stones, fire, water,
> flesh, iron, and the like things, which I name
> and discourse of, are things that I know. And
> I should not have known them, but that I
> perceived them by my senses; and things
> perceived by the senses are immediately
> perceived; and things immediately perceived are
> ideas; and ideas cannot exist without the mind;
> their existence therefore consists in being
> perceived; when therefore they are actually
> perceived, there can be no doubt of their
> existence. Away then with all that scepticism,
> all those ridiculous philosophical doubts.
> What a jest is it for a philosopher to question
> the existence of sensible things, till he hath
> it proved to him from the veracity of God: [So
> much for Descartes] or to pretend our knowledge
> in this point falls short of intuition or
> demonstration? [So much for Locke] I might as
> well doubt of my own being, as of the being of
> those things I actually see and feel.[27]

With that assertion of philosophical realism as emphatic
prelude, Berkeley turns to the task of meeting all the objections
to immaterialism that he knew of or could imagine. We cannot but
admire his honesty and courage; for there are, among the total of
twenty to thirty (depending on how we divide and organize them),
some that obviously made him uneasy; and among those some that
seem to render his metaphysics untenable.

Instead of reviewing all the objections and replies, we will
order and organize them to get a sampling of the different types
of objections and of Berkeley's typical replies. There are
objections from common sense, from modern philosophy, from modern
science, and from religion and theology. We will consider them in
roughly that order; but we will save the most difficult for last,
and postpone some of them until Part III.

One of the objections from common sense is that the plain man would not agree that to exist is to be perceived. The reply is that he would if he understood Berkeley's meaning, and understood the absurd philosophy of materialism this position opposes. Berkeley adds that any good Christian will readily agree that to be is to be perceived, so long as the perceiver is understood to be God.[28] And if it seems odd to say that only spirits and ideas exist (another objection), that is the fault of philosophers who have defined matter in such an untenable way.[29]

A little later Hylas notes that a majority opinion would reject immaterialism; and at the very end, after Philonous has met all the objections, still, says Hylas (speaking doubtless for many of us) there is an "unaccountable backwardness that I find in myself towards your notions." As for the "majority opinion," Berkeley is confident that it would be with him if materialism and immaterialism were adequately explained to all men. He adds, "...if by 'material substance' is meant only sensible body, that which is seen and felt (and the unphilosophical part of the world, I dare say, mean no more), then I am more certain of matter's existence than you or any other philosopher pretend to be."[30] Berkeley replies to the "unaccountable backwardness" with the passage we quoted from earlier[31] as evidence of Berkeley's aim to defend common sense. Berkeley will not quarrel with us for an expression. If we must, he says, retain the word "matter," but mean by it "sensible things."

Second are what we can label as objections from modern philosophy, or as typical problems in modern philosophy. The first is the problem of the knowledge of minds; the second is the problem of causality. The problem of the knowledge of minds is raised early in the third dialogue. The difficulty is this: Berkeley has presented ideas -- the immediate objects of our awareness -- as being inert, passive, having in themselves no power, efficacy, agency. The active beings are spirits. But because God is an agent, a purely active being, we can have no idea of Him. Or, if Berkeley maintains that somehow he conceives God without an idea of Him, then why cannot Locke, e.g., maintain that he conceives matter without an idea of it?

Berkeley's answer to the first question is first to grant that properly speaking we have no _idea_ of God or of any other spirit. But each one of us knows intuitively or immediately, albeit not perceptively, that he is a thinking substance. The _notion_ (or "'idea' in a large sense," says Berkeley) I have of God, granted it is inadequate, is obviously not through perception, but rather is based on reflection on my own mind, and on reasoning. I do not have an inactive idea, but rather "some sort of an active thinking image of the Deity." The answer to the second question is that matter is not known in any of these ways.[32]

That Berkeley was greatly concerned about this difficulty is evident by his pursuing it further in the third edition of the Three Dialogues. It is the same difficulty, put into different words: you say there is spiritual substance, although you have no idea of it; but deny that there is material substance, because you have no idea or notion of it; is that fair? The most interesting part of this objection is Berkeley's anticipation of Hume's[33] rejection of spiritual substance, through these words from Hylas: "Notwithstanding all you have said, to me it seems, that according to your own way of thinking, and in consequence of your own principles, it should follow that you are only a system of floating ideas, without any substance to support them. Words are not to be used without a meaning. And as there is no more meaning in spiritual substance than in material substance, the one is to be exploded as well as the other."[34] Berkeley of course does not accept the criticism, and insists that in fact we do have knowledge of ourselves as things which think, perceive, will, act -- in short, not existing as strings of ideas, but as substances. It is interesting to note that the majority of subsequent philosophers in this empiricist tradition seems to side with Hume rather than with Berkeley.[35]

The second of these modern problems is that of causality; and it arises because of the tendency of modern science and modern philosophy to treat all physical things as being inert, passive, unable of themselves to act. The problem is there in Berkeley, too; for although matter has been destroyed, the physical world has not; and that physical world is a system of ideas, each of which is inert. The problem basically is whether there is any sense, and if so, what, in speaking of cause in such a world. That is, given a world of completely inert things, none of which is capable of initiating action, how could anything ever happen? how could there be change? Descartes' answer is that God, having set matter in motion in the beginning, keeps it in motion through each succeeding moment. Berkeley's answer is the same, except of course that there now is no matter. But still there is nature, and God or finite minds are the causes of all effects in nature.

When Hylas pursues this problem by suggesting that this seems to make God the cause of such heinous sins as murder, sacrilege, adultery, Philonous counters by reminding Hylas that moral evil consists in an inner spiritual deprivation, not in outward acts; and that finite spirits are able to act. But notice how Berkeley puts it. "...I have nowhere said that God is the only agent who produces all the motions in bodies. It is true I have denied there are any other agents besides spirits, but this is very consistent with allowing to thinking rational beings, in the production of motions, the use of limited powers, ultimately indeed derived from God, but immediately under the direction of their own wills, which is sufficient to entitle them to all the guilt of their actions."[36]

We might wish that Berkeley had written more on this problem. Confronted with the problem of knowledge, his predecessors saying that our ideas represent material substance(s), Berkeley solves it, escapes skepticism, and saves common sense, by affirming that ideas, instead of being representative of things, are the things. But now, confronted with the problem of causality, Berkeley seems not to have avoided the dualism. Although he studiously dodges using the word "matter," he finds "body" to be a neat substitute. And although he would remind us that "body" means a bundle of ideas, still we find it difficult to imagine that bundle being moved about. Nor is it any wonder that Berkeley dared not put it that way.

Adding to the bothersomeness of this problem of causality is the puzzle as to how we, as spirits (or as knowers), come to be affected by ideas from without. In the subjectivist perspective, the mind, with respect to sensory awareness, is altogether passive -- not an active knower, but a passive receptacle of ideas. How do the ideas get there? For Berkeley of course the answer is easy: God puts them there. Indeed, as we will pursue more extensively in the next chapter, nature, understood as a system of ideas, can be looked upon as a language by which God, the Author, speaks to finite spirits.

Third are what we can call objections from physics. These, and Berkeley's replies, show both the separation that had already occurred between philosophy and the new science, and Berkeley's own theory of what might be expected from the new science of physics. The general objection can be stated as follows: in the light of the great successes in seventeenth century science, it is plausible to conclude that there is material substance. Berkeley's response, in essence, is that we should not confuse the philosophical issue of whether there is matter, as defined by Descartes et.al., with the work of natural scientists.

Specifically, the first objection is an appeal to the demonstration in Newtonian physics that the quantity of matter is proportional to the gravity of bodies. Berkeley's response is well-informed and precise. Philonous summarizes Hylas' point as follows. "You lay it down as a self-evident principle that the quantity of motion in any body is proportional to the velocity and matter taken together; and this is made use of to prove a proposition from whence the existence of matter is inferred. Pray is not this arguing in a circle?"[37] When Hylas avoids the circularity by substituting "extension and solidity" for "matter," Berkeley has made his point.

The next objection is blunter. What becomes of the science of physics, which seems to presuppose the existence of matter? The reply is that the science of physics explicates phenomena. The phenomena are appearances perceived by sense, which in turn are ideas. In short, physics does not presuppose matter, as that is defined by Descartes, et.al. Another way of putting this point is that the physicist _as_ physicist is uninterested in this philosophical dispute. For no matter how the dispute is decided, there is still the job of explicating the phenomena. As Berkeley puts it, "And yet, for all this [reduction of phenomena to ideas], it will not follow that philosophers [read "natural scientists"] have been doing nothing; for by observing and reasoning upon the connection of ideas, they discover the laws and methods of nature, which is a part of knowledge both useful and entertaining."[38]

Fourth are objections from theology,[39] which can be taken as questions of Berkeley's Christian orthodoxy. Whether we judge his replies to be altogether satisfactory or not, there really is no doubt of his orthodoxy. That is, Berkeley held to traditional Christian theology and supposed his philosophy to support it, not oppose it. The first of these four objections is that his philosophy does violence to the scriptural account of creation. Berkeley's reply is the nice one that Scripture speaks of the creation of the sun, moon, stars, earth and sea, plants and animals, but nowhere does it speak of the creation of an unknowable, unperceivable, unthinking, corporeal, material substance.

The second is a more subtle objection. Your account, Hylas says, demands men first in the order of creation, in order to perceive other objects, whereas in the Mosaic account man comes last. The reply is that at creation, the several parts of the world became gradually perceivable to finite spirits, but we are not required to suppose that men are the only finite spirits.

But, Hylas asks, do you not mean that since the existence of sensible things consists in their being in a mind, therefore they must have existed eternally in the mind of God, and hence were not created? In his reply Berkeley grants that the creation is in respect of finite spirits, not of God. Berkeley did not raise the obvious, next, embarrassing question: whence come the finite spirits, in respect of whom the creation is? They cannot be mere ideas in God's mind, because ideas are passive, whereas spirits are active.

The next, and last, of the objections from theology claims that the reply to the preceding objection argues change and imperfection in Deity. Berkeley replies that if so, it goes against any theory of creation, and hence is not an objection to the philosophy of immaterialism as being unorthodox.

Fifth, and the last to be considered now, are objections that raise the problem of unknowables. Even granting that Berkeley has satisfactorily answered all the other objections, there are difficulties here raised by Berkeley himself that seem to make his position untenable. The difficulties grow through a series of three objections and replies. The first objection is that if we grant that ideas are the real things, and not representative of real things, then how account for disagreement in sense perceptions? Berkeley's long reply may leave us wondering with what right he can still claim to be a defender of common sense. The second part of his reply is against the representative theory of perception; and it leaves us wondering whether he might not more plausibly have been a defender of common sense if he had given up entirely what he has in common with the representative theory of perception, that the immediate objects of awareness are ideas. For it is his clinging to that that makes the first part of his answer seem strange to common sense.

The first part of his reply is that strictly speaking the objects of different sense faculties are different; so likewise objects perceived by the same sense faculty from different perspectives are different. On the basis of observed coexistence or succession, we combine ideas, and for the sake of economy, use common names. So, for example, when I see a red color coexisting with a flavor I taste coexisting with a texture I feel, I use the one word "cherry," which users of the English language have come to call this combination of ideas. In short, the "things" of our common sense world are combinations of sensible things, or of ideas. Granted that our ideas are variable; it does not follow from this that our senses are not to be trusted, unless we presuppose that the "cherry," e.g., has some one single, unchanged, unperceivable, real nature. But common ordinary people presuppose no such thing. What they mean by "cherry" is not some single, unchanged, unperceivable real nature underlying what they perceive. Instead, they mean what they do perceive -- red, tart, soft, round qualities, associated together in observation.

The second part of the reply is worth quoting in full, as review and summary of Berkeley's position, although it is directly aimed at criticizing the representative theory of perception.

> It is your opinion, the ideas we perceive by
> our senses are not real things, but images, or
> copies of them. Our knowledge therefore is no
> farther real, than as our ideas are the true
> representations of those originals. But as
> these supposed originals are in themselves
> unknown, it is impossible to know how far our
> ideas resemble them; or whether they resemble
> them at all. We cannot therefore be sure we

118

have any real knowledge. Farther, as our ideas are perpetually varied, without any change in the supposed real things, it necessarily follows they cannot all be true copies of them: or if some are, and others are not, it is impossible to distinguish the former from the latter. And this plunges us yet deeper in uncertainty. Again, when we consider the point, we cannot conceive how any idea, or any thing like an idea, should have an absolute existence out of a mind: nor consequently, according to you, how there should be any real thing in Nature. The result of all which is, that we are thrown into the most hopeless and abandoned scepticism. Now give me leave to ask you, first, whether your referring ideas to certain absolutely existing unperceived substances, as their originals, be not the source of all this scepticism? Secondly, whether you are informed, either by sense or reason, of the existence of those unknown originals? And in case you are not, whether it be not absurd to suppose them? Thirdly, whether, upon inquiry, you find there is any thing distinctly conceived or meant by the absolute or external existence of unperceiving substances? Lastly, whether the premises considered, it be not the wisest way to follow Nature, trust your senses, and laying aside all anxious thought about unknown natures or substances, admit with the vulgar those for real things, which are perceived by the senses?[40]

The second objection is of the same sort, continuing to expose what is most vulnerable in Berkeley's position. The objection is an obvious one that we might well have thought of long before reading this far. It is: if each of us perceives only the ideas existing in his own mind, then how can you and I say that we perceive the same objects? Berkeley's reply is that taking "same" in its common meaning, there is no problem. Taking "same" to mean "exactly the same," or "identity," as some philosophers do, there may be a problem. But who knows what these philosophers mean by the abstract idea of identity? It seems to have nothing to do with our ordinary experience. Further, the same problem, if it is one, exists for those who believe in material substance, for they too hold that the immediate objects of awareness are ideas.

Can we be satisfied with this reply? Here is a real difficulty that Berkeley does not so much meet as to doubt whether it is a real problem; and it is lame to add at the end that if it is, then it is for his opponents as well. We might put the difficulty a bit more strenuously: if the immediate objects of my perception are my own ideas, how can I know that there is an external world, let alone know that my ideas are the same as yours? Berkeley perhaps never really seriously entertained this more strenuous form of the difficulty because he was certain that he was a defender of common sense, and that it is absurd to doubt the existence of a world external to the mind. However, it is nonetheless a legitimate objection to anyone who, like Berkeley, philosophizes with the subjectivist bias, and with an analysis of experience having ideas as the immediate objects of perception. As Gilson, the eminent historian of philosophy, has commented: "Everyone is free to decide whether he shall begin to philosophize as a pure mind; if he should elect to do so the difficulty will be not how to get into the mind, but how to get out of it. ...Berkeley's ... achievement was to realize ... that it was a useless and foolish thing even to try it."[41]

The last part of Gilson's statement is not the whole truth. It is true of course that Berkeley stayed "in mind" by denying material substance, but it is also true that he believed, with the plain man, that there is a world of things (ideas) independent of any finite mind, and perceived as they really are. The problem is, how can he do that? The next objection and reply show how he tried. That objection is still concerned with "sameness."

The third of these three objections is that believers in material substance suppose an external archetype (that is, suppose a real material thing) "to which referring their several ideas they may truly be said to perceive the same thing." Berkeley begins his reply by noting again that material substance has been shown not to exist. But then he adds: you may "suppose an external archetype on my principles; external, I mean, to your own mind, though, indeed, it must be supposed to exist in that mind which comprehends all things..."[42] Not only may we so suppose, but it seems we must so suppose, unless we are willing to give up common sense completely, and adopt a view that would have the external world either non-existent or changing with each different perspective in a finite mind.

Why, then, did not Berkeley raise the next obvious questions? If there is an external archetype (idea in the mind of God), are not your idea and mine the same or different by reference to that archetype? We could put the question another way, leaving out "sameness." If there is an external archetype, then how can I know that the idea in my mind corresponds to the archetype? Presumably the archetype is the real thing. Does not my perceiving the real thing, then, depend on my idea's corresponding to the archetype? But how can I get outside my own mind and its idea to tell whether my idea corresponds to the real thing, the archetype in the mind of God? Probably Berkeley did not raise these questions because he could not; to raise them would be to abandon his metaphysics. For here are again the problems of the representative theory of perception, which Berkeley thought he had so ingeniously avoided, come back to plague him. Here, it seems, is an insuperable difficulty, the one more than any other that makes his theory of reality untenable. The best we could possibly say for it now is that if it is true it is unknowable, for on Berkeley's own principles we can never get outside our own ideas to compare them with the archetypes in the mind of God.

The other "insuperable difficulties" we will take up where they can help us in our interpretive tasks. But before we leave Hylas and Philonous there is one more objection and reply that is appropriate here; for it may restore our sympathy with Berkeley's attack on materialism, or at least remind us of his aim. The objection is that the theory of immaterialism is too radical, and will unsettle men's minds. Berkeley replies that quite the contrary immaterialism is a return to common sense, and that it is the Cartesian notion of matter that will unsettle men's minds.

> But it is none of my business to plead for novelties and paradoxes. That the qualities we perceive, are not on the objects : that we must not believe our senses : that we know nothing of the real nature of things, and can never be assured even of their existence : that real colours and sounds are nothing but certain unknown figures and motions : that motions are in themselves neither swift nor slow: that there are in bodies absolute extensions, without any particular magnitude or figure : that a thing stupid, thoughtless and inactive, operates on a spirit : that the least particle of a body, contains innumerable extended parts. These are the novelties, these are the strange notions which shock the genuine uncorrupted judgment of all mankind; and being once admitted, embarrass the mind with endless doubts and difficulties. And it is against these and the like innovations, I endeavour to vindicate common sense.[43]

Chapter 6

Language and Signs

On the contemporary academic scene study of language and signs is thriving; among many professional philosophers it is regarded as the most important, and perhaps most fundamental, part of the philosophic enterprise. Although Berkeley was not preoccupied with the study of language, he certainly was deeply concerned about it; he devoted his Introduction to the Principles of Human Knowledge to a discussion of the nature and abuse of language. Moreover, Berkeley often spoke of nature as a language spoken to us by God its author.

Because the abuse of language, Berkeley thought, was caused chiefly by John Locke's doctrine of abstract ideas, we begin with a statement of that doctrine as Berkeley understood it. An account of Berkeley's substitute for Locke's doctrine will be preceded by a review of abstract ideas as understood in the classical philosophical tradition to which Berkeley felt so indebted. Finally, we review Berkeley's application of his account of language to his theory of vision and to the notion that nature is a language.

I Locke's Doctrine of Abstract Ideas

Because John Locke held that the immediate objects of knowledge are ideas, he was puzzled about material substance, concluding that it is a something-I-know-not-what underlying the sensed qualities of shape, extension, etc. Locke was equally puzzled about abstract ideas, and for the same subjectivist reason. Berkeley, in the Introduction to the Principles, quotes the crucial passage,

> Abstract ideas are not so obvious or easy to children or the yet unexercised mind as particular ones. If they seem so to grown men, it is only because by constant and familiar use they are made so. For when we nicely reflect upon them, we shall find that general ideas are fictions and contrivances of the mind, that carry difficulty with them, and do not so easily offer themselves, as we are apt to imagine. For example, does it not require some pains and skill to form the general idea of a triangle (which is yet none of the most abstract comprehensive and difficult) for it must be neither oblique nor rectangle, neither equilateral, equicrural, nor scalenon, but all and none of these at once. In effect, it is

something imperfect that cannot exist, an idea
wherein some parts of several different and
inconsistent ideas are put together. It is
true the mind in this imperfect state has need
of such ideas, and makes all the haste to them
it can, for the conveniency of communication
and enlargement of knowledge, to both which it
is naturally very much inclined. But yet one
has reason to suspect such ideas are marks of
our imperfection. At least this is enough to
shew that the most abstract and general ideas
are not those that the mind is first and most
easily acquainted with, nor such as its
earliest knowledge is conversant about.[1]

We cannot help sympathizing with Locke, and perhaps wonder
whether we can explain any better how we form abstract general
ideas. And yet this passage exemplifies that being "insensibly
drawn into uncouth paradoxes, difficulties, and inconsistencies"
that Berkeley, in the first paragraph of the Introduction, claims
is the result of departing from common sense and following "the
light of a superior principle."

Having quoted the above passage, Berkeley at once launches
into a severe criticism of it, pinpointing a number of Locke's
suggestions that seem paradoxical, if not unbelievable. Thus, for
example, he writes,

If any man has the faculty of framing in his
mind such an idea of a triangle as is here
described, it is in vain to pretend to dispute
him out of it, nor would I go about it. All I
desire is, that the reader would fully and
certainly inform himself whether he has such an
idea or no. And this, methinks, can be no hard
task for any one to perform. What more easy
than for any one to look a little into his own
thoughts, and there try whether he has, or can
attain to have, an idea that shall correspond
with the description that is here given of the
general idea of a triangle, which is, neither
oblique, nor rectangle, equilateral,
equicrural, nor scalenon, but all and none of
these at once.[2]

So telling is Berkeley's criticism that we feel there must be
some other way of explaining how we communicate with one another;
or if not that, then a better formulation of the doctrine of
abstract ideas. Therefore, before we consider Berkeley's other
way, it seems appropriate, given Berkeley's classical

124

predilections, to review the classical doctrine of abstract ideas.

II The Classical Doctrine of Abstract Ideas[3]

The difficulties Locke encounters seem inescapable, given that the immediate objects of knowledge are ideas which the mind passively receives. Thus Locke supposes that we as children receive into the mind, as particular ideas, a scalenon triangle, an equilateral triangle, an oblique triangle, etc.; and then through much mental huffing and puffing, magically produce the general triangle which is none and all of the above particulars. The mind, not allowed any of the action with respect to the particular ideas, is then called upon to do the mission impossible with respect to the general ideas.

As a possible way out of the puzzlements, we might suppose instead that not ideas, but cats, for example, are the immediate objects of knowledge; and that our minds or intellects are actively working to achieve knowledge of such things as cats, dogs, triangles, -- whatever. So far at least there is nothing contrary to our common sense.

The account of intellectual activity we will here review aims to be a refinement of common sense, as well as a safeguard against the snares and traps of subjectivism and skepticism. With respect to our coming to know _what_ things are, the intellectual activity is abstraction. When you and I say that we know what the fragrance of the rose is, or the size of a basketball, or the ways of the planets, what we have done (or have had done for us by another intellect whom we have no reason to mistrust) is to cut off or abstract some _one_ trait, or nature, or characteristic from _many_ particular roses, or basketballs, or planets, and to make that nature or essence an object of knowledge. To be sure, we have not materially cut that essence off; that of course is impossible. Rather, we have formally cut it off, we have conceptualized it.

My (or your) concept of the rose's fragrance is, to employ a technical term, a universal; an _unum versus alia_, a one with respect to, or over against, the many. By virtue of the intellectual activity of abstraction the fragrance of the rose, which is as "many" as there are roses, has become one before the intellect, or as an object of knowledge. If we call this an abstract idea, we then recognize that it is not "all and none" of the particulars; but instead a universal, a one (in intellect, as known) with respect to many (in reality, apart from being known). Thus, when I know "triangle" or triangularity, I abstract that essential feature from all the peculiar individuating traits of the many particular triangles that exist; when I know "rose" or roseness I cut off that essence from all the many individual roses

125

that have existed, are existing, or will exist in the real natural world.

Hence, on this view conceptualizing, or forming abstract ideas, is the intellectual activity by which we come to know what things are, in all their rich diversity. Ideas, concepts, are properly understood as instrumental to knowledge, not as immediate objects of knowledge. One philosopher in the classical tradition has employed a helpful analogy.[4] Artificial lenses are used by many of us for assistance in focussing objects. We see through the lenses; they are not the objects of sight, but instead are instrumental to it. Concepts, ideas, are not objects of knowledge, except when we think about them, as we are here doing. Again the analogy helps. We can remove our spectacles, in order to look at them; but when we do, we employ lenses which are not themselves at the same time objects of sight. So, when we come to know what concepts are -- that they are instruments of knowledge, e.g. -- we employ concepts in the knowing, which are not, and need not be, known before they reveal the nature of concepts.

Another way to put this realism is to say that our concepts (ideas) are significant of what things are. But they are peculiar signs, unlike traffic signs, or signs in nature (smoke being a sign of fire, e.g.), or even unlike words. Because of the crucial importance in that difference we must expand somewhat on this and hope that it will explain not only Locke's distortion of the classical notion of abstract ideas, but also indicate how and where Berkeley seems to have gone wrong in his response to Locke; and thereby give the clue to his account of language, theory of vision, and theory that nature is a language.

To begin let us consider a feature that all non-conceptual signs (barber poles, words, grimaces, lightning bolts, whatever) share. Before any of these signs can signify for us, we must be aware of the sign. We must know and recognize what the sign, in itself, and apart from its significance, is. Indeed, any one of these signs can be described: a barber pole, for example, is a pole with spiral stripes colored alternately red and white; a frown is a furrowing of the brow and a downturning of the mouth. Even though it be the case that such a sign (a stop sign, e.g., or a word) has no other reason or cause for existing but to signify something else, still the sign must be recognized before it can signify.

If what has been said about concepts is true, then they are peculiar in that they are not, and need not be, known or recognized before they signify. It is not only that their reason or cause for being is to signify, but also that their very being is nothing but a signifying, of the "what's" of things. Let us

126

call these signs _formal_ signs; and, at the risk of using a misleading term in this book about Berkeley, call the others material signs.

As Berkeley asked us to reflect on Locke's doctrine, so now the classical philosopher asks us to reflect whether we can reasonably deny that formal signs are constantly employed by each one of us in all his waking hours; that what is peculiarly human about us, if anything is, is this remarkable capacity to conceptualize, to know, to become formally other things. We might convince ourselves that there are formal signs when we consider the impossibility of our ever knowing anything if there are only material signs. If a material sign is to signify for us we must first recognize it: stop signs can not work if they are not materially present. If we supposed that there were no formal signs, then we could know any material sign (like a word, e.g.) only by way of another material sign; and that in turn by way of a prior material sign; and so on, to infinity. In other words, knowledge would be impossible, because it could never begin.

In the _Three Dialogues_ Berkeley tried to explain the passivity of the mind in sense perception: in plucking the flower, bringing it to the nose, inhaling, we can be said to be active; but then willy-nilly the mind is impressed with an odor, is the passive recipient of an idea. The response of the classical realist to this rests upon the distinction between knowing and sensing which Berkeley himself acknowledged, in one of the objections and replies we earlier bypassed. The objection is to Berkeley's notion of a perfect God: "...you have asserted that whatever ideas we perceive from without, are in the mind which affects us. The ideas therefore of pain and uneasiness are in God; or in other words God suffers pain: that is to say, there is an imperfection in the divine nature, which you acknowledged was absurd. So you are caught in a plain contradiction."[5] Berkeley escapes the contradiction by observing the distinction between suffering pain and knowing what pain is.[6] If we apply that distinction to human experience we certainly would agree with Locke and Berkeley that we cannot know what pain is, or know about cats, dogs, and triangles without experience. Thus we must feel the pain, see the cat, pet the dog, in order to have knowledge of them. But granted that, still our coming to know what pain is, and how dogs and cats look and feel and act, is the result of the intellect's activity we have just reviewed.

Berkeley's account of the passivity of the mind is commonplace among thinkers convinced of the skeptical conclusion that we do not and cannot know the natures and causes of things.[7] But notice what happens in that sort of analysis. We are told that our minds are impressed with colors, sounds, shapes, and other such particular ideas; and that these ideas are said to be representative of an external reality. Already the analyzer has made over ideas into material signs (to use our terminology); and into signs we cannot even be said to know, but only impressed with. We then cannot even begin to ask sensibly whether the world I come to "know" corresponds to that series of impressions.

All the while, of course, the analyzer of our experience presupposes that we all know and understand what he is talking about; that we know what colors, sounds, and shapes are; that we are aware of what it means to "be impressed with"; that we are conscious of the difference between "internal" and "external"; that we know the significance of "significance." Thus Berkeley assumes that his reader knows what plucking, flower, nose, inhaling, activity are. In short, it seems that none of us can write or speak one meaningful sentence without utilizing formal signs, without conceptualizing, without forming and using abstract ideas. How could the skeptic convince us that we can not come to know things? or that we can not know the world as it really is? To do it, he must argue, and for that he must already presume a remarkable amount of intellectual, rational awareness that he and we share about the world, including ourselves.

It does need to be emphasized, however, that the classical realistic theory of knowledge does not claim that men know all there is to know, or even that men know very much, or even that all of the knowledge that we have is incorrigible. No, the claim is only that men have the capacity to know things, and know them as they really are. Given this, a plausible theory of knowledge must aim at describing the tools of knowledge in such a way that the description of them does not turn us toward skepticism. Because Berkeley claimed to be defending common sense and arguing against the reality/appearance dichotomy, we must keep this aim in mind as we review his account of ideas and language.

III   How Particular Ideas and Words Become Universal

Locke distorted the classical account of abstract ideas by taking ideas to be the immediate objects of our knowledge, instead of being instrumental to our knowing what things are. Because Berkeley has the same subjectivist bias as Locke, his response to Locke's doctrine was bound to be different from the classical response. Even so, he came very close to that response, as is evident in his writing that "...it must be acknowledged that a man may consider a figure merely as triangular, without attending to the particular qualities of the angles, or relations of the sides. So far he may abstract: but this will never prove, that he can frame an abstract general inconsistent idea of a triangle."[8] Berkeley recognized that so far we do indeed abstract. But subjectivism kept him from acknowledging that thereby the intellect knows triangularity; and it accounts perhaps for his guarded language, his writing "consider" instead of "conceptualize." Again, he writes, "...all knowledge and demonstration are about universal notions, to which I fully agree: but then it doth not appear to me that those notions are formed by abstraction in the manner premised [by Locke] ; universality, so far as I can comprehend not consisting in the absolute, positive nature or conception of any thing, but in the relation it bears to the particulars signified or represented by it:..."[9] The classical philosopher cannot help wondering what if; if only Berkeley had thought through that peculiar cognitive relationship the concept bears to what it signifies.[10] But instead, for Berkeley, the problem is how a particular thing, name, or notion can be rendered universal.

The problem can be put this way. For Locke, the word "triangle," having a definition like "a plane surface comprehended by three right lines," must signify one abstract general idea; which idea in turn represents all and no particular triangles. Berkeley's response is to note that the very definition shows the uselessness of such abstract general ideas; that is, the definition says nothing about the individuating traits of particular triangles -- their color, the length of the lines, the degree of the angles. No, the definition, and hence the particular word or name "triangle," signifies all triangles, by leaving out the peculiarity of each one. If we are inclined to say to this, "But do you not mean that in conceptualizing 'triangle' we are abstracting or cutting off that nature from all the individuating traits of particular triangles?", Berkeley's response is that now we, like Locke, are supposing some one abstract idea mysteriously formed. And given his subjectivism he cannot but respond that way. For Berkeley, the immediate objects are ideas, particular ideas or sensible qualities. If the mind uses a particular idea to signify many or all like ideas, then it becomes in the use general; the particular thus becomes universal.

Words, Berkeley tells us, become general in the same way. Frame in your mind a triangle idea; you must admit that that is a particular idea. You can, however, if you will, let it signify all triangles, e. g., if you want to recall the difference between triangles and circles. Likewise we must admit that the word "triangle" is, taken in itself, particular; but if we will it, we can let it denote or signify all triangles. Words so understood and properly used are indispensable for the communicating of knowledge among human beings. However, if we fall into the same trap as Locke, supposing that words, or common names, signify abstract ideas, we will spend our efforts in idle disputes about things that do not exist.

We can not help wondering whether there might not be something amiss here. Granted that the word "dog" (to change the

129

example) can and does signify or denote any dog, past, present, or future; still "dog" is but a material sign. And the intellectual power, by virtue of which I recognize the word "dog" when written or spoken (so that it can and does signify for me), is presumably the same intellectual power by virtue of which I recognize dogs. Further, without that power of knowing I could come to recognize neither "dog" nor dogs. In other words, ideas, things, words, so long as they are taken, as Berkeley takes them, as material signs, cannot be sufficient to knowledge. With material signs only, we can never come to know anything.

But for the moment, let us put this wondering aside, and try to follow through Berkeley's account of language. Berkeley does seem to agree with classical philosophy that human languages, even when properly used, are insufficient for knowledge. At the end of his Introduction to the Principles, he says that "...we need only draw the curtain of words, to behold the fairest tree of knowledge, whose fruit is excellent, and within the reach of our hand."[11] Then he entreats the reader "to make my words the occasion of his own thinking, and endeavor to attain the same train of thoughts in reading, that I had in writing them. By this means it will be easy for him to discover the truth or falsity of what I say. He will be out of all danger of being deceived by my words, and I do not see how he can be led into an error by considering his own naked, undisguised ideas."[12]

By now we should guess that for Berkeley those naked, undisguised ideas speak the language of nature, of which of course God is the author. We will move to that, as Berkeley did, by way of his theory of vision.

IV   Berkeley's Theory of Vision

Let us suppose that nature is a set of material particles, of various sizes and shapes and configurations, moving about in accordance with mechanical laws; in short, that nature is a mechanism. Given this we would explain the phenomenon of sight as part of the mechanism. We have already noticed how the transmission theory of light lends credence to that explanation. Supposing also that men are minds as well as machines, we will go on to explain that those mechanical causes produce pictures, in the mind, of external material things; and add that the pictures are copies or representations of the material things; not necessarily of things as they really are, but nonetheless representations of them.

As we have already discovered, for Berkeley there are at least three things wrong with this theory: 1) the supposed matter is inert, and hence cannot be sensibly said to cause anything; 2) the mind is asked to do the impossible: compare the pictures it

130

has with the reality pictured; 3) furthermore, an idea can be like nothing but another idea, or can represent nothing but another idea.

The predominant theory of vision in Berkeley's time did suppose that material causes produce images on the retina and thus cause vision; it did suppose that by some magical powers we compare the pictures produced with the reality, and declare that reality is far different from the pictures of it; it did suppose that nonetheless those visible objects represented something external to the viewer, without the mind.

Berkeley's theory of vision effectively and compellingly counters all that. We will not take the time or space to explore the technical details of it. But the reader who does examine An Essay Towards A New Theory Of Vision, first published in 1709, cannot but be impressed by the wealth of scientific and mathematical learning that the then quite young George Berkeley displays. He shows comfortable familiarity with the remarkable work in science that made Whitehead label the century that had ended not long before Berkeley was writing, the century of genius.

When Berkeley composed A New Theory of Vision, his immaterialism was well in mind, needing only to be worked out in publishable form. In other words, the two theories grew together. However, we can take the theory of vision as a step on the way to the idealism of the Principles and The Three Dialogues, for the following reason.[13] Berkeley's aim, in the theory of vision, is to show how colors and light (visible objects) are to be understood as signs, rather than as effects of material causes; and as signs of other ideas, namely, tangible ideas. In the Essay he does not suggest or argue that the tangible ideas, too, are significant of some other reality. Instead, he gives the impression that touch is a privileged sense faculty, by virtue of which we know an external world. In short, in the Essay he did not aim to establish immaterialism.

The logic of his argument is simple, trying to explain how it is that in ordinary experience we take the objects we see to be the same objects we feel. It is argued first that in fact we do not see the same objects that we feel. The only immediate objects of sight, Berkeley insists, are light and colors. The sense of touch is aware of neither light nor color. Having established the difference between visible and tangible objects, Berkeley argues that it is by virtue of experience from our infancy up that we learn to read the visual language as significant of the objects of the tangible world. So used are we to this language, and so comfortable with it, that we see right through the visible objects, as signs, to the tangible objects; and hence typically say and suppose that we see rough or hard or smooth or close or

131

distant objects. Now, says Berkeley, that is true, in the same sense as we might say, in reading Tom Jones, that we see Squire Western and Sophia. But in fact, as we are all well aware, to one who does not know the English language, the squire and his daughter must remain unknown.

Furthermore, just as we can ponder the obstacles to our understanding in Fielding's using words we are not acquainted with, or words (particularly in giving voice to the peculiar temper of Squire Western) with letters blanked out, so are we aware of the errors in judgment we make by misreading visible signs: the tower in the distance looks round, but in fact is square; the stick partially submerged in water looks bent, but in fact is straight; etc. Berkeley's aim is not, as was Descartes', to conclude total distrust of the senses, but rather to show, in the theory of vision, that visible objects are signs of tangible objects; signs that we, as mental beings, spirits, are capable of reading and understanding. Far from being a mechanical process, caused by matter in motion, seeing is a mental occurrence, conducted by minds or spirits.

V Nature is a Language

Once again, let us suppose, with the predominant scientific philosophy of Berkeley's time, that nature is a set of material particles, moving about in accordance with mechanical laws; in short, that nature is a mechanism. Given that, we would explain not only seeing, but every other sort of sense experience as part of the mechanism. If we still suppose that men are extranatural, i. e., minds as well as machines, we will go on to explain that material, mechanical causes produce all of our sense experience. If instead we come to regard ourselves as wholly natural, i. e. as complex machines, our account will be that much simpler; for now we need no longer worry about how it is that mental causes can effect material changes, and vice versa.

And again, we have already discovered with Berkeley how unsatisfactory either version of that theory is. It is unbelievable, and it is unintelligible. We cannot believe that reality (matter in motion) is so different from what we experience of a world full of colors, sounds, etc. Nor can we make sense of an unexperienced material substance, defined as inert and passive, causing changes in the world. Materialism, either as part of a dualism that also includes mind, or by itself, pure and simple, is an untenable position. Nature cannot be either matter or mechanism.

The clue to an intelligible alternative lies, for Berkeley, in his theory of vision. We need only expand the notion. Nature, we are taught by Berkeley, instead of being a mechanical system of material particles, is a system of ideas. Nature, so understood, can be ultimately explained only by concluding a Mind, a Superperceiver, a providential God. If we already understand that vision is a language, that visible objects are signs, we need only add that so it is with all other sensible objects, all other ideas. Together they constitute a language spoken by Supermind to finite minds.

If we still worry about the fate of science in this metaphysics, Berkeley reassures us.

> ...Hence it is evident, that those things which under the notion of a cause co-operating or concurring to the production of effects, are altogether inexplicable, and run us into great absurdities, may be very naturally explained, and have a proper and obvious use assigned them, when they are considered only as marks or signs for our information. And it is the searching after, and endeavouring to understand those signs instituted by the Author of Nature, that ought to be the employment of the natural philosopher, and not the pretending to explain things by corporeal causes; which doctrine seems to have too much estranged the minds of men from that active principle, that supreme and wise spirit, in whom we live, move, and have our being."[14]

What a blow has been struck against materialism, and all its attendant corrupting and evil tendencies. For surely, if men of science are made to understand that nature is a language, and not a material process, they will be inclined to honor and praise its Author, rather than to be childishly distracted by a new mechanical toy. And we would expect, then, that all the marvelous and magnificent technological fruits of science would be directed toward man's spiritual welfare; surely, the Author of nature could have intended nothing else.

VI Where Have All the Causes Gone?

It seems appropriate now to consider the implications of the notion that a world of nature can be bereft of causes. That a nature composed of inert matter is powerless is clear enough. But that Berkeley should oppose it with another nature equally powerless is cause for wonder, especially because he is the proclaimed spokesman for common sense. Berkeley's plain man presumably takes nature to be composed of a variety of kinds of colorful, noisy, odoriferous, tasty, and tangible things; moreover, he understands some of those things, and not only men,

133

to be agents, i.e., to have within themselves the power(s) to bring about change(s). The plain man never doubts that when that furry, chattering thing skitters across the lawn, picks up an oval object in its teeth, and hurries away with it, that it is really the squirrel that is acting, so as to effect changes in itself and in the acorn. Nor does the plain man doubt that if the acorn falls into fertile soil and sprouts, it is the acorn becoming oak, or the oak growing. In short, the plain man sees the world, although he may not articulate it as refinedly as his classical philosophical spokesman, as so many potentialities being actualized, so much matter being formed -- a world made up of changing things acting and being acted upon, interacting with one another, causing and being affected.

Furthermore, the man who so sees the world is not likely to have his mind estranged from the supreme active principle. Quite the contrary; being daily aware not of matter in motion, but of activity, he is inclined to regard God as being the actor or agent par excellence.

Moreover, if the plain man is also familiar with Scripture, it would not be unfair of him to suggest that when the apostle, Paul, spoke of the God in whom we live, move, and have our being, he was waxing poetic; and that if Berkeley means for us to take it literally, it is difficult to see how he can avoid being charged with the corrupting heresy of pantheism.

A number of times hitherto we have insisted that Berkeley was not opposed to science, and did not see religion and science as opposed to one another. Now we need to add, to explain his apparent desertion of the plain man, that Berkeley was understandably awe struck by seventeenth century science; so much so that although he could not allow natural science (or natural philosophy, as he and others at that time still called it) to be a study of corporeal (material) causes, that being unintelligible; at the same time he could not but allow that nature is a most remarkable uniform system the operations of which were being discovered as never before in the history of man by this new science. Then, when his subjectivist bias decreed to him that nature is composed of ideas, each one of which is inert, inactive, he had no recourse but to conclude that all power and acting in reality belong in minds, not in nature. The dualism of mind and matter that Berkeley kicked out the front door has sneaked in the back. It was bound to, because Berkeley saw nothing amiss in a science of nature that recognizes no power, efficacy, energy in nature itself. No wonder then that he urges upon the men of science that what they really are doing is "searching after, and endeavouring to understand those signs instituted by the Author of Nature."

It could be that nature is a language, but if so it is goodbye to common sense, all of Berkeley's assurances to the contrary notwithstanding. Strip nature of power and causes, and the plain man no longer recognizes the skeleton.

VII A Farewell to Realism

For all that, Berkeley in fact tries to mollify the plain man by insisting that he does not want to deny that sensible bread nourishes us; and that he does deny that insensible, inactive material can nourish us. And further, he wants us, recognizing this, to give the glory to God.

But for what should we give Him the glory? If we speak now for the very practical plain man, we may agree that he is mollified. Yes, he might say, we do give Him the glory, three times a day, before meals. And if that is all you mean, good Bishop, then fine, there's an end of it.

And apparently, albeit surprisingly, that is all that Berkeley means. Let us suppose that nature is a language. Still, Berkeley tells us, language has more than one use. It can be and is used to inform, to communicate knowledge. Thus, when someone reads a book about Plato he expects to be informed about who the man was, what his philosophy is, why it is that philosophy and not some other, and so on. But language also can be and is used to direct or command. Thus, when a parent wishes to praise or admonish his child, he will use language aimed not so much at informing as at guiding. The drill sergeant, barking his commands, is not so much informing as he is ordering a line of march. The language of the manual on how to repair the kitchen sink directs our actions without informing us of the principles.[15]

Moreover, as Berkeley warned us in the Introduction to his Principles, words have a capacity to deceive us. Thus, a language intended for one use primarily, say directive, if taken as informative, may well mislead us to a distorted account of reality. So it seems is the case with the language of nature! Toward the end of his theory of vision Berkeley writes, "I think we may fairly conclude that the proper objects of vision constitute an universal language of the Author of nature, whereby we are instructed how to regulate our actions in order to attain those things that are necessary to the preservation and well-being of our bodies, as also to avoid whatever may be hurtful and destructive of them."[16] Twenty-four years later, Berkeley put it this way, in a publication of 1733: "In the contrivance of vision, as in that of other things [which are, we now know, hearing, smelling, tasting, touching] , the wisdom of Providence seemeth to have consulted the operation, rather than the theory, of man; to the former things are admirably fitted, but, by that

135

very means, the latter is often perplexed."[17]

However distressing this might be to our realistic propensities, and to our desire to read Berkeley as a defender of common sense and a philosophical realist, it is difficult to see how Berkeley could have concluded otherwise, given his subjectivist bias. Any language, even in its informative function, in a certain sense stands between us and what we would know. That is to say, before the words can signify, we must recognize the words; a person speaking or writing in a language foreign to us cannot inform us. Hence, if nature is indeed a language, then we seem to be in the hopeless position we noted already in the problem of archetypes or of unknowables. God speaks to us by way of ideas; but whether those ideas, the immediate objects of knowledge, have any resemblance or correspondence to the supposed archetypes in the mind of God, we have no way of knowing. If nature is a language, then we have no more reason to suppose that visible or tangible, etc., objects are like the archetypes in the mind of God, than we have to suppose that the word "dog" is like dogs.

Although Berkeley shies away from this conclusion in The Three Dialogues, he offhandedly reaches it in his theory of vision, in 1733 as well as in 1709. But whether he shies away from it, or openly acknowledges it, the conclusion is inevitable: the instruments of knowing (ideas as "material" signs) turn out to be such as to keep us from knowing. We must begin to strongly suspect that the cause for Berkeley's failure is his subjectivist bias. If anyone starts to philosophize in his mind, supposing that the immediate objects of knowledge are ideas in the mind, it is difficult to see how he can argue for either common sense or a philosophical realism aimed at refining common sense.

Those sympathetic with Berkeley's lifelong warfare against materialism and its attendant corrupting evils, and with his concomitant crusade for theism, religion, good morals, public spirit, and a sound body politic, cannot but be saddened by Berkeley's failure. They can hold to Berkeley's demonstration that materialism cannot be proved; but Berkeley has not, and cannot, show that its contrary, immaterialism (or idealism), is true.

By contrast, those who are antipathetic to Berkeley's aims can now rejoice, if Berkeley is right in maintaining that materialism is at the root of so much he disapproved of. Materialism's strongest modern enemy has done his best to prove the contrary, and has failed. Who, then, can gainsay those who freely choose to believe that there is no God, and that any moral or political system which prevents our freely seeking whatever

136

ends we please is one to which we can give no allegiance?

In short, Berkeley failed to provide the metaphysical and epistemological system he hoped would provide the underpinning for the classical education, morals, and politics he favored. Given that failure, he would not be surprised at the growth subsequently of skepticism, atheism, and irreligion.

PART III

Interpretations of Berkeley

Chapter 7

The Kantian Turn:
Metaphorics and/or Linguistic Analysis

There is another passage, in the literature of Berkeley's time, beside the ones we have quoted from Berkeley, about what nature teaches. It begins, "This nature effectively teaches us to avoid things which produce in me the feeling of pain and to seek those which make me have some feeling of pleasure and so on." A page later the author goes on in a less hedonistic vein; "...I am accustomed to misunderstand and misconstrue the order of nature, because although these sensations or sense perceptions were given to me only to indicate to my mind which objects are useful or harmful to the composite body of which it is a part, and are for that purpose sufficiently clear and distinct, I nevertheless use them as though they were very certain rules by which I could obtain direct information about the essence and the nature of external objects, about which they can of course give me no information except very obscurely and confusedly."[1] The author of these lines is none other than Rene Descartes. No wonder Gilson wrote of the unity of philosophical experience. Given the same starting point great thinkers, no matter what bypaths they take, will arrive at the same conclusion. So it is that, given the starting point of subjectivism, we have seen Berkeley confess, albeit reluctantly, that the universal language of nature does not teach us what things are, but instead instructs us on how to cope. So pervasive has this notion become in the modern intellectual world that it is now commonly supposed that "rationality" means "problem-solving." Whether the problem be landing a man on the moon, or having both guns and butter, or cleaning up our environment, "reason" can solve it. But to suppose that reason can also come to know the essences and natures of things, be they men, moons, guns or butter, is to lapse into antiquated, naive, and (so it is thought) thoroughly discredited rationalism. "Empiricism" is the cry of our time: study the facts, order the phenomena, discover the laws; and thereby solve the problems. More than that reason cannot be expected to do.

And if, in the education that accompanies this scheme, there still are "courses" and "majors" in the humanities, i. e., in poetry, drama, music, painting, etc., it is not because it is supposed that there reason might come to know what man, nature, supernature are. Such study is required or recommended for the sake of developing, as it is often expressed, well-rounded citizens. A more sophisticated explanation is that one of the perennial problems man faces is his own stubborn penchant for values. True, we know now, so the argument goes in this enlightened scientific age, that what any one of us takes to be good or beautiful is utterly subjective, with no empirical foundation. But today's typical "humanist" urges us to take advantage of both the stubborn penchant and the subjectivity by creating our own values. And why not? If reason is no good for discovering what is good and beautiful, perhaps at least it can make them up; and in the bargain, put a good face on the bad deal by labeling the activity "being creative." We become like God, not by knowing good and evil, for that is impossible, but by creating good and evil. And with each of us being thus a creator and a god, the great God is no longer the Lord Almighty, but instead Who's-To-Say.

In his account of the present condition of moral philosophy, Alasdair MacIntyre notes the prevalent view that "all moral, indeed all evaluative, argument is and always must be rationally interminable."[2] Given the split between fact and value, between scientific judgments based on carefully controlled experience and value judgments based on subjective attitudes and preferences, the prevalent view seems inevitable. As MacIntyre notes, the philosophical theory expressive of this view is emotivism, according to which "all moral judgments are nothing but expressions of preference, expressions of attitude or feeling, insofar as they are moral or evaluative in character."[3] After arguing that emotivism fails as a theory of meaning of a certain type of sentence, MacIntyre disregards emotivism's claim to universality of scope, and instead treats it as the outcome of trends in modern moral philosophy.[4]

For the sake of understanding recent modern interpretations of Berkeley,[5] we will review trends in modern philosophy from Berkeley's time to ours. Some of the review will pay attention to metaphysics, some to moral philosophy. Such a review is bound to be oversimplified, and should not be taken as facile dismissal of all modern thought.[6] By focussing on what seems to be the inexorable logic of subjectivist philosophy, it tries to show how the inability of modern thought to provide a rational foundation for morality has led to the prevalence in our time of emotivism on the one hand and existentialism on the other. If successful, it will show the consequences of Berkeley's failure to complete his project, and show why recent modern interpretations of Berkeley are as they are.

I   Hume's Skepticism

If we are sympathetic to Berkeley's enterprise, we might at this point conjecture that there is still at least one stone we might turn over, hoping to find the clue to a realistic metaphysics, if not a science of nature. Even granting that we cannot know nature as it really is, can we not maintain still that it is a system of ideas, not of material particles; and also that we know ourselves, through reflection and introspection, to be mental substances, thinking, willing, acting; and with that, hold to there being an infinite Mind? In short, can we not still salvage the metaphysics of "to be is to be perceived or a perceiver," even though our perceived ideas do not disclose to us the really real? and perhaps thereby provide a foundation for classical moral philosophy?

With that stone overturned we find not the clue to a realistic metaphysics, but instead the ticket to skepticism. Berkeley saw the problem, and wrestled with it early in the third dialogue. In the midst of grappling with the question as to how we can know active things, if ideas are passive, and are the immediate objects of knowledge, Berkeley has Hylas assert that, "...to me it seems, that according to your own way of thinking, and in consequence of your own principles, it should follow that you are only a system of floating ideas, without any substance to support them."[7] We before commented that Berkeley anticipated David Hume. The latter did indeed so argue, and in every bit as compelling and convincing a way as did Berkeley to explode the notion of material substance.

The logic is as inexorable as it is simple. Starting with the subjectivist bias, the immediate data of conscious awareness are impressions, to use Hume's word. But just as we have no sense impression of material substance, so we have no impression of mental substance. The very first step in Descartes' rationalism was a misstep. Not "I think (or doubt), therefore I am." That is a _petitio principii_, a begging of the question, an assuming the very thing to be proved. How prove that ego, that "I," as substance? We can say from experience, or from the sort of reflection possible for Descartes, Berkeley, and ourselves, that there is thought -- or rather a thought, then another, then maybe a willing, etc. But from this sort of analysis it should be evident that there is no impression of spiritual substance, anymore than there is, in experience, an impression of material substance. Given the subjectivist bias, the logic of the analysis of experience atomizes the experienced world, whether of the supposed external nature or the supposed internal mind, into a succession of discrete data.

Hume goes on to practically reassure us. Through experience we accustom ourselves to living in and coping with this welter of data. We all note certain regularities in events, both in those called by us "external," those "internal," and those of apparent interaction between the external and the internal. But we are not in a position to claim knowledge of material substances that have within themselves powers and energy. Likewise we cannot know that we are spiritual substances possessing such powers. All we know, says Hume, is our profound ignorance. The moral is that we in fact get along well enough by way of custom and experience, but that we should eschew metaphysics. Dualisms, materialisms, idealisms, are all vain enterprises. Instead, the proper tasks for philosophers, Hume counsels, recognizing the limitations of human knowledge and being healthily skeptical, are on the one hand to achieve as systematic and orderly an account of nature as experience will allow, without speculating about such things as substances, powers, causes, forces; and on the other hand to achieve a similar account of man's moral behavior. Indeed, Hume announced in his major work, A Treatise of Human Nature, that his aim was to accomplish in moral philosophy what Newton had accomplished in natural philosophy.

A striking feature of many post-Berkeleyan attempts to establish morality is the maintenance of at least some of the values our modern Western civilization has inherited from the classical and Judeo-Christian traditions. Thus Hume does not doubt (he is not fanatical in his skepticism), for example, that justice is good for men. He empirically reports that virtually all men, all societies, all cultures approve of just behavior, and disapprove of injustice. However, we can have no rational insight into such values as justice, courage, honor, love, etc. In reason's stead Hume puts moral sense or sensibility. Just as normal men are equipped with five senses for experiencing the world of nature, so normal men possess a moral sense of right and wrong. Reason's function, then, is not to discern good and bad, right and wrong, not to direct the individual in his moral quest, but instead is to function pragmatically, usefully, in the attainment of values in the existence of the individual or polis that the moral sense discerns. Should someone try to upset our system of morals, we cannot argue with him, but can only appeal to his moral sense. Should that be lacking, there is no other appeal, save presumably to force.

II   The Kantian Turn

In The Theory of Vision Vindicated, Berkeley wrote, "How comes it to pass that a set of [visible] ideas, altogether different from tangible ideas, should nevertheless suggest them to us, there being no necessary connexion between them? To which the proper answer is, That this is done in virtue of an arbitrary connexion, instituted by the Author of nature."[8] Supposing that to be the case, there is cause for wonder that we are able to read the language. Clearly, we can do so only because God has constructed our own minds so that we can do it. We can extend the question and the wonder. Taking nature, the whole system of ideas, to be a language, how is it that we, as minds, can read the language?

If not exactly that question, then similar questions are what Immanuel Kant (1724-1804) must have asked himself when he was thinking through the skeptical conclusions of Hume, which had, as Kant himself put it, awakened Kant from his dogmatic slumber. The answer Kant gave has in large measure determined the course of modern philosophy ever since. We can put the question in Hume's terms: given that experience provides a welter of discrete, atomic data, how is it that the mind is able to order the data? The data themselves provide no principles of order. And if Hume says that we do it from custom or habit, fine; but that needs explication. The critique of reason that Kant produced aimed to show that we understand nature as we do because the mind itself provides the structure. To begin with, we take nature to be spatial and temporal because space and time are _forms_ of our _sensibility_, not data of experience. Then, we understand nature to be composed of substances causally related because substance and cause are _categories_ of our _understanding_, not data of experience.

In short, Kant tells us, heretofore philosophers have supposed that knowledge is mind's conforming to reality. No wonder that Hume concluded that we have a profound ignorance. But henceforth, following the critique of reason, we mean that knowledge is reality's conforming to mind. To be sure, our knowledge of nature is then phenomenal; that is to say, we cannot claim that it is a knowledge of the way things really are apart from our sensible awareness and categorial understanding of them; but nonetheless it is knowledge. Furthermore, it is a knowledge that reached its culmination in Newtonian physics. Nature may not really be a lawfully determined order, but we cannot help understanding it that way.

If that suffices as an explanation of science, metaphysics has yet to be accounted for. Taken as a demonstrated account of noumena (of things as they really are, independent of us as knowers) metaphysics is impossible, Kant tells us. However, there are important kinds of human experience -- aesthetic, moral, religious -- which suggest to man's _speculation_, beyond his scientific understanding, regulative ideals, such as the existence and providence of God and the immortality of the soul; and also suggest archetypal images of what reality, viewed as a whole, and not piecemeal, or ectypally (as is done in scientific understanding), might be. For example, in aesthetic experience, our enjoyment and appreciation depend on our viewing the painting, say, as a whole. We can, to be sure, focus attention on the brush strokes, wondering how the painter did it, and so on; but then we lose archetypal awareness. Consquently, as wonderer about the whole, man can only speculate; but there is no danger in that, so long as he does not confuse it with scientific knowledge.

Without in the least bit denigrating Kant's magnificent _tour de force_, we can perhaps recognize that he did what was inevitable in the logic of subjectivism. Berkeley had already hinted at it. Hume perhaps forced the conclusion. If mind, screened off from reality by ideas or impressions, cannot come to know the archetypes, at least it can come to read the language of nature. In the construction of the reader of that language, "the wisdom of Providence seemeth to have consulted the operation, rather than the theory, of man." Henceforth, it seems, theory, which can be at best well-educated speculation, is an altogether different enterprise than is scientific understanding. The philosopher, as speculator, must be guarded, carefully hedging, remembering always not to try to transform his speculative ideals into dogmatic truths. The philosopher, as carefully analytic critic, can assist scientific understanding by clarifying, making more coherent and consistent, the logic and language of science.

Despite this tentativeness in metaphyics, Kant thought to establish morals on firm, rational ground. Viewing human behavior ectypally, we would naturally look, as we do in explaining planetary behavior, for example, for patterns and laws that determine the behavior. Another way of putting it is that Kant sees us as animals, as subject to all the pushes and pulls of inclination, compulsion, and temptation. However, as rational beings, we escape the determinism ruling phenomena; and can come to recognize that we can dictate moral duty to ourselves, despite our desires and impulses. Kant formulates a moral categorical imperative (thou shalt, with no ifs, ands, or buts) from the demand of pure practical reason. Honesty, justice, courage, etc. are well enough established when we recognize that we cannot will their opposites to be universally practiced among men. Hence, in Kant's scheme, the virtues become rationally willed duties. Where classical moral philosophers, like Plato, Aristotle, and Berkeley, conceive the primary moral task to be ordering and directing the desires and appetites which move us, to the end of happiness, Kant so sharply bifurcates the rational and the animal that he sees no relevance of desire or appetite, pleasure or pain, to moral issues. Aristotle's ideal man, whose character is such that he finds pleasure only in acting virtuously (courageously, temperately, etc.) is for Kant suspect: to the extent we are inclined to do good, or find pleasure in it, we cannot be sure we are behaving from a moral principle. Kant's position, however, is bound to appeal to us when we consider how far we are from Aristotle's ideal. As often as not we are tempted or inclined to perform the vicious act, but are restrained...by what? Hume would say a moral sense, Kant a sense of duty. Perhaps many of us today would say conscience. (The cynic would say, as we have seen, by fear of punishment.) None of these views is grounded in a metaphysics. Neither Hume nor Kant thinks it possible to discover an account of reality that will support the value system they pretty much take for granted.

III   Utilitarianism

Jeremy Bentham (1748-1832) was morally indignant especially about injustices being done to workers in industrializing nineteenth century England. Because he rejected traditional moral philosophy -- a blend of the classical and the Judeo-Christian -- as being superstitious, he must have wondered why he was indignant. His answer, and the basis of social reform, is found in the pleasure principle. The only motives for human behavior are the attraction of pleasure and the repulsion of pain. In this he found a guiding moral principle: do that which will promote the greatest amount of pleasure and the least amount of pain for the greatest number of people. Surely the pain being suffered by the working people outweighs the pleasure enjoyed by the captains of industry. And yet, how does it follow from my awareness of either the pleasure principle or the suffering of my fellows that I am obligated to help them?   Moreover, there are obvious differences in pleasures, from those we share with other animals to those unique to humans.

The latter consideration led John Stuart Mill (1806-1873) to revise the utilitarian position, as it had come to be called, by distinguishing the higher from the lower pleasures. When Mill goes on to suggest that some of the great thinkers in the Western tradition, including even Jesus Christ, have really been utilitarians, he has really exposed the inadequacy of the pleasure principle for grounding morality. Nonetheless, utilitarianism has been, in modified forms, the principal antagonist since Mill's time to the deontologism (morality of duty or obligation) fostered by Kant. Replacing, or supplementing, the pleasure principle is the notion that our moral acts should be guided by considering the consequences of our behavior. Thus, for example, while most of us would readily agree that we ought to tell the truth, we can all easily think of circumstances where lying would lead to more desirably moral consequences.   (Hence, a better label, consequentialism, has emerged for this line of thinking.)

But why ought we ever be obliged to tell the truth? Or why, in some circumstances, considering the consequences, should we lie?   What is there in the nature of things, including human nature, that would lead us to either conclusion? To this last question, at least, utilitarianism has no answer. The split between fact and value, or between man as part of nature and man as morally responsible, has become too great for an answer to be forthcoming. The traditional values have not yet disappeared -- a Bentham can still become morally indignant; but the metaphysical underpinning has disappeared.

147

IV   The Heroic Will

As MacIntyre summarily puts it, "modern moral utterance and practice can only be understood as a series of fragmented survivals from an older past....the deontological character of moral judgments is the ghost of conceptions of divine law which are quite alien to the metaphysics of modernity...the teleological character [consideration of ends or consequences] is similarly the ghost of conceptions of human nature and activity which are equally not at home in the modern world...."[9] MacIntyre goes on to mark the historic achievement of Friedrich W. Nietzsche (1844-1900) in understanding "more clearly than any other philosopher...not only that what purported to be appeals to objectivity were in fact expressions of subjective will, but also the nature of the problems that this posed for moral philosophy."[10] That is to say, Nietzsche, as MacIntyre points out,[11] destroys the illusion of the modern project to discover a rational foundation for objective morality. Nietzsche's conclusion is that morality is not grounded in reason or in moral sense (conscience), but instead in will. Thus each man is conceived as a purely autonomous agent, who by an heroic act of will can create his own morality, and thereby create himself.

Obviously, not all of us do that. Many of us still cling to what Nietzsche labels slave-morality, inherited by us from our Judeo-Christian and classical traditions. Nietzsche argues much as Alciphron and Lysicles had in _Alciphron_, only more forcefully, against priestcraft and superstition. Another way to put it is that Nietzsche sees no metaphysical underpinning for morality. Given that, and given the failure of the modern project, the only conclusion Nietzsche can see is that will alone can produce genuine morality.

Many readers will recognize Nietzsche to be a forerunner of contemporary existentialism. The fame of thinkers like Jean-Paul Sartre and Albert Camus rests in large measure on their stories of characters placed in moral quandaries, who after reasoning with themselves or others, finally realize that if the rational weighing back and forth is not to go on interminably, they must willfully choose and act; in so doing, the heroes of the stories make themselves and achieve moral authenticity. So strongly is this emphasized that any of us who either claims that his choice is grounded on rational insight into the nature of things or simply chooses not to choose, instead going along with prevailing mores, is a total moral loss, is not truly human. Moreover, there is no metaphysical support for our choosing; indeed, to the existentialist the world is absurd, because, apart from our freedom and willing, reality is only the hurrying of matter endlessly, meaninglessly. We must choose, then, in a word; in our choosing, in the commitments we make, the acts we perform, we produce our moral characters. If we do not so choose, we become less than human. But after all there is no point in it, nothing in the nature of things that underwrites our doomed moral enterprise.

V   From Speculation to Analysis

Modern subjectivist philosophy has forced a number of radical dichotomies: matter/mind or nature/man; phenomena/noumena or appearance/ reality; fact/value; is/ought; metaphysics/science; speculation/analysis. The ever present temptation to modern philosophers is to overcome one or more of the splits by denying the existence of one of the parts. Thus, we have seen Berkeley denying matter and denying that reality is different from appearance. Kant we can interpret as counseling us to face up to the pairings as being inevitable, grounded in the split between knower and known; and advising us never to suppose that men in this life can repair the breaks.

G.W.F. Hegel (1770-1831), the most remarkable philosopher of the nineteenth century, could not resist the temptation to bring things back together. Kant himself had suggested that ultimately things must harmonize; or at least we cannot help thinking so. The soul we must think to be immortal; for it is impossible that in this life duty can ever be totally harmonized with happiness. But if so, Hegel mused, why should we suppose that heaven and earth are forever separated? or that we must forever oppose time and eternity? Might it not be that Ultimate Reality, call it Spirit, or the Absolute, is itself "growing," developing; that history is not just a succession of events, but a working out, a progression, of ultimate spiritual reality? Hegel's strategy for overcoming the dichotomies was to polarize the split pairs. Or better -- Hegel claimed to have uncovered the Absolute's strategy, which is to develop itself through a process in which polarized or contradictory forces or powers are synthesized into higher unities. In turn the new syntheses give rise to new antitheses; and ultimately out of that polarized opposition come yet other higher syntheses; and so on. The history of philosophy might be read that way, for example. The objectivism of ancient philosophy has become polarized through the emergence of modern subjectivism. Eventually a synthesis of these polar opposites will emerge; thus does Spirit progress.

Hegel believed that this dialectical process was nearing its completion in the nineteenth century, and would perhaps culminate in individuals achieving their highest freedom and purpose as members of a unified state. Morality, then, for Hegel, is a function of the stage of development of the Absolute. Whether or not the development is near its completion, still what truth, beauty, or goodness are, at any stage, is a function of that stage. There is no point in finding fault with barbarians or savages, or lamenting, as Berkeley did, the decadence of Europe. Seen as steps in the dialectical process, all these periods of human history are understood as inevitable and as necessary to Spirit's development.

Given Berkeley's enmity to materialism we should note here the dialectical materialism of Karl Marx (1818-1883), which so often has been read as Hegelian speculation turned upside down, with matter replacing spirit. The inevitable process and progress are there; the inevitable struggle of opposing forces, issuing in higher syntheses. Likewise, Marx saw the denouement of the material and economic struggling to be in the offing, with the crushing of the bourgeoisie class, the dictatorship of the proletariat, and then finally the withering away of the state and the introduction of heaven on earth. The continuing and lasting appeal of Marxism is apparently the practical and revolutionary program outlined to achieve for all mankind freedom and equality. We have long since reviewed Berkeley's critiques of those ideals.

The twentieth century has witnessed a philosophical revolt against what have been labelled the excesses and futilities of ivory tower speculation. All the while that Hegel and his emulators were speculating, science had been growing apace. Evolutionary theory in biology, relativity and quantum theory in physics, atomic theory in chemistry, the coming into being of new social sciences -- all that apparently without philosophy's guidance and assistance. The revolt may be said to have been announced by the declaration of a criterion of meaningfulness from a group known as the Vienna Circle; and the establishment of a new philosophical regime guaranteed by the prolific and effective labors of that same group. The criterion of meaningfulness aimed to undermine idle speculation by declaring that for any statement to be meaningful (that is, either true or false) it must be subject to empirical verification, either by direct observation or by the more sophisticated experimental procedure of exact science. So, for example, the statement, "The Absolute develops itself in a dialectical way" is declared unworthy of serious attention, because it can be neither verified nor falsified.

The aim of this growing body of logical positivists or logical empiricists has not been to destroy speculation, but rather to unify the sciences, by careful and precise analysis and critique of the logic and language of scientific investigation. More recently such philosophers have offered their services also to moralists, theologians and religionists, historians, litterateurs; and even to philosophers themselves. That is, the developing techniques of logico-linguistic analysis can be applied to the works of the old masters, like Plato and Aristotle and

Berkeley, as well as to more recent scientific and humanistic endeavors.

Alongside this movement, and again in revolt against speculation there has come into being what is called phenomenology, which aims at a more radical empiricism than earlier modern philosophers, like Hume e. g., achieved. William James (1842-1910), the famed American philosopher, is a forerunner of this empiricism. To understand religion, for example, we must get back to the phenomena, the actual experiences of men in all their richness and diversity. Hence James' book, The Varieties of Religious Experience. And hence the replacement of theology -- study of God --, by religious studies -- study of man.

Finally, such speculative philosophy as has continued has quite consciously placed itself back under the Kantian strictures. Thus, the sympathetic surveyor of this speculative scene, acknowledging man's desire to see things steadily and see them whole, will at the same time note that there are alternative world hypotheses to be entertained, or different stances on the philosophical compass, so to say, from which we can try to get our bearings. But no one of these perspectives can be proclaimed as the truth about reality. So, some of us may be satisfied with picturing the world as a mechanism, others may make more sense of it viewed as if it were a work of art, perhaps others will be pleased by taking it as a mathematical grid, maybe as a language. And while we may fruitfully speculate, by carefully and constructively weighing the pros and cons of these possible alternatives, metaphysics in the old style, as coming to know what and why things are, is forbidden.

A contemporary American philosopher, Richard Rorty,[12] has given a new twist to this. He distinguishes between two styles of philosophy: systematic and edifying. The former has been the predominant style in Western thought since the time of the ancient Greeks, and supposes that philosophy's aim is to come to know what's what, and to live accordingly. By contrast, edifying philosophy's aim is to promote conversation. Knowing on this latter view can be said to be believing, in accordance with the most sophisticated current standards. The philosopher's task is to defend what he believes against all antagonists in the interminable conversation; and if persuaded by an antagonist, to modify his beliefs. So called objective truth is nothing but belief about which there is general agreement. The interesting twist is that Rorty accuses the systematic philosopher with having a moral defect in thinking he must bow before some ineluctable truth he has seen. That is, he is avoiding his responsibility to choose among competing views. By contrast, the edifying philosopher, recognizing that we humans cannot come to know objective reality, becomes heroic in choosing and defending belief

151

in the continuing conversation. Hence, important features of existentialism are introduced into speculation: moral commitment and authenticity, choosing despite the conviction that there can never be a firmly established warrant for our so choosing; in sum, there is no possible metaphysical underpinning for our endeavors.

We cannot help noticing that scientific philosophy in one form or another seems to be the loadstone for all this modern intellectual activity. If nineteenth century speculation went its idealistic way, it was because it supposed that science had pre-empted study of material nature. If twentieth century linguistic and logical analysis has become handmaiden to the sciences (and lately to other disciplines) it is because it is supposed that science, not philosophy, is the proper studier of nature (or theology, of God; literature, of poetry and drama and novel, etc.). If phenomenology has returned to the phenomena, it is because it wants to emulate in its way empirical, scientific investigation. If twentieth century speculation is tentative and cautious, it is because of the conviction that subjective mind, when it ventures beyond a scientific ordering of the phenomena, can too easily fall into nonsense.

Further, it appears that the speculative, analytic, empirical or phenomenological tasks modern philosophy has set for itself are virtually inexhaustible, leaving no time either in the species or in the individual for what Berkeley took to be the true business of the philosopher.

Given the overwhelming preponderance in our world of modern philosophy, in one or other of these forms, it is not to be wondered at that interpretations of Berkeley tend to ignore or even scorn his classical predilections, and instead see him as exclusively a modern philosopher. First, then, we will see Berkeley interpreted as speculative philosopher; second, as forerunner of the linguistic analyst.

VI   It's Only a Paper Moon....

In Science and the Modern World Whitehead argues that perhaps the most important use of philosophical speculation is that it stimulates and makes possible advances in scientific knowledge. Colin Murray Turbayne, an eminent contemporary philosopher and Berkeley scholar, agrees with Whitehead; and also supports Whitehead's contention that philosophical speculation must aim at doing justice to other aspects of human experience: the religious, the moral, the aesthetic. Further, Turbayne's book, The Myth of Metaphor, suggests that we post-Kantians should certainly all be aware by now that metaphysics is passé, having been replaced by speculation. For Turbayne, the model or metaphor is an extraordinarily successful speculative device for illuminating areas of human experience that might otherwise remain obscure.[13] His purpose, then, is to help bring clarity to both science and philosophy by showing that while philosophical metaphors can be and are helpful and illuminating, they can be and have become pernicious and confusing when taken as metaphysics.

Thus, Turbayne proposes, in the spirit of Berkeley, to "explode the metaphysics of mechanism." Descartes and Newton, those "two great [metaphysicians of mechanism] of our modern epoch have so imposed their arbitrary allocation of the facts upon us that it has now entered the coenesthesis of the entire Western World. Together they have founded a church, more powerful than that founded by Peter and Paul, whose dogmas are now so entrenched that anyone who tries to re-allocate the facts is guilty of more than heresy; he is opposing scientific truth."[14] But because Turbayne wants to explode metaphysics, as well as mechanism, he proposes to show that we can dispense with mechanism by first explaining that it is only a metaphor, and then that a better metaphor can be put in its place.

The better metaphor is that nature is a language. Turbayne's teacher in this is Berkeley. The difference is that where Berkeley came to take his metaphor literally, and hence proposed a metaphysics, Turbayne, having followed through the logic of subjectivism, with such as Hume and Kant leading the way, recognizes it as only a metaphor. Turbayne leads us to serious consideration of the metaphor in the same way that Berkeley led us to serious consideration of the metaphysics of immaterialism, by way of the theory of vision.

Berkeley's theory of vision, and its difference from the then predominant theory of vision, can be understood well enough for our purposes by reference to the famous Molyneux problem. Suppose a man born blind, who by the sense of touch has come to know cubes and spheres; and suppose that in maturity he is made to see, and is presented for visual observation a cube and a sphere, of like size and of like material. Would the man know at first, or even repeated, sight which is the cube and which the sphere? In Berkeley's theory of vision the answer is that he would not. The man must learn from experience that the colors he is now aware of through sight are signs of what he has already come to know through touch. Berkeley's theory has subsequently received repeated confirmation. According to the opposed geometrical theory of vision, which is "the core of all subsequent representative, copy, or picture theories of perception,"[15] the man should know at first sight which is the sphere, which the cube.[16]

When this theory of vision is expanded to include all sense perception, we say that the ideas received by the mind are signs, and we escape all the difficulties accompanying the representative theory of perception, where, in the case of sight, e. g., the eye is taken to be like a camera and the mind is asked to do the impossible: compare the pictures with the originals. "Signs do not copy or picture undiscoverable causes; these signs are tied to the world, for they convey meanings which, in the form of hypotheses, we can reject or retain; and the questions we ask of the external world, such as, 'What does this mean?' and 'Is this a dagger which I see before me?' are answerable within the rich context of further experience."[17]

Turbayne concludes that if we thus theorize that visual data are signs, not pictures or copies, and if all sense data are so to be understood, then it seems appropriate to say that nature is a language, not a machine, so long as we understand that we use metaphor. The question then becomes not which metaphysics is right, but which metaphor is better. Turbayne's reasons for concluding that the language metaphor is better appeal not only to scientific experience and epistemology, but also to religious experience (the language metaphor fits with our religion; the machine does not), and to aesthetic experience (the language metaphor has a greater charm).[18] Underlying all the reasons is the subjectivist bias.

VII   "...a philosopher should abstain from metaphor."[19]

Turbayne's transformation of Berkeley's metaphysics into metaphorics is impressive, understandable, and perhaps inevitable. However, there is a crucial difficulty in this proposed metaphorics that is foreseen by Berkeley. We have alluded to it already in pondering the problem of unknowables and in wondering what ideas, taken as signs, could be signs of. We will renew a review of Berkeley's puzzlement by another in the set of objections and replies. Hylas raises the following objection: what can it mean to say that ideas are in a mind? How can trees, animals, other extended things be in an unextended thing? Philonous' reply is that they can not be, if "in" is taken in its gross literal sense. But Hylas wonders whether Philonous is not thus abusing language. Philonous is confident that he is not. He notes that he has been using common language; and that we use language metaphorically quite often when speaking of mental operations by analogy to sensible things.[20] All that so far seems not only unobjectionable in reply, but also on the way to a theory of knowledge appropriate to a defense of common sense and a philosophical realism.

Why, then, did Berkeley not have Hylas raise the next obvious question? Do the ideas (sensible things) exist in God in the gross, literal sense? And if not, then apparently they do not exist anywhere in the gross, literal sense. To say that the

154

immediate objects of knowledge exist literally in God would not only rescind Berkeley's credentials as a defender of common sense, but also would make him, the orthodox Christian, guilty of the heresy of pantheism. But then, if the objects of knowledge do not exist anywhere in the gross, literal sense, where is the analogy? where is the metaphor? In other words, Berkeley, as a defender of common sense, knows what the literal sense of "in" is; but given his subjectivist bias, there is no room for the "in" in him.

Turbayne's metaphorics falls victim to the same difficulty. Harking back to the theory of vision, let us recall the cubes and spheres. Turbayne says that the same name, e. g., "roundness," is given to the two different objects, the object of touch and the object of sight. There is no common nature, he says; but note how he puts it: "...no common nature between this fixed size and shape, etc., of the physical object and the fluctuating sizes and shapes of the visual signs,..."[21] So far as the theory of vision goes, the physical object with its fixed size and shape is evidently the object as known by touch. The theory is that we learn to identify things by sight in the way that we identify things by words: the visual image is a sign by means of which one becomes aware of something. But just as words -- in an ordinary language, e. g. -- are artificial and conventional signs, and not resemblances, of what they signify, so visual images are artificial and conventional signs, not resemblances, of what they signify. If we now ask what they are signs of, the answer is that they are signs of objects known by touch. So far, so good. This theory, or metaphor, seems at least as good as the picture or copy theory of vision. However, its plausibility rests on the tacit assumption that touch is a privileged sense, that sense by means of which I know roundness, squareness, etc.

When Turbayne introduces the other metaphor, that nature is a language, the privileged status of touch disappears; tangible data as well as visible data must be regarded as signs analogous to the signs of an ordinary language like English. That being so, a visible image is not properly speaking a sign of roundness, say, in the tangible object; for that tangible object is itself a sign. If we say it is a sign of roundness, where is the real roundness that it is a sign of? In the mind of God? Well, here we are again. In the mind of God in the gross, literal sense?

Another way of exposing the difficulty is by wondering, given metaphorics, just how we can choose between rival metaphors. "An obvious way to choose," Turbayne tells us, "...like the way we choose between different portraits of the same subject, is by their degree of likeness to the thing illustrated...We know that the world is not a machine with ghosts in it [Descartes' theory], nor is it a language. But which is it more like?"[22] An obvious answer to that would be that if we know that the world is neither a machine with ghosts in it, nor a language, that is because we know it is a world of men, animals, plants, planets, etc. And why not develop and refine that knowledge instead of playing around with metaphors? In other words, if there is knowledge which enables us to say which of the metaphors is better, then that is metaphysical, or on the way to being metaphysical, knowledge. Given that, why settle for the metaphor? Furthermore, if it is claimed that the world is unknowable, that metaphysics is impossible, then no metaphors are possible either. In case metaphysics is not possible, asking us to compare rival metaphors is like asking us to compare portraits of a subject who is unportrayable.

At the beginning of his book, Turbayne writes, " Metaphor's use involves the pretense that something is the case when it is not."[23] Suppose, then, we convince Turbayne that using metaphor depends on our knowing what the reality is. Might he not still propose his metaphor as a model for science? Another way to put it, rather sharply, is: how can it be that philosophers presume to present models for science? If they are pretending, then why not cut out the games, and get down to business? If they are not pretending, then we have metaphysics, for good or ill.[24]

After Turbayne asks the question, "But which is it more like?", he begins his answer with two more questions. "Which is closer to the natural process as we found it to be after stripping it of the metaphysical disguises put on it by Newton and Descartes? First, is the relation that we observe to obtain between events more like that of cause-effect, or more like that of sign-thing signified?"[25] Evidently, then, what we know the world to be, and is the basis for comparing the metaphors, is the world as disclosed by the strict empirical analysis of David Hume. The world, really, is succession of events, or of atomic impressions. Hume concluded that, given this subjectivist analysis, we have in fact not a knowledge that encourages or even allows attempts at metaphor, but instead a profound ignorance.

It seems that Berkeley would reject Turbayne's interpretation not only on the ground that the philosopher should abstain from metaphor, but also because metaphorics provides no basis for morality. Perhaps it is not accidental that Turbayne provides no moral reason, independent of religion, for preferring the language to the machine metaphor. But more importantly, if we cannot come to know what reality, including man, is, than we have no support for the classical or traditional moral philosophy defended by Berkeley.

VIII   Philosophy as Dust Settling

In the preceding chapter we noted that although Berkeley

could not allow natural science to be a study of material causes, that being unintelligible, he nonetheless concluded that all power and causal activity in reality belongs in minds, not in nature. At the same time, awe struck as he understandably was by the new science, Berkeley had no doubt that however much it is the business of first philosophy (or metaphysics) to study the real causes, it is the business of science, and not philosophy, to study nature.[26] In other words Berkeley had no doubt that in itself nature is powerless and causeless; that all power lay in mind and that all change is effected by God or finite spirits.

Suppose we agree that it is physics, chemistry, et. al., that study nature, discovering laws and ordering the phenomena. And at the same time suppose we agree that any attempt to "know" or understand beyond that yields only either metaphorics or an untenable metaphysics. Surely, then, we would say that in taking nature to be a language, Berkeley goes too far. However, what Berkeley does say about language seems insightful to men generally, and instructive and helpful to the scientific enterprise.

Such is the interpretation of Berkeley that comes from the contemporary professionals who take philosophy's task to be the analysis of the logic and language used by various investigators into nature, man and supernature. That interpretation is ably and brilliantly presented by G. J. Warnock in his book, Berkeley. T. E. Jessop, one of the editors of the definitive edition of Berkeley's works, writes that "Berkeley's system...was plainly a piece of religious apologetics, the outline of a constructive natural theology, of a theistic metaphysic."[27] On Warnock's interpretation, Berkeley instead "set before himself as his primary concern the task of simplification, of clearing the air."[28] That task is performed by analyzing language. Thus, "This Introduction [to the Principles] is in many ways his most original and lively contribution to philosophy." Warnock expands: "In the first few paragraphs of his Introduction Berkeley enunciates with vigour and clarity a view of the nature of philosophical inquiry which would be widely accepted today, and which is in fact sometimes taken to be wholly modern."[29] In that Introduction Berkeley had aphorized that we have first raised a dust and then complain we cannot see. Warnock properly interprets that "the dust we raise is the dust of linguistic confusion."[30] Hence, the philosopher's task is not solving or giving answers to real problems, but instead diagnosing and removing puzzles of our own making.[31]

As an instance of the value of philosophy, so understood, to science, Warnock notes that Berkeley showed physicists the proper meaning of "force" and "motion;" and hence relieved them from looking for some entities that do not exist. That is to say, "force" and "motion" do not name entities, but instead are words used to explain or speak about how things move. In other words, Berkeley at his best was forerunner of today's logical empiricist who aims to assist scientific investigation by his second-order analyses (the scientist himself conducting the first-order analyses).

Warnock is not unaware that Berkeley aimed to explain reality, to engage in metaphysics. However, he regards this "over-ambitious" inclination as being caused by wanting to remove with a single blow the problem of the unknowables, raised, as we have seen, by Descartes and Locke.[32] Warnock does not suggest that this subjectivism might be overcome by a more satisfactory theory of knowledge. Instead, he proposes that Berkeley was on the right track when he suggested that the real meaning of language lies in its use. Hence philosophical analysis should be directed toward explaining the uses of language, not toward understanding reality.[33]

Not only is such interpretation plausible, but also it is invited by Berkeley himself. We have seen him reluctantly confess that language, whether that which God speaks to us in nature, or that contrived by man, seems intended more for the operation than the theory. And given that interpretation it is no wonder that Warnock's only attention to Berkeley's deep and life-long moral, political, and religious concerns is a brief but severe criticism of Alciphron. His interests at the time of writing, Warnock claims, had turned in a different direction. The book has a "disconcertingly polemical tone." Berkeley was "probably ill-advised in attempting the dialogue form." And finally, "the disputes have by now lost most of their interest."[34]

There can be no doubt that Berkeley would be utterly dumbfounded by that last judgment, because its author is a leading professional philosopher in a society beset by all the evils that Berkeley saw coming into being: excessive luxury, gambling, corruption in politics, partying and whoring widely practiced and accepted, religious and family institutions in steady decline, etc., etc. If the disputes have lost their interest it must be because either minute philosophy has won the day, or because professional academic philosophers have other interests, or both. As parents, as interested citizens, such professional philosophers doubtless are concerned about private and public virtue, about the health of the body politic, etc. But they look upon themselves, as philosophers, as specialists in an exacting and worthwhile enterprise, but with no special expertise or insight into the pressing moral, political, and religious problems of our time.

None of this is to say that Warnock is guilty of gross

158

misinterpretation of Berkeley. No, not only is Warnock's interpretation grounded in what Berkeley clearly and forcefully wrote, but also philosophy, taken as linguistic analysis, is an outgrowth from roots that Berkeley (and others) planted in European philosophic soil. We can read Warnock's giving Alciphron short shrift in the following way. On the strength of Berkeley's own counsel about and practice of linguistic analysis Warnock's counterpart in Berkeley's time could have admonished the well-intentioned man: "When you follow your own advice and clear the scientific air by acute and telling analysis of mathematical and physical language, you help us all. But when you forget yourself, and lapse into polemical and interested moralizing, as you have done in Alciphron, the doctor himself becomes patient. If only you had brought the same brilliant analysis to moral, political, and religious language that you gave us in physics and science, your own controlling convictions of theism and political virtue might have been better served. At least, clarity, coherence, and consistency in moral and religious language would have increased, so that the moralists and religionists might have received a fairer hearing."

What might Berkeley have replied to that? More than one writer[35] on Berkeley has suggested that Berkeley's failure to write the other three parts of what had been planned as a series of volumes on the Principles of Knowledge was caused by his awareness of apparently insoluble difficulties in his immaterialism and idealism. We might put the problem this way. We have seen that from the time of his earliest major philosophical writings Berkeley was in essential agreement with classical philosophers like Plato and Aristotle about education, morals, politics, the role of religion in the polis, and about philosophy as pursuit of wisdom. But the metaphysics he devised to underlie and support the moral, political, and religious philosophy not only could not bear the burden, but also (to change the metaphor) directed bright thinkers to transform philosophy from metaphysics and pursuit of wisdom into linguistic analysis. Berkeley's search for meaning and significance in nature and nature's author is thus transformed into something like, "How am I using language, and thus what if anything can I mean, when I say things like, 'Official support and encouragement of gambling is wicked,' or 'Excessive luxury tends to corrupt the moral fiber of the nation,' or 'Responsible men and women ought not to engage in the masquerade,' or 'Public officials ought not to take bribes or abuse power'?" In short, the philosopher's attention is turned from substantive, "first-order" issues to linguistic, "second-order" puzzles. Once the puzzle-solver has determined whether there is any meaning in such statements, and if so what it is, then presumably the moralist and political scientist and religionist can better address the substantive issues.

159

Who are these moralists? political scientists? religionists? Evidently, minute philosophers. Not all of them frivolous, to be sure; many of them serious, without a doubt. But whether our judgment is that it is better or worse to have philosophers in the classical mode or free-thinkers addressing the substantive moral and political issues, there is no doubt what Berkeley's judgment is. If he had had the slightest suspicion that his own attempts at clearing the air, of settling the linguistic dust, would have contributed to the predominant role of minute philosophers in today's world, the thought would have broken his heart.

Chapter 8

Completing Berkeley's Project

Berkeley was right, I believe, in opposing libertinism, irreligion, and atheism. He was right, I believe, in seeing religion as the main stay of the body politic. He was right, I believe, in opposing classical philosophy to free-thinking. He was right, I also believe, in seeing the metaphysics of materialism as being at the root of misdirected morality and politics. His attack against materialism is, I believe, unanswerable on modern subjectivist principles. He was right, I believe, in attempting to provide a metaphysical foundation for a morality of virtue; for without that, the emotivism and existentialism of our present era seem inevitable. However, his metaphysics of immaterialism, I believe, fails; and fails because it is based on subjectivism. Moreover, even though we suppose the metaphysics sound, it does not seem to provide the foundation Berkeley wanted. One cannot help thinking that Berkeley himself realized it. Was Part II of the Principles, the manuscript he lost in Italy, on the moral philosophy following from immaterialism? If so, did he not perhaps ever rewrite it because he saw it did not suffice? At any rate, none of Berkeley's defenders or interpreters has heretofore seemed interested in completing his project.

Finally, I believe that completion of Berkeley's project requires rejection of modern subjectivism in favor of a classical realistic metaphysics and epistemology. Hence, we will review what seem to be three crucial notions -- substance-accident, matter-form, and intentional logic --, and show how with them we can have a metaphysics on which to build a classical moral philosophy. Because Berkeley occasionally came close to these notions, we will engage in some speculation contrary to fact.

I Hierarchy

Berkeley's plain man, as the plain man of any era, understands reality to be multi-leveled, including inanimate things and materials, plants, animals, men, and supernature, or God. To say that there is a hierarchy of substances is to note that beings at higher levels are able to organize the things and materials of lower levels. Thus plants organize and utilize the soil in which they grow, animals organize and utilize living matter, and so on. It is striking that Berkeley, a defender of common sense, oversimplifies the hierarchy. Descartes had divided the world into material and mental substances, with the latter having some control over the former. Berkeley divides the world into spirits and ideas. Gone from Berkeley's world, as much as from Descartes', are plants, animals, and men, so far as we understand men as animals.

Berkeley's staunchest contemporary defender, A. A. Luce, is sensitive to this deficiency. In a rather moving article he writes,

> Can we believe that there is nothing powerful or operative in yonder sycamore which pushes or pulls its sap higher than where you or I are sitting, ... and incidentally is striving to endure and propagate its kind? I am not blaming Berkeley. He was wise in his generation, and took the problem of his day, and refuted matter for good and all; he rightly plumped for 'the two kinds, entirely distinct and heterogeneous' [the reference is to Section 89 of The Principles of Human Knowledge], viz, active minds and passive sensa; but why should not we in our day use Berkeley, and go on to find room in the perceptual situation he outlined for the living thing, the living mind of man, and the living God?[1]

The obvious answer to Luce's latter question is that we cannot use Berkeley for this purpose because of the subjectivist analysis of our experience, which denies our common awareness of things or substances. It denies reason's power to recognize plants, animals, and men.[2]

Luce goes on to note that in later writings, in Alciphron and Siris, Berkeley tried to do better by living things, with "a serious attempt to isolate life, as a unique reality, midway between mind and the sensible."[3] But what a hopeless attempt, given that living things are active, the sensible are ideas, and the ideas are the real things of nature and are passive. It is also interesting that Luce's reference to Alciphron (VI, 14) is to a passage in which Lysicles, the more frivolous of the free-thinkers, is speaking.

In another article Luce writes, "Living things,...have a principium individuationis of their own; they contain semi-spiritual or vitalist elements that as such cannot be seen or touched."[4] That is probably true, but one wonders how we could ever learn it from subjectivist empiricism. Luce adds, "Berkeley nowhere treats the organic adequately. The knowledge of his day did not permit it."[5] Say rather that the theory of knowledge of his day did not permit it. Luce almost admits as much when he adds, "Does Berkeley's account of the thing of sense also agree with common sense? I devoutly hope it does; for if it is not common sense, then it is nonsense; there are no two ways about

162

it."[6] Finally Luce makes an appeal for philosophy as a refinement of common sense. His heart is in the right place, as was Berkeley's; but his mind, as was Berkeley's, is misled by subjectivism.

Berkeley, then, in his later years realized that with living things excluded from the hierarchy, there was a deficiency in his theory of reality. Did he also recognize, however dimly, that man, in the hierarchy of living things, is an animal, albeit a rational one? At any rate, defense and promulgation of the classical moral philosophy depends on our realizing that. Talk about developing virtuous habits can make no sense for a Descartes, who has so sharply sundered mind and body. Can it for Berkeley, who has apparently done the same, even though body is now understood as ideas? Apparently not. Hence, to complete Berkeley's project, we must replace man in the hierarchy as an animal, a rational animal.

II Substance-Accident

Despite Luce's misgivings about Berkeley's treatment of living things, he was a convinced Berkeleyan, or immaterialist. Hence, his comments about matter and material substance are revealing.

In his introduction to Berkeley's _Philosophical Commentaries_,[7] Luce writes, "Berkeley wrote the _Commentaries_ as a study in 'ye immaterial hypothesis.' ...All turns on his view that you can have a true philosophy of the world without the traditional Greek notion of material substance."[8] From what we have discovered in Chapter 5 about Aristotle's account of matter, we can imagine Aristotle seconding Luce's statement about the traditional Greek notion of material substance. Indeed, Aristotle himself presented a plausible account of change by correcting the traditional Greek notion of matter. For Aristotle matter is not a substance, but is instead a principle or source of changing substances.

However, that this is not what Luce means is evident from what he writes elsewhere. "There is no intrinsic difficulty in Berkeley's view of the external world. Great thinkers, great artists, great men of action lived before Aristotle invented matter and coined a word for it. It is not the facts of life, but the history of thought that makes immaterialism hard to expound and understand. The scales are weighted against Berkeley."[9] What is particularly striking is that Luce writes this lament in a paragraph that takes off from the following quotation from Berkeley's _Commentaries_: "I differ from the Cartesians in that I make extension, Colour, etc. to exist really in Bodies & independent of Our Mind. All ys carefully & lucidly to be set

163

forth."[10]

That Luce's lament is misdirected can be seen by our introducing another classical realistic insight. Once more, it is to Aristotle that we turn, and once more it is our common ordinary understanding that we seek to make clear and to refine.[11] Surely the plain man holds that height, color, etc., do exist really in bodies, and independent of our minds. Furthermore, just as surely, the plain man comes by this opinion from his experience of the world of nature as a world of changing things. The leaf which was a pastel green in spring, a dark green in summer, is now brown; but it is the same leaf. The thing (leaf) has abided through the states of green and brown that have succeeded one another. The water in the lake was liquid in summer, and now in winter is solid; but it is still water. The man who yesterday was sad is today joyful; but it is the same man. States come and go; things persist through the coming and going.

The words Aristotle used to articulate and refine this common knowledge are usually translated into English as substance and accident, "substance" signifying that which is changing and persists throughout the change, "accident" that state which is characteristic of the changing thing at the beginning of the change or at the end of the change, or at some intermediate state in between (the steak is raw at the beginning of the frying; the end can be at the rare, medium rare, etc., stage).

Aristotle goes on in his articulation by observing that any thing that can be said to be must be either substance or accident. "Substance," then, means that which exists in itself, and not in another (the man, e. g.); "accident" means that which exists but only in another (the color of the man's skin, e. g.; or his sadness or joy). Furthermore, of these senses of being, substance is the primary sense, for accidents (qualities, quantities, places, etc.) can exist only in or with reference to substances, or things existing in themselves. However, accidental existence is very real (consider, e. g., the useless space in a circular, as opposed to a rectangular, field house). Nor do we regard accidents as some (substantial) things tacked on or added to the substances (the circularity, or rectangularity, are modes of fieldhouses' existing, not spread on as paint is spread on the walls).

Hence it is that substance-accident provides the most basic classification of entities. Whatever is, is one or the other. No matter what we come to theorize about reality, we all agree to begin with, that being in the most proper sense is substance, and that all other beings are accidents of substances. There is nothing terribly profound here; but yet it is the sort of insight that needs tending and care. That modern philosophy has been

164

inclined to neglect the insight is perhaps evident in Luce's accusation of Aristotle and his supposition that the traditional and only notion of material substance is the one Berkeley sought to reject. At least, we can here note the importance of the substance-accident distinction to our making sense.

To make this clear, suppose that we theorize with the characteristic scientific philosophy at the end of the seventeenth century, according to which, and to quote Whitehead again, "nature is a dull affair, soundless, scentless, colorless; merely the hurrying of material, endlessly, meaninglessly." If we employ our basic concepts of substance and accident, we say then that what is substantial (and hence really real) in nature is the matter which is hurrying about. It could be. The point here is not to decide whether that theory is true, but rather to note that if it is, then our notions of substance and accident force the conclusion that In nature there is no meaning, but only the play of atoms. In other words, all the different arrangements of the material (matter alone, in this theory, is really real) are only modes or accidents of the substantial. There is then no real substantial difference between a rock and a worm, an ape and a man, but only an accidental arrangement of the matter; much as we might say that there is no real difference between an automobile and a clock, but only a difference in the arrangement or ordering of the elemental parts.

If we suppose, as Luce evidently has, that "matter" has only this one possible meaning, then we too must conclude that the best -- the only -- strategy for a philosopher who believes that there is meaningfulness or purpose in nature, or disclosed in nature, is to prove that such "matter" does not exist. Luce's evident mistake is to suppose that "matter" can only be defined and understood as that stuff which occupies space. If instead we define "matter" as the principle of changeability or potentiality, and then add that in nature all substances (things existing in themselves) are material substances, all we are saying is that everything in nature is subject to change. And thus we are articulating the common sense of the plain man: all natural, material substances are subject to change.

So far we have not closed the door to meaningfulness or purpose in nature. It could just be that the plain man is right -- that men, e. g., are neither naked apes nor machines, but men; i. e., substances, existing in themselves, and not as accidental wholes. Then when we add form to matter as a principle of changing things, in order to clarify our experience of change, we make intelligible the possibility that men are indeed men, and that they as natural substances, along with other animals, and plants, and elements, are significant, purposeful, meaningful. Moreover, we are now no longer in the desperate position of trying to prove that matter does not exist, but instead seem to be "carefully and lucidly setting forth" how height, color, etc., exist in bodies -- namely, as accidents of substances.[12]

To continue posing the refinement of common sense as an attractive alternative to subjectivism, let us consider one final criticism of Berkeley; and do so by once more recalling materialism's view that nature is "merely the hurrying of material, endlessly, meaninglessly." Some of what the plain man and Aristotle take to be accidental being -- colors, sounds, et. al. -- have in the materialist and/or subjectivist theory only subjective existence in the minds (or brains) of perceivers; or are only appearances, not realities, not even accidental realities. Against this Berkeley levelled his devastating criticism, showing that in this account there is neither evidence in our sensory experience for there being material substance, nor reason to postulate it as explanatory of our sensory experience. On the contrary, Berkeley concludes, all the items in our sensory awareness seem to be what Aristotle calls accidents and Berkeley calls qualities, "primary" or "secondary". For Berkeley, in other words, the world is as it appears to be, full of colors, sounds, and other qualities.

There is a contemporary classical realist who has succeeded in showing that Berkeley's failure to make sense of that world comes from his neglect of the concepts of substance and accident. In the quotations that follow Richard J. Connell has Locke and Hume in mind, but it is clear that Berkeley is included because he too is a subjectivist.

> Let it be supposed that Hume [or Berkeley] is right: there is no substratum underlying the qualities which we perceive. If it is given, then, that the qualities do exist outside the knower, it follows that they cannot be accidents according to the Aristotelian definition; for accidents are understood to exist in another as in a subject. Thus, if substance does not exist, neither do accidents. However, it is a fact of experience that these qualities do exist; therefore, if it is denied that they exist in a substratum, the only alternative is to maintain that they exist independently of a subject -- they exist but not in another as in a substratum. But this is the definition of substance; hence, these qualities are themselves substances in the Aristotelian sense. Thus, the position of Hume and Locke is, in fact, a denial of the reality of accidents rather than substances. Hume

166

explicitly concedes this when he says: "Every quality being a distinct thing from another, may be conceived to exist apart, and may exist apart not only from every other quality, but from that unintelligible chimera of a substance."

From this further consequences follow, for if "substances" (things) are in truth collections of qualities, and if qualities are in point of fact substances, then a thing is a collection of qualities become substances, each of which is exterior to the other. Hence, an elephant would be an aggregate consisting of a shape that is a substance, a color that is a substance, a motion that is a substance, a density that is a substance, etc., all gathered together like marbles in a heap. But this is plainly false. Whatever an elephant may be, it is not an aggregate of that type.[13]

Let us imagine a Berkeley not only convinced, as he of course was, that part of philosophy's task is to defend the plain man's experience of the world, not explain it away as scientific philosophy has done, but also sensitive to this critique of the empiricist analysis of our experience. Can we not suppose that at the very least he would suspect that something was radically wrong in his account of reality? and that this insight into substance and accident might point the way to a correct analysis?

III Form-Matter

What makes substances to be what they are? The inescapable answer, if we leave aside the efficient cause(s) of substances, is form, not matter. Even the hard-nosed materialist agrees. When Descartes, for example, decreed that nature is matter, he went on to define and describe that substance, to give its form. Descartes' successors continue the search for the definition of matter, taken always by the materialist to be the building block from which all else in nature is made. No materialist supposes that matter, or material substance, is formless. From the materialist's perspective science continues its search for the form of all matter.

The plain man, supported by the classical philosopher, knows better. Material, changing things (substances) are multiform. There are levels of being, and within some levels there is variety of form. But it is still form that makes substances to be what they are. Form is a principle or source of changing things, concomitant with matter. Here matter signifies changeability, or

167

potentiality, rather than an unchanging building block. The materialist's search for matter, or the form of matter, appears to be a will-o'-the-wisp. At least it has not yet been found, and if our philosophically refined common sense is right, it never will be found. For form and matter are instead concomitant principles of changing things, and there is nothing in our common or scientific experience of nature that forever abides. Whatever we recognize in nature is what it is (form), but is subject to change (matter).

When we earlier spoke of Aristotle's account of matter, we did not emphasize substantial form. Now, given the substance-accident distinction, we need only note that there are substantial forms. Thus, plants are substantially different from minerals, animals from plants, men from other animals. There are powers in plants not present in minerals, in animals not present in plants, in men not present in other animals. The substantial form of any entity, then, is what makes it what it is, empowers it to do what it does.

IV Human Logic

Among the powers possessed by man, and the one that sets man off from other animals, is the power to know the natures and causes of things. As we have seen, the logic appropriate to man is intentional; that is to say, ideas (concepts) are understood as instrumental to our knowing forms or natures, but not themselves the immediate objects of our knowing. Let us tie this logical point to the substance-accident point by imagining a Professor Turbayne rejuvenated in his campaign to rid us moderns of the notion that we are machines. In his chapter on ordinary language, Turbayne writes:

> Since Aristotle, ordinary people have had the view that the world is full of things or substances that own properties or qualities. We notice the corresponding fact that most sentences of the Indo-European languages lend themselves to the subject-predicate analysis. This has been the main and obvious way to analyze them. Thus either we have made our language to fit the facts or we have made the facts to fit the obvious structure of our language. What makes us suspect that the latter alternative is true is that there are more languages in existence that are incapable of the subject-predicate analysis than otherwise. The people who speak them do not suppose the world divisible into subjects and predicates.[14]

168

Doubtless Turbayne's last sentence is accurate. But neither do we Indo-European language users suppose the world divisible into subjects and predicates. This can help us to better understand the difference between language as a system of <u>material</u> signs and logic as a system of <u>formal</u> signs, as well as to help shed light on the substance-accident distinction.

It should take but a moment's reflection for us to become aware of the distinction between the <u>real</u> relation of substance-accident and the <u>linguistic</u> relation of subject-predicate. Consider the two sentences, "Turbayne is a brilliant writer" and "Turbayne's brilliant writing is persuasive." Because the plain man takes Turbayne to be a substance (he exists in himself, and not in another; he persists through innumerable changes in him), and his brilliant writing an accident (it exists in Turbayne, not in itself), he might suppose a one-to-one correspondence between that and the first sentence, where "Turbayne" (but not Turbayne, note) is the subject, and "a brilliant writer" is the predicate. But any tendency to confuse the two relations should be removed as soon as we ponder the second sentence. Surely no plain man would take Turbayne's brilliant writing to be a substance, however much he would readily acknowledge that "Turbayne's brilliant writing" is the subject of the second sentence.

If we add to this the point that the <u>logical</u>, <u>not</u> the linguistic, relation of subject-predicate is an instrument by means of which we all come to know the ways in which things exist (whether they be substantial things, or accidental, real, logical, fictional, natural, supernatural, or whatever), just as the concept is the <u>logical</u> relation of universality; then we are no longer in any danger of confusing logic or language with metaphysics. In other words, propositions, as well as concepts, are formal signs by means of which we come to know.[15] Given these insights, our rejuvenated Turbayne might well find his way out of the maze of metaphors, and get back to metaphysics, to a discovery and description of the way things really are. In other words, when we have an account of the tools of knowledge, such as the classical realist gives us, which enables us to intelligibly say and argue that it is the real world we know, and not just our own ideas, we perhaps have rid ourselves of the threat of subjectivism.

V   What If...?

Berkeley neglected what we might call the substance-accident truism, most likely because of his subjectivism. However, at least late in his life he showed awareness of the classical Aristotelian notion of matter as potentiality. He also realized that in refuting the philosophers' matter he had not refuted matter understood as potentiality; nor did he display any desire

169

so to do.[16] Moreover, we have seen how, in his criticism of Locke's doctrine of abstract ideas, he came close to divining the secret to the intelligible logic and epistemology he needed for his desired philosophical realism.[17]

Suppose he had grasped the classical realistic insight regarding formal signs. Instead of departing so quickly from common sense by asserting that the immediate objects of knowledge are ideas, he might well have argued instead that it is by way of ideas, propositions, arguments, understood as formal signs, that we men can and do come to know, however haltingly and limitedly, the natures of things, the ways in which they exist, and the causes for their so existing. Furthermore, had he been able to clearly distinguish between logic as a system of formal signs and language as a system of material signs, he might well have praised God for making us knowers and not mere readers of language. And thus he could have regarded us as able not only to cope with nature, but also able to come to knowledge of what and why things in nature are.

Suppose also that early on he had clearly grasped the import of Aristotle's "matter" as the principle of potentiality, and of Aristotle's "natural substances" as composites of matter and form, and of Aristotle's definition of change as the actualization of the potential, or the forming of matter. Then, instead of taking nature to be a system of inert, passive ideas, stripped of all causal powers, he might well have elucidated it as changing substances causing and being effected, interacting with one another. Nor can we doubt that had he gone this far he would have stopped short of Aristotle's conclusion of God as the Pure Form, the Uncaused Cause, the Final Cause of nature; or of Aquinas' conclusion that God is not only Final Cause, but also Efficient Cause of nature.

Finally, and getting to the real point of all this supposition contrary to fact, had Berkeley done all this, surely he would have not only defended and refined common sense and theism, but also have built a firm foundation for morality and religion.

VI Morality

Suppose it really is the case that nature is comprised of a variety of kinds of changing things, and of innumerable individuals within the kinds. Then, to take but one example, our judgment that a particular, individual oak tree is good or bad need not be based on our subjective desires or whims, but on an objective understanding of whether or not that oak tree has come to actualize its potential. If it has reached maturity, is thriving, weathers the storms, and produces crops of acorns, we can sensibly call it good; if its growth has become stunted, so that it does not produce acorns, we can sensibly call it bad, or deficient.[18]

And so with man. He, too, is a changing natural substance. Given the power of knowing, we can know not only what oaks and acorns are, but also what men are. Moreover, we also can then come to know what a really good man is -- namely, one who has actualized his human potentiality. There need be no more whimsy, sentiment, or subjective value judgment in that knowledge than in the judgment about the oak's being good or bad. At any rate, the point is that classical moral theory stands or falls with classical metaphysics. If we can not say that we know what and why things in nature are, we are in no position to say that we know what and why men are; and hence can make no objective value judgments regarding human behavior.

Given this classical realism, it is relatively easy to describe the good man. Plato, for example, does it in The Republic, by first describing man understood as a rational animal. There are three basic parts in the human soul, the human substantial form: reason, spirit, appetite (he left out the vegetative part, I take it, as having no import for his theory of morality). The appetites move us, the spirited part spurs us, and reason knows. Hence the good man is the one in whom the most god-like part, reason, directs his activities, with support from the spirited part. Plato goes on to locate the cardinal virtues of prudence, courage, temperance, and justice by showing the proper inter-relationships of these parts.

However, as Plato and all other classical philosophers see, while it is easy enough to describe a good man, the real problem is to become one. Is it within our power? As living things we, like the oak and the otter, are somewhat at the mercy of environment; and include in that term, if you will, such things as our genetic structure and our temperament. However, and again similarly to plants and animals, we are agents. Are plants capable of initiating activity? Probably not, but they do direct activity. Few of us believe that they do it consciously; but none of us doubts that if the acorn grows, the activity will be directed to the development of an oak tree, and not a rose bush or ten story building. Do our pet dogs and cats initiate as well as direct activity? Only those of us schooled in a materialistic, deterministic perspective could seriously doubt it. Our pets seem clearly capable even of eliciting, if not initiating, activity in us.

Still, very few of us will hold the pet dog morally responsible for biting the postman, while virtually all of us do hold ourselves and our fellow humans morally responsible for much

171

of our activity, both as to its origin and its direction. Why is this, except that we, unlike our pets, are <u>rational</u> agents. We know, or are capable of knowing, what we do and why we do it. In one of his travels Gulliver visits the land of the Houyhnhnms, discovering these horses to be perfect rational animals. Gulliver has difficulty explaining peculiar habits of civilized Yahoos (the name given by the Houyhnhnms to the human species), such as lying. How can a rational animal not say what is truly the case? In his satire, Swift does not mean to convince us we are not rational -- how could we recognize and appreciate the satire if we were not --, but does convey how far we fall short of the ideal. The point might be taken to be that for any of us Yahoos to achieve anything near the perfection that is easily enough described for rational animals, we need much training and education.

That seems clear enough. What we must also recognize is that the rational part of our souls, understood now as the power to know what's what and to act accordingly, is the most exalted part of our souls, and should be master and not servant. Plato spoke of the rational part as being the most god-like; in our Judeo-Christian tradition we commonly suppose that it is the rational part of our functioning that is meant when scripture declares that we are created in God's image. If instead we come to regard reason as mere calculator, serving the appetites and inclinations that pull us hither and thither, there can be no rational or metaphysical basis for morality; and finally no morality at all, but just an incessant power struggle between man and man, nation and nation. Because anyone who has read this far will agree that we are not by nature calculating <u>animals,</u> but instead <u>rational</u> animals, I will in what follows assume that.

Because we are rational animals, we need education. Our reason is not given to us full blown, as apparently it was with the Houyhnhnms. It requires nurturing. Such nurturing can only come in a community of rational men, where elder generations take responsibility for the education of the young. Our needs, most emphatically our rational needs, can be met only by our living in community, in a polis. Because man is rational, he is also political; he cannot thrive outside the polis. Hence, the primary educational responsibility in any polis is to instruct the young on what the good, or properly human, life is; and to provide the means for achieving that goodness, or virtue.

Aristotle articulated the wisdom of the ages by emphasizing the necessity of young people developing the moral habits of courage, temperance, and the like. So important and obvious is this that we all tend to agree with Aristotle that if these habits do not become part of one's character by age seventeen or so, they probably never will. Development of the virtues does not mean

172

that we give up a pleasurable existence for a painful one. Quite the contrary, the most satisfying existence is the one in which moral character is fully developed. Acquiring the proper moral, and intellectual, habits is painstaking; but similarly to an accomplishment like piano playing, once the mastery is achieved, the activity is pleasurable. Berkeley poignantly expressed this in the passage we quoted at the end of Chapter Three: the minds of young people before it is too late "should be formed and accustomed to receive pleasure and pain from proper objects, or, which is the same thing, to have their inclinations and aversions rightly placed. This, according to Plato and Aristotle, was the ... right education."[19]

It needs to be added that because few if any of us reach moral perfection there must be laws. As we have seen in our discussion of Berkeley and Shaftesbury, in Chapter 3, from the classical perspective law exists not primarily to protect us from one another, but to provide guidance for us. Whether or not the law in fact does that depends upon the law makers. Accordingly, the classical philosophers, including Berkeley, have seen an essential task of education to be making possible the emergence of genuine moral and political leaders. Would we not all have more confidence in our democracy if we had greater assurance that our educational system was drawing out wise leaders?

In sum, Berkeley's unfinished moral project has its proper foundation in a classical realistic metaphysics, with its leading notions of substance-accident, form-matter, act-potency, etc.

VII Religion

If one is skeptical about man's power to come to know the natures and causes of things, then if one holds to religious belief(s), the religion seems clearly a matter of blind faith, and apt to become fanatic. For given skepticism, there is no philosophic or scientific, no rational account of the world that will at least buttress the faith. By contrast, the logic of the metaphysics we have outlined pushes us to conclude that there is a God, and that ultimate explanation of our changing world lies in supernature, and not in matter or nature. That far at least we have support for the Christian faith that Berkeley held to.

Moreover, as the greatest medieval Christian theologian, St. Thomas Aquinas, held, there is nothing in the Christian faith contrary to the wisdom of the ages, or to common experience philosophically refined. God as Creator, Redeemer, and Paraclete adds to our metaphysical picture of God as Uncaused Cause; it does not go contrary to it.

Nor does God as law giver subvert the morality of virtue.[20]

The Mosaic Law makes better sense to us when we understand the law giver by analogy to a loving parent rather than by analogy to a pruning, jealous of authority general. We should not steal, covet, murder, commit adultery, etc., because a loving God knows what activities and habits will and will not lead to happiness and well being for us as individuals and as members of a polis. When Jesus Christ appeared to make the law even sterner by forbidding us to even look in an adulterous or lustful way, we can interpret that as in accord with the morality of virtue. That is, the ideal is to so form one's character that one is no longer even tempted. So is the self-controlled person distinguished from the merely continent one.

The virtues of faith, hope, and love, granted that they depend on more than naturally developed moral character, namely on direct divine intervention in one's life, still do not contravene or even replace such virtues as prudence, courage, temperance, etc. Indeed, those familiar with so-called situation ethics, where anything can be done, in some circumstances or other, so long as it is done lovingly, will recognize that such an ethics is at best a desperate attempt to salvage some morality from a modern philosophy bereft of metaphysical or rational foundation.

As for religion and politics, perhaps enough has been said in Chapters 2 and 3. However, given Berkeley's desire to establish a metaphysical foundation for politics, as well as religion, and given the current debate on religion in politics, a bit more will be added. Many today interpret the Constitutional principle of separation of church and state to mean that no church should interfere with or influence political matters, particularly if the church's doctrines or practices take issue with the liberal establishment's view on morals and politics. Indeed, the Supreme Court has come to read the Constitution that way, and has in a variety of ways banned the influence of religion in public education. I believe that those who so interpret the Constitution do so because they believe, much as did the free-thinkers in Berkeley's day, that traditional religion is priestcraft and superstition. They are also convinced that there is no metaphysical or rational foundation for belief in God. Hence, their beliefs are, deep down, anti-religious. Given the great gains of secularism in recent times, they are content to tolerate religion, if only it will keep its nose out from under the moral and political tent.

I believe these beliefs and attitudes will persist until Berkeley's project is completed; that is, until such people come to understand that there is in fact metaphysical foundation for belief in God, and for religion. When that happens, such people will return to the views of such as Washington and Jefferson, quoted in Chapter 3, Section X, as well as Berkeley, on the

importance of religion to the body politic. At such time, such
people will interpret the Constitutional principle as meaning that
there should be no establishment of a particular religion by the
government. Again, I believe Berkeley was right in stressing the
crucial importance of metaphysics -- theory of reality -- to
morals, education, religion, and politics.[21]

VIII The Moral

Finally, we must ask why Berkeley rejected the path of
classical realism, and ventured instead the idealism we have seen
to fail. We cannot of course mind read. But yet, what Berkeley
and other philosophers of the seventeenth and eighteenth century
wrote is sufficient to force this conclusion: the new science
developing through the late middle ages and the Renaissance, and
reaching its culmination in Newtonian physics was so impressive,
astounding, and successful that it tended to be taken by all
intellectuals of Berkeley's time as the account of nature, as a
given in one's theorizing about reality.

And so it was with Berkeley. To remind ourselves of this, we
need only recall that Berkeley's attempt to overcome the
appearance/reality dichotomy, and to thus reconcile science with
common sense and philosophy, was to substitute inert, passive
ideas for inert, passive matter. He could not substitute changing
things, some of which at least were active and possessing causal
powers, because Newtonian physics was an indubitable given. When
we add to this that it was out of that same new science that the
transmission theories of light and sound came, to provide the
impetus for both the appearance/reality dichotomy and the
subjectivism characteristic of modern philosophy, we can not help
concluding a certain inevitability about Berkeley's rejection of
classical metaphysics and epistemology.

The moral then seems obvious. If Newtonian physics is the
account of nature, then neither Berkeley nor anyone else can
convincingly argue idealism or materialism, or any other
philosophical ism, save only, it appears, skepticism. In other
words, if Newtonian physics is the account of nature, then the
appearance/reality dichotomy is absolute and irreparable. And if
that is the case, then philosophy and science will not and cannot
get together; and philosophy will not be the pursuit of wisdom.

There is a corollary moral. Any thinker who wants to argue a
philosophical realism, or a philosophic defense and refinement of
common sense, must suppose that Newtonian science is not the
account of nature. If we still have some hope that such an
enterprise (namely, philosophical realism) is possible, we at
least can be encouraged by the fact that no longer is Newtonian
science taken to be the account of nature. Indeed, recent work in

both philosophy of science and philosophy of nature leads us to conclude that although Berkeley's attempt to defeat materialism, skepticism, immorality, and irreligion failed, it is still possible and intellectually responsible to try to complete Berkeley's project. In the appendix we had occasion to remark on the suggestive and thoughtful reflection, in the last chapter of Professor Ardley's book, on the place of modern science in our world. Professor Ardley concludes: "...we know what the world is like, at least in essentials, quite independently of organised scientific investigation. Such an investigation adds a wealth of subordinate detail, corrects accidental deformities, enlarges our views, assists our technical mastery; it builds, in a stylized way, what we might call the infra-structure of our knowledge of nature."[22]

Certainly it is as clear to us as it was to Berkeley that we cannot settle for any facile or naive realism that either obscures or ignores the advances in knowledge in physics, physiology, and psychology. At the same time, ridding ourselves of subjectivism depends on our remembering that if there is increase of knowledge in these fields, it is increase of knowledge. And with removal of the threat of subjectivism, it is not too much to hope that philosophy will be put in its proper place in the curriculum, and education become what Berkeley, learning from the ancients, proposed that it be. "And those who, in their own minds, their health, or their fortunes, feel the cursed effects of a wrong [education], would do well to consider they cannot better make amends for what was amiss in themselves than by preventing the same in their posterity."[23]

176

Appendix

Berkeley as a Modern Plato

Preparatory to his interpretation of Berkeley, Professor Gavin Ardley[1] explains what classical thinkers, beginning with Plato and Aristotle, take philosophy to be. The love of wisdom (philosophy) comes into being because men wonder about the mysterious universe. Furthermore, metaphysics for the classical philosopher is not, as it tends to be for moderns like Descartes, a system building arising out of a science or a physics; but rather has its origins in and grows out of the common ordinary experience we all have. As Ardley puts it, "Philosophic reflection does not discover wholly new truths; rather it enables each man to clarify and articulate old truths; it enables him to possess the old truths more fully."[2]

Ardley characterizes Plato as the prototype of this kind of philosopher. Plato mistrusted the professional philosophers of his day (who were, we might note, using Berkeley's term, minute philosophers; some serious, the first scientists, and some frivolous, the first moral free-thinkers or sophists); he believed that corruption in philosophy was rooted in moral corruption; he was convinced that philosophy grows from a sense of playful wonder, and that it thrives only in dialogue, the way of all genuine love; and finally, he saw the origin of philosophy in common piety and good sense.

Ardley's interpretation of Berkeley, then, is that although he and Plato "run very different courses in their intellectual analyses, as a consequence of their very different circumstances,"[3] still Berkeley's intentions were the same as Plato's. Berkeley intended to pursue wisdom, not to build a metaphysical system called idealism; indeed, one of the primary aims of the Principles is to turn men away from trifling speculations. Furthermore, Berkeley's major works are dialogues (Three Dialogues between Hylas and Philonous, and Alciphron) or dialectic (Principles of Human Knowledge). Finally Berkeley finds the origin of philosophy in common sense, and not in modern science.

Ardley's book is important for our understanding Berkeley's intentions as a classical philosopher. It makes those intentions clearer than the present work, because Ardley has profounder insights into the nature of classical philosophy. Furthermore, the last chapter of Ardley's book presents much suggestive and thoughtful reflection on the place of modern science in our world; and quite appropriately, for that of course was one of Berkeley's major concerns.

177

Our criticism of the notion of Berkeley as a modern Plato is that Ardley shows what Berkeley intended, or should have intended to do, rather than what he actually did. Let us consider some instances of this. First, in previewing Berkeley's concern about Newton's mechanical physics being taken as an adequate account of nature, Ardley writes: "... [Berkeley] shows how we can fully appreciate the work of Newton, without losing our confidence in the primacy of the world of Plato and Aristotle."[4] If he has, there are very few aware of it. More importantly, those who do know of Berkeley's theory of nature as a language rather than as a mechanism find it, as we have seen, unsatisfactory. Moreover, and again, Berkeley himself confessed that, so understood, nature does not disclose to us what and why things are, but only teaches us to cope.

Second, Ardley writes that "...in place of the attitude of mere exploitation of natural resources encouraged by the new philosophy, Berkeley revived the sense of joyful intercourse of man with Nature as with his home."[5] There is no doubt that Berkeley wanted to do that; but also no doubt that he failed, and not simply because we are slow learners, but more because Berkeley's teaching is not convincing. After all, if nature is a system of inert, passive ideas, we as active beings are not likely to find in it much occasion for joyful intercourse with it.

Third, when Ardley comes to write of the difficulties in Berkeley's immaterialism he says, "Berkeley would admit [in Dialogue III, as we have seen, he did admit] the propriety of all these questions;...But he would deny that these questions are of any crucial importance....to attribute an excessive importance to these questions is a symptom of a fundamentally wrong orientation. (Like...the man who refuses to speak until he is fully informed about grammar.)"[6] But those questions are of crucial importance. Moreover, it is incredible that Berkeley would have written two major works to answer them if he thought them not to be of crucial importance. Ardley implies that trying to puzzle out answers to the epistemological problems that Berkeley wrestled with takes us away from the pursuit of wisdom. He is probably right; and it is regrettable. But whose fault is it? In part, it is Berkeley's fault. And while, as we suggest in Chapter 7, Berkeley would be heartbroken to know it, nonetheless that is the fact.

Fourth, Ardley claims that Berkeley did not propound a metaphysical system; "he has instead 'plain common sense together with an application and eagerness to discover the truth.'"[7] But we have seen how radically Berkeley, despite his intent, departs from common sense when he declares ideas to be the immediate objects of knowledge, and when he rules causality out of nature. Ardley goes on, "The proper end of metaphysics, as Berkeley understands it, is the furtherance of morality and piety."[8] Doubtless; but Berkeley's does not do it. And again, "For the time being, he banishes subtleties and the allure of system; recalls these sophisticated children to their patrimony; directs their attention to the things that matter; urges them to relax from fervour, and to cultivate that astonishment from which alone wisdom may grow."[9] Again, the <u>Principles</u> and the <u>Three Dialogues</u> just do not read that way. Instead, Berkeley is convinced, and is trying to convince us, of a theory of reality. Moreover, Berkeley did not succeed in directing the attention of philosophers to what he took to be the true business of a philosopher. However true it may be that "by mastering the way of ideas he can exhibit its paradox in such a way that no reasonable man will thereafter want to defend it,"[10] still it is true that Berkeley did go on defending it, as Ardley himself acknowledges,[11] and did so because he saw no other way to frustrate the steady growth of materialism.

To sum this up, let us note an uncompleted analogy that Ardley presents in trying to convey the importance of Berkeley. "It was left for Aristotle to complete Plato's work,... to direct his energies to the detailed examination of the world order, to found sciences on sound principles. There could be no Aristotle without a Plato to prepare the way and give life to the enterprise....Berkeley was the new Plato, exhorting in terms appropriate to his times, and conveying a similar message; and again like Plato, the second phase, of system, is left as sketches and hints."[12] Thus, $\frac{\text{Plato}}{\text{Aristotle}} = \frac{\text{Berkeley}}{\text{X}}$. Can not the tragedy of Berkeley's story be summed up, as well as the failure of Ardley's interpretation, by noting that in late twentieth century that fourth figure in the proportionality remains an X? Instead of a new Aristotle, we have had Hume and Kant, continuing philosophy on its apparently inexorable modern subjectivist way. Moreover, that it went that way was in some measure, as we have seen, the responsibility of George Berkeley.

It seems that Berkeley would reject Ardley's interpretation because he meant to destroy materialism <u>and</u> to establish an alternative metaphysics, immaterialism. Moreover, if Berkeley's metaphysical and epistemological writing is seen as only a kind of Platonic dialectic designed to expose the inadequacy of materialism and skepticism, it at the same time leaves us with no metaphysical support for morality. Ardley might retort that even if we suppose Berkeley was serious about his immaterialism and further suppose that his immaterialism is sound, we still do not have a metaphysical foundation for classical morality. From a world of active spirits living amidst passive ideas, how can we reconstruct a morality of virtue? Men seem to fit into this world no better than into Descartes'. Would not Berkeley then have been constrained to ground traditional morality in some such way as

Hume or Kant or Bentham grounded it, appealing to conscience or duty or utility,[13] instead of to actualization of potential, or development of right habits, or reason's direction of appetite?

Notes and References

All references to Berkeley's writings are to The Works of George Berkeley, 9 volumes, edited by A. A. Luce and T. E. Jessop. The titles of the works referred to have been abbreviated as follows, and in the order of their being referred to:

Alc   Alciphron

Si   Siris

MM   A Discourse Addressed to Magistrates and Men in Authority

AT   Advice to the Tories Who Have Taken the Oaths

RGB   An Essay Towards Preventing the Ruin of Great Britain

PO   Passive Obedience

Gu   Essays in the Guardian

TV   Essay Towards a New Theory of Vision

TVV   The Theory of Vision, or Visual Language...Vindicated and Explained

An   The Analyst

DM   De Motu

Pr   A Treatise Concerning the Principles of Human Knowledge

HP   Three Dialogues Between Hylas and Philonous

Alciphron is comprised of seven dialogues. Each dialogue has numbered sections. Each reference to Alciphron contains in parentheses a Roman numeral and an Arabic numeral, referring respectively to the number of the dialogue and the number of the section of that dialogue. Siris and A Treatise Concerning the Principles of Human Knowledge have numbered paragraphs. Each reference to either of these works contains in parentheses an Arabic numeral, referring to the paragraph(s). So with TV, TVV, and DM.

Preface

1. If there is any contemporary deserving that stature it is, in my opinion, Edward Pols, in the philosophy department of Bowdoin College. The three books in which this twentieth century version of classical philosophy is expressed are The Recognition of Reason (Carbondale, 1963); Meditation on a Prisoner (Carbondale and Edwardsville, 1975); and The Acts of Our Being (Amherst, 1982). The first is a response to the challenge of skepticism; the second a response to the challenge of materialism; the third a prolonged reflexive defense of man as a rational agent and primary being.

2. William A. Wallace has outlined, by way of ten theses, a classical realistic program, informed by modern science, and including moral philosophy and natural theology, in "The Intelligibility of Nature: a Neo-Aristotelian View," The Review of Metaphysics, Vol. XXXVIII, No. 1 (1984), pp. 33-56.

3. Alasdair MacIntyre, After Virtue (Notre Dame, 1981).

4. Gilbert C. Meilaender, The Theory and Practice of Virtue (Notre Dame, 1984).

Introduction - A Life Against the Current

1. Quoted in G. R. Cragg, The Church and the Age of Reason (Baltimore, 1960), p. 247.

2. A.A. Luce, The Life of George Berkeley (London, 1949), p. 25.

3. Works, Vol. 8, p. 127.

Chapter One - Free-thinking

1. J. M. Robertson, A Short History of Freethought (New York, 1957), p. 5.

2. ibid., pp. 5-6.

3. G. M. Trevelyan, History of England (London, 1926), p. 474.

4. J. M. Robertson, op. cit., pp. 376-382. But see Wilson, Clyde, "Calhoun and Community," Chronicles of Culture, July,

1985, 17-20.

Chapter Two - Religion and Politics

1. Alc, Works, Vol. 3, p. 217. (V,35)

2. Works, Vol. 7, Essays VIII and IX. All essays in the Guardian were originally anonymous. Berkeley's authorship of the twelve essays printed in the Nelson edition of the Works has been established by A. A. Luce in his article, "Berkeley's Essays in the Guardian," Mind, Vol. 52, 1943, pp. 247-263.

3. Works, Vol. 8, p. 28.

4. Si, Works, Vol. 5, p. 164. (368)

5. MM, Works, Vol. 6, p. 218.

6. AT, Works, Vol. 6, p. 53.

7. RGB, Works, Vol. 6, p. 84.

8. ibid., p. 69.

9. MM, op. cit., p. 208.

10. loc. cit.

11. ibid., p. 210.

12. loc. cit. See also Wilson, op. cit., Note 4, p. 182.

13. PO, Works, Vol. 6, p. 20.

14. ibid., pp. 24-25. Incidentally Berkeley is still taking happiness to be the end of human living, and truth, et. al., to be instrumental to that happiness.

15. ibid., p. 25.

16. The reader familiar with Plato might consider the Socrates of Apology, Crito, Phaedo as exemplifying what Berkeley argues.

17. PO, op. cit., Vol. 6, p. 18.

18. RGB, op. cit., p. 71.

19. ibid., p. 74.

20. ibid., p. 76. See Plato, The Republic, Books 2-4, for a thorough criticism of the luxurious polis.

21. ibid., p. 78. Our "supposed" polis is so enlightened and liberated as to forego the wearing of masks.

22. ibid., p. 83.

23. loc. cit.

24. ibid., pp. 69-70.

25. ibid., pp. 70-71.

26. MM, op. cit., p. 201.

27. For a compelling recent articulation of this contention, the reader might be interested in Henri Bergson's The Two Sources of Morality and Religion (New York, 1935).

28. MM, op. cit., p. 215.

29. ibid., p. 216.

30. RGB, op. cit., p. 70.

31. MM, op. cit., p. 218.

32. loc. cit.

Chapter Three - Classical Philosophy vs. Minute Philosophy

1. A. A. Luce, The Life of George Berkeley (London, 1949), p. 96.

2. ibid., Chapters VIII and IX.

3. Alc, Works, Vol. 3, p. 31. (I,1)

4. Works, Vol. 3, p. 2.

5. Alc, Works, Vol. 3, p. 33 (I,1)

6. ibid., pp. 34-43. (I,2-7)

7. ibid., p. 44. (I,9)

8. ibid., pp. 45-7 (I,9-10) See the argument of Thrasymachus in Plato, The Republic, Bk. 1.

9. ibid., pp. 46-7. (I,10)

10. ibid., p. 47. (I,10)

11. ibid., pp. 55-8. (I,14)

12. ibid., pp. 58-9. (I,15)

13. ibid., pp. 60-4. (I,16)

14. ibid., pp. 80-1. (II,11)

15. ibid., p. 83. (II,13)

16. ibid., p. 66. (II,2)

17. ibid., p. 69. (II,3)

18. ibid., pp. 71-83. (II,5-12) Mandeville himself agreed with this evaluation. But he insisted that Berkeley mistook his emphasis. Instead of arguing for vice, he was arguing against it; but showing that if we are to give it up, we must also give up being a great, luxurious, and flourishing nation. See his A Letter to Dion (Liverpool, 1954).

19. ibid., p. 83. (II,13)

20. ibid., p. 84. (II,13)

21. ibid., p. 116. (III,3)

22. Stanley Grean, "Introduction," Shaftesbury's Characteristics (Indianapolis, 1964), p. xiii.

23. Shaftesbury, "The Moralists," Characteristics (Indianapolis, 1964), p. 137.

24. ibid., pp. 135-7.

25. ibid., pp. 47-55.

26. Alc, Works, Vol. 3, p. 122. (III,7)

27. ibid., p. 133. (III,13)

28. Shaftesbury, "The Moralists," op. cit., pp. 55-6.

29. Shaftesbury, "A Letter Concerning Enthusiasm," op. cit., pp. 28-30.

30. Shaftesbury, "An Inquiry Concerning Virtue or Merit," op. cit., pp. 275-7.

31. Shaftesbury, "Advice to an Author," op. cit., pp. 225-7. These citations are given because, although other writers on Berkeley have said that Berkeley is unfair to Shaftesbury, none of them, as far as I know, has argued that Berkeley could have enlisted Shaftesbury's aid in his campaign against minute philosophy.

32. Shaftesbury, "Miscellaneous Reflections," op. cit., pp. 352-369.

33. Shaftesbury, "A Letter Concerning Enthusiasm," op. cit., p. 11.

34. Shaftesbury, "The Moralists," op. cit., p. 150.

35. Alciphron seems to, at Alc, Works, Vol. 3, p. 117. (III,3)

36. Both statements are quoted from Virgil C. Blum, S. J., "Shinto Catholics and the Right to Life," Supplement to the Catholic League Newsletter, Vol. 11, No. 9, 1984, p. 2.

37. Shaftesbury, "The Moralists," op. cit., pp. 53-4.

38. Alc, Works, Vol. 3, p. 160. (IV,14)

39. ibid., p. 170. (IV,21)

40. ibid., pp. 36-7. (I,3)

41. ibid., pp. 214-5. (V,34)

42. ibid, p. 182. (V,9)

43. See, for example, Dean Wooldridge, Mechanical Man (New York, 1968).

44. See, for example, B. F. Skinner, Beyond Freedom & Dignity (New York, 1972).

45. Alc, Works, Vol. 3, p. 310. (VII,16) Berkeley, in pp. 309-318 (VII,16-20), entertains and responds to a number of variations on the deterministic theme.

46. In <u>The</u> <u>Two</u> <u>Sources</u> <u>of</u> <u>Morality</u> <u>and</u> <u>Religion</u>. See note 27, Ch. 2.

47. Alc, <u>Works</u>, Vol. 3, pp. 201-218. (V,23-36)

48. <u>Gulliver's</u> <u>Travels</u>, Part III.

49. Alc, <u>Works</u>, Vol. 3, p. 50. (I,11)

50. ibid., p. 47. (I,11)

51. ibia., p. 48. (I,11)

52. loc. cit.

53. ibid., p. 50. (I,11)

54. Quoted by permission of the author, whose name, along with that of the college newspaper in which this article was published are being suppressed, out of consideration for the college of which the author was dean.

55. Gu, <u>Works</u>, Vol. 7, pp. 203-4.

56. ibid., p. 203.

57. ibid., p. 205.

58. Alc, <u>Works</u>, Vol. 3, p. 54. (I,13)

59. ibid., pp. 328-9. (VI1,31)

Chapter Four - <u>Scientific</u> <u>Philosophy</u>

1. TV, TVV, <u>Works</u>, Vol. 1.

2. An, <u>Works</u>, Vol. 4.

3. DM, <u>Works</u>, Vol. 4.

4. Pr, <u>Works</u>, Vol. 2, p. 25. (Introd.,1)

5. Rene Descartes, Meditation VI, <u>Discourse</u> on <u>Method</u> and <u>Meditations</u>, trans. L. J. Lafleur, (Indianapolis, 1960), p. 134.

6. op. cit., pp. 5-6.

7. op. cit., pp. 7-8.

8. op. cit., pp. 45-6.

9. op. cit., p. 46.

10. op. cit., pp. 46-7.

11. Si, Works, Vol. 5, pp. 150-1. (331)

12. T. A. Kantonen, "The Influence of Descartes on Berkeley," The Philosophical Review, September, 1934, pp. 483-500.

13. Descartes, op. cit., pp. 82-3.

14. It is true that Descartes had some reservations about animals being unfeeling. See his letter to Henry More, 1649, Descartes, Selections, (New York, 1927), pp. 358-360. But his principles require his overcoming the reservations.

15. Descartes, Discourse on Method and Meditations, p. 94.

16. In the three books cited in Note 1 of the Preface.

17. There is indication in Locke's writings, however, that he is willing to entertain the possibility that man is thinking matter, rather than a mind in a machine.

18. John Locke, An Essay Concerning Human Understanding, Bk. II, Ch. XXIII, Sec. 2.

19. loc. cit.

Chapter Five - Immaterialism

1. Alfred N. Whitehead, Science and the Modern World (New York, 1960), pp. 77-80.

2. HP, Works, Vol. 2, p. 171.

3. ibid., pp. 210-211.

4. ibid., p. 261.

5. The major source for this account is Aristotle's Physics. See also his Metaphysics. Because of the notorious difficulty in reading some of Aristotle's works, the

beginner might do well to become acquainted with this venerable tradition by way of one or more contemporary interpretations. Of the many available I recommend John Wild, _Introduction_ to _Realistic Philosophy_, (New York, 1948), Part II of which includes explication of "matter;" and Henry B. Veatch, _Aristotle_, (Bloomington, 1974), a brief but very readable and helpful introduction.

6. This account is not meant as a substitute for, much less an improvement on, the modern physico-chemical explanation of H_2O changing from solid to liquid to vapor, or vice versa. Contemporary philosophers in the Aristotelian tradition acknowledge that water is not an element, but instead a compound of hydrogen and oxygen; that when water is heated, the H_2O molecules move faster; etc. But still, the question at issue here is whether "matter" should be construed as a substance, the stuff of hydrogen and oxygen, and all else, or as potential, as the changeability of all natural things. Philosophers (scientists) in the materialist tradition are always looking for the unchangeable stuff from which all else is made; philosophers (scientists) in the Aristotelian tradition regard that as a will-o'-the-wisp, --- hold that nothing in nature, no matter how elemental, is .ichangeable.

Moreover, Aristotle, while holding that locomotion is the most pervasive sort of change, it seeming to be present in all other kinds of change (for example, motion of H_2O molecules in heating of water), does not reduce other kinds of change (growth, for example) to locomotion. For a most persuasive argument against the reduction of change to locomotion, the reader is referred to Edward Pols, _Meditation_ on _a Prisoner_. See Note 1, Preface.

Finally, the soundness of the modern physico-chemical explanation of the changes in H_2O presupposes the capacity of the human intellect to grasp the natures and causes of things, and gives the lie to the subjectivism reviewed in Chapter 4, and Section IV below.

7. For pro-abortionists I note that Aristotle was not anti-abortion; he regarded the foetus as going through vegetable and animal stages before becoming human. Biological evidence today makes that view untenable. If Aristotle is right about substantial form, the foetus is human from the moment of conception. See Chapter 5, Section III, and Chapter 8, Section II.

8. Si, _Works_, Vol. 5, p. 146. (317)

9. See above, Chapter 4, Sec. I.

10. See Francis Parker, <u>The</u> <u>Story</u> <u>of</u> <u>Western</u> <u>Philosophy</u> (Bloomington, 1967), for an insightful explication of objectivism vs. subjectivism.

11. Pr, <u>Works</u>, Vol. 2, p. 41. (I,1)

12. <u>Works</u>, Vol. VIII, p. 28. It might be noted that in Socrates' time and place both materialism and subjectivism were prominent views among the intelligentsia.

13. Against this one might cite Berkeley's <u>De</u> <u>Motu</u> (<u>Works</u>, Vol. 4), last paragraph. "Allot each science its province; assign its bounds; accurately distinguish the principles and objects belonging to each. Thus it will be possible to treat them with greater clarity." John Earman, in defense of Newton's natural philosophy, criticizes Berkeley for separating philosophy from science, in "Who's Afraid of Absolute Space?", <u>Australian</u> <u>Journal</u> <u>of</u> <u>Philosophy</u> 48 (1970): 287-319. As will be argued in a later chapter, Berkeley hoped that science henceforth would be done under the aegis of immaterialism, rather than materialism.

14. HP, <u>Works</u>, Vol. 2, p. 196.

15. ibid., p. 175.

16. ibid., pp. 187-8.

17. However, A. A. Luce points out that not all of Berkeley's predecessors had been so inconsistent. See <u>The</u> <u>Dialectic</u> <u>of</u> <u>Immaterialism</u> (London, 1963), pp. 70-1.

18. HP, <u>Works</u>, Vol. 2, pp. 188-194.

19. ibid., pp. 203-4.

20. ibid., pp. 205-6.

21. ibid., p. 206.

22. ibid., p. 217.

23. loc. cit.

24. For a helpful account of our experience of color (and by inference, of other sensible qualities) see William A. Wallace, <u>Causality</u> <u>and</u> <u>Scientific</u> <u>Explanation</u>, Vol. 2 (Ann Arbor, 1974), pp. 251-2.

25. Etienne Gilson, _The Unity of Philosophical Experience_ (New York, 1937), pp. 194-5.

26. An extreme case is Dean Wooldridge, _Mechanical Man_ (New York, 1968), who argues that consciousness makes no difference to any thing or event, but yet writes a well organized book to convince us that only matter and laws of nature are real, and that man is a machine. For him the "ideas" in our "minds" are data fed into computers, our brains.

27. HP, _Works_, Vol. 2, pp. 229-30.

28. ibid., pp. 234-5.

29. ibid., pp. 235-6.

30. ibid., pp. 237-8.

31. See above, Chapter 5, Sec. I.

32. HP, _Works_, Vol. 2, pp. 230-2.

33. David Hume (1711-1776) was a British philosopher who followed the subjectivist way to its ultimate skeptical conclusions: not only can we not know matter, but also we cannot know mind, and we cannot know causal necessity. See Chapter 7, Section I.

34. HP, _Works_, Vol. 2, p. 233.

35. Whether on this issue we tend to side with Berkeley or with Hume, we cannot help wondering whether there may not be something radically wrong with a theory of knowledge which defines ideas at the outset in such a way that this difficulty appears. This is one of the more important difficulties, not only in Berkeley's philosophy, but in the whole modern subjectivist tradition which begins by regarding ideas ("perceptions" is Hume's word) as the immediate objects of human awareness. See Chapter 6.

36. HP, _Works_, Vol. 2, p. 237.

37. ibid., pp. 241-2.

38. ibid., p. 243.

39. ibid., pp. 250-6.

40. ibid., p. 246.

41. Etienne Gilson, op. cit., pp. 196-7.

42. HP, _Works_, Vol. 2, p. 248.

43. ibid., p. 244.

Chapter Six - Language and Signs

1. Pr, _Works_, Vol. 2, pp. 32-3. (Introd.,13) The passage is from Locke's An _Essay_ on _Human Understanding_, Bk. IV, Ch. 7, Sec. 9.

2. Pr, _Works_, Vol. 2, p. 33. (Introd.,13)

3. The sources of this classical view go back as far as Plato and Aristotle. For a readily accessible account of the logic of this position the reader is referred to this textbook of it: Francis Parker and Henry Veatch, _Logic as a Human Instrument_ (New York, 1959). For the student who is acquainted with modern mathematical logic, Henry Veatch's _Intentional Logic_ (New Haven, 1951) will be most enlightening. There Professor Veatch shows how different the logic of classical realism is from the logic of modern subjectivist scientific philosophy.

4. Francis Parker in Parker and Veatch, op. cit.

5. HP, _Works_, Vol. 2, p. 240.

6. Berkeley concludes the response by claiming that God is different from us in knowing pain without suffering it. Why God did not make us the same way, -- in other words, Berkeley's theodicy -- however, is not here our concern.

7. As we shall see shortly, in Section VII, Berkeley himself is forced to a skeptical conclusion.

8. Pr, _Works_, Vol. 2, p. 35. (Introd.,16)

9. ibid., pp. 33-4. (Introd.,15) First emphasis added.

10. For a definitive realistic account of the cognitive relationship of concept to what it signifies, see Veatch, _Intentional Logic_, Chapters 1 and 2, or Parker and Veatch, _Logic as a Human Instrument_, Ch. 2. Against this realistic logic we should cite Harry M. Bracken. In his _Berkeley_ (New York, 1974), he shows awareness of intentionality as an option to the views promulgated by Descartes, Locke, Berkeley, and others. After reviewing the matter-form notion of substance, he writes, "The same form thus exists

192

in two ways: materially in the object and immaterially in the mind. Moreover, the objectivity of our knowledge is thereby guaranteed, or one might say, presupposed. Sometimes identity is replaced with resemblance. In either case the tie or relation is usually described as 'intentional'. That hardly helps as an explanation. The temptation to interpret concepts as literal likenesses is ever present. By the time of Descartes, a variety of efforts to analyze and explicate the nature of the relation between concepts and material things had been found wanting. In Descartes the implications of the mind/body dualism implicit in scholastic philosophy are taken seriously." (p. 44) For another account of intentional logic, the reader might consult the Material Logic of John of St. Thomas (Chicago, 1955). John of St. Thomas was a contemporary of Descartes.

11. Pr, Works, Vol. 2, p. 40. (Introd.,24).

12. loc. cit. (Introd.,25)

13. What follows will repeat the review we gave of this theory in Chapter 3, Sec. VI.

14. Pr, Works, Vol. 2, pp. 69-70. (I,66)

15. I cannot resist noting, however, that mine adds gratuitously a philosophical essay in the Cartesian spirit, congratulating our age for its enlightenment -- that is, for its hygienic plumbing systems. Well, who could be against indoor plumbing! Moreover, no right thinking person, even apart from the convenience of the indoor toilet, could wish a return to the plagues and epidemics that inevitably distress people who lack good plumbing systems. Nonetheless, here is one more voice added to the Cartesian chorus, as though heaven could be reached by a tower of modern plumbing fixtures. Berkeley would probably lament that the essay, instead of praising God whose language disclosed how to build the systems, places the plumber on a pedestal, as though he were the creator of the nature that made the systems possible.

16. TV, Works, Vol. 1, p. 231. (147)

17. TVV, Works, Vol. 1, p. 263. (36)

Chapter Seven - The Kantian Turn

1. Descartes, Meditation VI, op. cit., pp. 136 and 137.

2. Alasdair MacIntyre, After Virtue, p. 11.

3. loc. cit.

4. ibid., pp. 12ff.

5. For another, non-modern, interpretation of Berkeley, see the appendix.

6. Both Edward Pols, in The Recognition of Reason, and Francis Parker, in The Story of Western Philosophy, do more than justice to modern subjectivism. Mortimer Adler, in Ten Philosophical Mistakes (New York, 1985) is, by contrast, more outspoken in criticism of modern philosophy.

7. HP, Works, Vol. 2, p. 233.

8. TVV, Works, Vol. 1, p. 266. (43)

9. After Virtue, pp. 104-5.

10. ibid., p. 107.

11. ibid., pp. 107-8.

12. Richard Rorty, Philosophy and the Mirror of Nature. (Princeton, 1979).

13. My paraphrase of the second sentence of Turbayne's "Introduction," The Myth of Metaphor (New Haven, 1962), p. 3.

14. ibid., p. 5.

15. ibid., p. 203.

16. Turbayne presents thorough detail and justification of this, ibid., pp. 159-171.

17. ibid., p. 207.

18. ibid., pp. 213-7.

19. DM, Works, vol. 4, p. 31. (3)

20. HP, Works, Vol. 2, pp. 249-250.

21. Turbayne, op. cit., p. 119.

22. ibid., p. 213.

23. ibid., p. 3.

24. See William A. Wallace, "The Intelligibility of Nature," op. cit., pp. 44-54, for a classical realistic account of modeling.

25. Turbayne, op. cit., p. 213.

26. DM, Works, Vol. 4, pp. 51-2. (71-2)

27. T. E. Jessop, "Berkeley as Religious Apologist," New Studies in Berkeley's Philosophy, edited by Warren C. Steinkraus (New York, 1966), p. 98.

28. Warnock, Berkeley (London, 1953), p. 12.

29. ibid., pp. 58-9.

30. ibid., p. 59.

31. ibid., pp. 59-60.

32. ibid., p. 245.

33. ibid., pp. 245-6.

34. ibid., pp. 229-30.

35. E. g., I. C. Tipton, Berkeley (London, 1974), p. 260.

Chapter Eight - Completing Berkeley's Project

1. A. A. Luce, "Berkeley and the Living Thing," Hermathena 123 (1977), pp. 19-25.

2. See Edward Pols, The Recognition of Reason, for what is perhaps the most telling recent statement and defense of reason's powers.

3. A. A. Luce, op. cit., p. 23.

4. A. A. Luce, "Sensible Ideas and Sensations," Hermathena 105 (1967), p. 79.

5. ibid., p. 80.

6. loc. cit.

7. The Philosophical Commentaries are notes preparatory to the writing of Berkeley's Essay Towards a New Theory of Vision and The Principles of Human Knowledge.

8. Works, Vol. 1, p. 5.

9. Luce, The Dialectic of Immaterialism (London, 1963), p. 132.

10. loc. cit.

11. The reader is referred once more to the works cited in note 5 of Chapter 5. To that list add Aristotle's Categories, and Richard J. Connell's Matter & Becoming (Chicago, 1966), pp. 16-36.

12. Berkeley perhaps would be pleased to find in Luce such a staunch defender of immaterialism. However, it is striking that Luce nowhere goes on to show how Berkeley's project succeeded, i.e., to show that Berkeley has provided a metaphysical foundation for the classical moral theory of virtue. Could that be because Luce sees that the immaterialism provides no such basis? At any rate Luce seems to have no interest in presenting and/or defending Berkeley's moral philosophy.

13. Richard J. Connell, Matter and Becoming, p. 29. The quotation from Hume is from A Treatise of Human Nature (Oxford, 1888), p. 222.

14. Turbayne, op. cit., p. 94. The first sentence of this quotation should read, "Since before Aristotle,..." Aristotle no more invented the substance-accident distinction than he invented "matter," or invented logic. What he did, in the former case as in the latter two, was to philosophically refine knowledge that all of us have.

15. See Henry B. Veatch, Intentional Logic, Chapter Five, for the definitive account of the proposition so understood, as against the modern scientific philosopher's meaning of "proposition."

16. See Note 8, Chapter 5.

17. Descartes was sixteen when he rejected classical learning in favor of developing his own brand new system. Berkeley was in his teens when his ultimate solution to the problem of

materialism occurred to him; and in his twenties when he published the metaphysical and epistemological books on which his fame rests. I believe the moral of this is that philosophical precociousness ought to be discouraged. Sit on it a while, maybe for years, should be the advice; think it through.

18. For a thorough explication of the notion of natural value in Aristotle's thought, see Kenneth L. Schmitz, "Natural Value," The Review of Metaphysics, Vol. XXXVIII, No. 1 (1984), pp. 3-15.

19. Alc, Works, Vol. 3, p. 329. (VII,31)

20. For a recent thoughtful harmonizing of the traditional morality of virtue with the Judeo-Christian religious tradition, see Gilbert C. Meilaender, The Theory and Practice of Virtue.

21. Recently I read a review, by Chilton Williamson, Jr., in National Review, Vol. XXXVII, No. 1 (Jan. 11, 1985), p. 58, of a book by Richard E. Morgan, Disabling America: The "Rights Industry" in Our Time. After reviewing Morgan's account of how the enterprise of creating new rights has adversely affected religion and education, Williamson concludes: "...Morgan invites us to ask of the rights-industry personnel: 'Who are these people?' Well, institutionally they are the ACLU, NAACP, National Council of Churches, American Jewish Congress; they are activist lawyers and committed academics -- members of what Morgan calls 'the talking class.' Personally, they are individuals with an ideal hitched to a grudge, who don't like the United States very much, and aren't concerned in the slightest by the degree to which the imposition of their whims disables American society and the American polity. The best way to fight them, Morgan believes, is to rip off their collective mask of 'compassion,' thus revealing them for the self-interested gentry they really are."

It probably is true that ACLUers and the like have replaced a morality of virtue with a morality of rights and liberty. However, it is a mistake to accuse them of being self-interested. They write and behave as they do, sincerely and disinterestedly, because their metaphysics rules out the supernatural, and hence the religious. The way to fight them is to convince them that their metaphysics is mistaken. That fight seems endless. For now, minute philosophy has the upper hand. How long it will remain so depends on the strength of the current revival of classical philosophy.

197

22. Ardley, *Berkeley's Renovation of Philosophy*, (The Hague, 1968), p. 176. See also the recent book by Edward Pols, *Meditation on a Prisoner*. Pols' aim is to properly place modern scientific knowledge in a realistically refined defense of common sense. He improves on Ardley's locution by suggesting that scientific knowledge is not so much "the infra-structure of our knowledge of Nature" as it is knowledge of the infra-structure of nature.

23. Alc, *Works*, Vol. 3, p. 329. (VII,31)

Appendix

1. Gavin Ardley, *Berkeley's Renovation of Philosophy* (The Hague, 1968).

2. ibid., p. 70.

3. ibid., p. 72.

4. ibid., p. 6.

5. ibid., p. 7.

6. ibid., p. 113.

7. ibid., p. 62.

8. ibid., p. 63.

9. loc. cit.

10. ibid., p. 135.

11. loc. cit., but at the bottom of the page.

12. ibid., p. 73.

13. Paul J. Olscamp, in his *The Moral Philosophy of George Berkeley* (The Hague, 1970), reading Berkeley through modern glasses, and missing his classical predilections, so interprets him; as does also J.O. Urmson, *Berkeley* (Oxford, 1982), pp. 72-6.

Selected Bibliography

The most complete bibliographies of Berkeley available are T. E. Jessop's A Bibliography of George Berkeley (The Hague: Nijhoff, 1973), and Colin M. Turbayne, A Bibliography of George Berkeley, in Colin Turbayne (ed.), Berkeley: Critical and Interpretive Essays. Minneapolis: University of Minnesota Press, 1982, pp. 313-29.

Primary Sources

The collected works of Berkeley appear in the definitive edition of A. A. Luce and T. E. Jessop, The Works of George Berkeley, nine volumes (London: Thomas Nelson & Sons Ltd. 1948-1957).

The following list gives selected contents, volume by volume.

Volume   I -   Philosophical Commentaries
               An Essay Towards a New Theory of Vision
               The Theory of Vision ... Vindicated and Explained

Volume II -   A Treatise Concerning the Principles of Human Knowledge
               First Draft of the Introduction to the Principles
               Three Dialogues Between Hylas and Philonous
               Philosophical Correspondence Between Berkeley and Samuel Johnson

Volume III -   Alciphron, or the Minute Philosopher

Volume IV -   De Motu
               The Analyst
               A Defense of Free-thinking in Mathematics

Volume   V -   Siris: A Chain of Philosophical Reflexions and Inquiries

Volume VI -   Passive Obedience
               Advice to the Tories Who Have Taken the Oaths
               An Essay Towards Preventing the Ruin of Great Britain
               The Querist and other Writings on Economics
               A Discourse Addressed to Magistrates and Men in Authority

Volume VII -   Sermons
               Berkeley's Essays in the "Guardian"

> Berkeley's Journals of Travels in Italy
> A Proposal for the Better Supplying of Churches in
> our Foreign Plantations

Volume VIII - Berkeley's Letters

Volume IX - Notes to Berkeley's Letters
Addenda

These volumes are now out of print, but the same works are available in three volumes from Kraus Reprint Co., Millwood, New York.

There are numerous editions, including many paperback, of Berkeley's A Treatise Concerning the Principles of Human Knowledge, and Three Dialogues Between Hylas and Philonous. The only other complete works in print now, apart from the collected works, are Essay Toward a New Theory of Vision, and The Theory of Vision, or Visual Language ... Vindicated and Explained; both included in Works on Vision, edited by Colin M. Turbayne, (Indianapolis: The Bobbs-Merrill Co., Inc., 1963).

Secondary Sources

Books

ADLER, MORTIMER, Ten Philosophical Mistakes. New York: Macmillan, 1985. From the standpoint of classical realism, a correcting of mistakes made by (mostly modern) philosophers in metaphysics, epistemology, human nature, morals, and politics.

ARDLEY, GAVIN, Berkeley's Renovation of Philosophy. The Hague: Martinus Nijhoff, 1968. Berkeley interpreted as a modern Plato. Contains insightful material on the relation of philosophy to science. See Appendix.

BRACKEN, HARRY M., Berkeley. New York: St. Martin's Press, 1974. Berkeley interpreted as a Cartesian, rather than as a Lockean. Bracken considers and rejects intentionality, in my judgment because he fails to appreciate the point of classical hylomorphism, and takes matter to be a substantial kind.

_____, The Early Reception of Berkeley's Immaterialism. Revised Edition. The Hague: Martinus Nijhoff, 1965. A careful review of how and why Berkeley's immaterialism was interpreted by his contemporaries.

BROWNE, J. W., _Berkeley's Intellectualism_. Jamaica, N.Y.: St. John's University Press, 1975. Makes a case that Berkeley moved in the direction of classical (Platonic) epistemology, without foreswearing his immaterialism.

BUCHDAHL, GERD, _Metaphysics and the Philosophy of Science_. Oxford: Blackwell, 1969. Chapter 5 shows Berkeley's contributions to philosophy of science. Berkeley's motivation - to provide the ultimate solution to the problem of materialism - does not figure into Buchdahl's analysis.

CONNELL, RICHARD J., _Matter and Becoming_. Chicago: The Priory Press, 1966. Resolution of the problem of matter and change, given the insights of classical realism.

GAUSTAD, EDWIN S., _George Berkeley in America_. New Haven and London: Yale University Press, 1979. A scholarly and readable account, by an historian, of Berkeley's years in America.

GILSON, ETIENNE, _The Unity of Philosophical Experience_. New York: Charles Scribner's Sons, 1937. Shows how similar philosophical errors have led to the breakdowns of medieval, Cartesian, and modern philosophy.

HICKS, GEORGE DAWES, _Berkeley_. New York: Russell and Russell, 1968. Reprint of 1932 edition. Hicks notes, without recognizing it, the classical caste of Berkeley's writings on ethics. Also catches Berkeley's misconstrual of Mandeville and Shaftesbury.

LUCE, A. A., _The Dialectic of Immaterialism_. London: Hodder and Stoughton Ltd., 1963. As the subtitle reads, "An account of the making of Berkeley's _Principles_." Aims to show the internal consistency, the intelligibility, and the plausibility of Berkeley's immaterialism.

_____, _The Life of George Berkeley_. London: Thomas Nelson and Sons Ltd., 1949. A definitive and sympathetic biography.

MACINTYRE, ALASDAIR, _After Virtue_. Notre Dame: University of Notre Dame Press, 1981. In considerable detail traces the failure of modern moral philosophies; and hopes for a return to a philosophy of virtue, but without the underpinning of classical realistic metaphysics or the support of religion.

MEILAENDER GILBERT C., _The Theory and Practice of Virtue_. Notre Dame: University of Notre Dame Press, 1984. Harmonizes Judeo-Christian teaching with the classical moral philosophy of virtue.

OLSCAMP, PAUL J., The Moral Philosophy of George Berkeley. The Hague: Martinus Nijhoff, 1970. Berkeley did not write a book on moral philosophy. This book attempts to construct Berkeley's moral philosophy from his principles, and from suggestions about morality in his writings. It is written from the perspective of modern, rather than classical, philosophy.

PARKER, FRANCIS, The Story of Western Philosophy. Bloomington: Indiana University Press, 1967. Reads the history of Western philosophy in terms of objectivism vs. subjectivism.

PARKER, FRANCIS, and VEATCH, HENRY, Logic as a Human Instrument. New York: Harper & Row, 1959. The best textbook of intentional logic, the logic appropriate to classical realism.

PITCHER, GEORGE, Berkeley. London: Routledge and Kegan Paul, 1977. In his effort to read Berkeley sympathetically, Pitcher approaches Turbayne's interpretation. (See Chapter 7, Section VI). Pitcher's devastating critique of Berkeley's Passive Obedience misses, I believe, the spirit of the moral philosophy of virtue.

POLS, EDWARD, The Recognition of Reason. Carbondale: Southern Illinois University Press, 1963. A response to the challenge of skepticism, by invoking and evoking reason's powers.

_____, Meditation on a Prisoner. Carbondale & Edwardsville: Southern Illinois University Press, 1975. A response to the challenge of materialism, wherein scientific accounts of man find their proper place within a classical philosophical realism.

_____, The Acts of Our Being. Amherst: University of Massachusetts Press, 1982. A prolonged reflexive defense of man as a rational agent and primary being.

RAND, BENJAMIN, Berkeley's American Sojourn. Cambridge: Harvard University Press, 1932. A brief and informative account of the why and wherefore of Berkeley's visit to new England.

SHAFTESBURY, Characteristics (Stanley Grean, ed.). Indianapolis: Bobbs-Merrill, 1964. A reading of Shaftesbury reveals how Berkeley could have enlisted his aid in fighting minute philosophy.

TIPTON, I. C., Berkeley. London: Methuen and Co. Ltd., 1974. The book attempts to understand Berkeley's metaphysics in his own terms, rather than those of contemporary thinkers; and concludes that Berkeley's reconciliation of idealism and common sense is at least questionable.

TURBAYNE, COLIN M., The Myth of Metaphor. New Haven: Yale University Press, 1962. Following his conviction that men cannot know what reality is, but nonetheless can fruitfully speculate about it, Turbayne urges the carefully guarded use of philosophical metaphors; and transforms Berkeley's metaphysics into metaphorics. See Chapter 7 of the text.

VEATCH, HENRY B., Intentional Logic. New Haven: Yale University Press, 1951. A detailed and thorough examination of the logic employed by all of us as knowers, as over against the limited modern mathematical logic.

_____, Aristotle: A Contemporary Appreciation. Bloomington: Indiana University Press, 1974. A brief but very readable and helpful introduction to classical realism, a la Aristotle.

WALLACE, WILLIAM A., Causality and Scientific Explanation, 2 vols. Ann Arbor: University of Michigan Press, 1972 and 1974. This great historian and philosopher of science shows how the categories of refined common sense, first worked through by Aristotle, have continued to permeate modern scientific investigations right up to the present day.

WARNOCK, G. J., Berkeley. London: Penguin Books Ltd., 1953. U.S. edition by the University of Notre Dame Press, 1983. An interpretation of Berkeley's metaphysics and epistemology from the perspective of contemporary linguistic analysis. See Chapter 7 of the text.

WILD, JOHN, Introduction to Realistic Philosophy. New York: Harper & Brothers, 1948. Remains a classic exposition in our time of classical realism.

Articles

ALLTSON, HENRY E., "Bishop Berkeley's Petitio," Personalist 54 (1973): 232-45. A reflective argument, showing that Berkeley's epistemological troubles are rooted in his acceptance of the Cartesian theory of ideas.

ARMSTRONG, ROBERT L., "Berkeley's Theory of Signification," Journal of the History of Philosophy 7 (1969): 163-76. Interesting evaluation of the bankruptcy of modern empiricism (through Berkeley and Hume); hints that pragmatism is the best alternative to it.

AYERS, MICHAEL R., "Substance, Reality, and the Great Dead Philosophers," American Philosophical Quarterly 7 (1970): 38-49. Argues for taking philosophers in context. Berkeley should be read as a serious metaphysician, wrestling with "substance." Berkeley's non-metaphysical interpreters rake in his ashes for phenomenalist ore. See below, Day's article.

BRACKEN, HARRY M., "Berkeley on the Immortality of the Soul," Modern Schoolman, 37 (1959-60): 77-79, 197-212. Argues that Berkeley's immaterialism was motivated by a sincere desire to preserve immortality of the soul. Also wrestles with the problem of archetypes.

_____, "Berkeley's Realism," The Philosophical Quarterly, 8 (1958): 41-53. Distinguishes between common sense Berkeley and rigorous Berkeley. Shows how, despite his good intentions to avoid skepticism, Berkeley got himself into impossible difficulty with the spirit-idea dichotomy.

BUSH, ERIC, "Berkeley, Truth, and the World," Inquiry 20 (1977): 205-25. An argument for Berkeley's epistemology and against phenomenalism, by appeal to biological and behavioral science.

CUMMINS, PHILIP D., "Perceptual Relativity and Ideas in the Mind," Philosophy and Phenomenological Research 24 (1963): 202-14. Careful analysis of Berkeley's (and other's) attacks on distinction between primary and secondary qualities. Concludes that Berkeley's argument is valid.

_____, "Berkeley's Likeness Principle," Journal of the History of Philosophy 4 (1966): 63-69. Shows that Berkeley's arguments against representationalism and matter do not require Berkeley's "ideas." Concludes the truth of Berkeley's claim that the issue between him and the materialists is not a verbal one.

_____, "Berkeley's Ideas of Sense," Nous 9 (1975): 55-72. Shows how Berkeley's immaterialism follows from subjectivism.

DAVIS, JOHN W., "Berkeley and Phenomenalism," Dialogue 1 (June, 1962): 67-80. Argues against the phenomenalist interpretation of Berkeley (see the annotation of the article by Day, J. P. de C.), on the grounds that Berkeley meant what he said.

DAY, J. P. DE C., "George Berkeley, 1685-1753," The Review of Metaphysics, 6 (1953): 83-113, 265-86, 447-69, 583-96. Interpretation of Berkeley as phenomenalist. Phenomenenalism is a variation of subjectivist philosophy. It is the contention that all our paradoxical talk in an object language about a material world can be resolved in talk about sensations, in a meta-language. The article typifies a tendency among some contemporaries to be condescending to past greats. In this instance, strip Berkeley's thought of its sentimentality (notions of God and immortal soul), equip it with the latest (so-called) logical techniques, and lo and behold we have an up to date philosophy worthy of some serious consideration by us twentieth century super-sophisticates. (Incidentally, the reader of this study will find an antidote to the language-meta-language poison in an article in the very same issue of The Review of Metaphysics, entitled "Metaphysics and the Paradoxes," pp. 199-218 by Henry Veatch and Theodore Young.)

GELBER, SIDNEY, "Universal Language and the Sciences of Man in Berkeley's Philosophy," The Journal of the History of Ideas 13 (1952): 482-513. An excellent and sympathetic treatment of Berkeley. Gelber argues that Berkeley's contention was that although in natural philosophy we cannot know the nature of things, still in first philosophy the intellect can, slowly and with difficulty, achieve genuine knowledge of ultimate reality.

GRAVE, S. A., "The Mind and Its Ideas: Some Problems in the Interpretation of Berkeley," Australasian Journal of Philosophy 42 (1964): 199-210. Gets to the heart of Berkeley's difficulties by reviewing the incompatibility between Berkeley's idealism and his defense of common sense.

GREY, DENIS, "The Solipsism of Bishop Berkeley," The Philosophical Quarterly, 2 (1952): 338-349. Acute argumentation showing that once Berkeley begins to philosophize in the mind, he cannot consistently work his way out. Can be taken as a criticism of all subjectivist philosophy.

GUZZO, AUGUSTO, "Berkeley and 'Things'," New Studies in Berkeley's Philosophy, edited by Warren E. Steinkraus (New York: Holt, Rinehart and Winston, Inc., 1966), pp. 72-84. Interesting comments on two of Berkeley's most stubborn difficulties: mind's activity in sense perception; and the causal relations among "things" of common sense.

JESSOP, T. E., "Berkeley as Religious Apologist," New Studies in Berkeley's Philosophy, pp. 98-109. Jessop sees the whole Berkeley, but sees him through the lenses of modern philosophy; and hence altogether misses his classical predilections.

KANTONEN, T. A., "Influence of Descartes on Berkeley," The Philosophical Review, 43 (1934): 483-500. A scholarly and insightful evaluation of the tremendous impact of Descartes' thought upon Berkeley's.

LASCOLA, R. A., "Ideas and Archetypes: Appearance and Reality in Berkeley's Philosophy," Personalist 54 (1973): 42-59. Argues for the archetypes as God's understanding of the world, and is willing to give up Berkeley's realism and defense of common sense.

LEWIS, DOUGLAS, "Some Problems of Perceptions," Philosophy of Science 37 (1970): 100-13. Defends Berkeley's realism and defense of common sense by arguing that secondary qualities are not private perceptions. Relevant to the "same" problem; see Chapter 5, Section VII of the text.

LUCE, A. A., "Berkeley and the Living Thing," Hermathena 123 (1977): 19-25. Shows a touching sensitivity to Berkeley's failure to do justice to living things, indicating that in his later works Berkeley too was sensitive to the failure.

MABBOTT, J. D., "The Place of God in Berkeley's Philosophy," The Journal of Philosophy (now Philosophy), VI (January, 1931), 18-29. Reprinted in A Treatise Concerning the Principles of Human Knowledge, with Critical Essays, edited by Colin M. Turbayne (Indianapolis: The Bobbs-Merrill Co., Inc., 1970), pp. 201-219. A successful effort to read Berkeley in his own terms, to discover what he really believed about God, finite minds, and ideas. Points to difficulties in the system, but does not exploit them.

MARC-WOGAU, KONRAD, "Berkeley's Sensationalism and the Esse Est Percipi Principle," Theoria, 23 (1957): 12-36. Brilliant analysis and criticism of Berkeley's argument to God to escape solipsism. Undermines this subjectivist argument for the existence of God.

OLSCAMP, PAUL J., "Does Berkeley Have an Ethical Theory?," A Treatise Concerning the Principles of Human Knowledge, with Critical Essays, pp. 182-200. The essay forces Berkeley's thoughts about morals on to the procrustean bed of contemporary theorizing in ethics, which theorizing eschews the classical insights of such as Plato and Aristotle.

PETRELLA, FRANK, "George Berkeley's Theory of Economic Policy and Classical Economic Liberalism," Southern Economic Journal 32 (1966): 275-84. Argues that Berkeley, like his fellow Britishers Adam Smith and Edmund Burke, presupposed that a good economy rests on strong moral standards, and those in turn on strong religion.

POPKIN, RICHARD H., "Berkeley and Pyrrhonism," The Review of Metaphysics, 5 (1951-2): 223-246. Shows how Berkeley's theory of reality was thought out as an answer to the prominent skepticism in the philosophy of Berkeley's time.

ROME, S. C., "Berkeley's Conceptualism," The Philosophical Review, 55 (1946): 680-686. Argues that Berkeley's account of notions vs. ideas contains the germ of a realistic (intentional) theory of knowledge.

SCHMITZ, KENNETH L., "Natural Value," The Review of Metaphysics 38 (1984), 3-15. A thorough explication of the notion of natural value in Aristotle's thought.

SMITH, JANET, "Can Virtue be in the Service of Bad Acts?," The New Scholasticism 58 (1984): 357-373. Relevant to Berkeley in that it shows the difficulties a typical twentieth century modern philosopher gets into in trying to make sense of virtue without the classical conceptual baggage.

TIPTON, I. C., "Berkeley's View of Spirit," New Studies in Berkeley's Philosophy, pp. 59-71. Are mental beings substances, following Locke? Or does Berkeley mean to say that they are persons? Is the mind altogether passive in sense perception? Or is there some activity, some agency, present? The essay helpfully explores these crucial questions.

TURBAYNE, COLIN M., "Berkeley and Russell on Space," Dialectica, 8 (1954): 210-227. Very important article for the understanding of Berkeley, for the student who wonders whether the intellect is really passive in sensory cognition. This article shows how Berkeley, supposing that it is, was led to his theory of vision and theory of reality.

_____, "Berkeley's Metaphysical Grammar," A Treatise Concerning the Principles of Human Knowledge, with Critical Essays, pp. 3-36. Tests and appraises the hypothesis that Berkeley uses the same language model in the Principles that he does in the Essay Towards a New Theory of Vision. The article's claims are partially vitiated by the fact that the meanings given by Aristotle (the antagonist) and Berkeley to the crucial terms are too different to warrant the comparisons Turbayne makes.

TUSSMAN, JOSEPH, "Berkeley as Political Philosopher," in Adams, George P. (ed.), George Berkeley. Berkeley and Los Angeles: University of California Press, 1957, pp. 122-140. Catches Berkeley's intention to be a moral and political philosopher; but misses the classical orientation. Likens Berkeley to

Rousseau and Dostoevski - country boys, who upon becoming acquainted with corruption in the city, prophecy.

WALLACE, WILLIAM A., "The Intelligibility of Nature: a neo-Aristotelian View," The Review of Metaphysics 38 (1984), 33-56. An outline, by way of ten theses, of a classical realistic program, including moral philosophy and natural theology as well as philosophy of nature and epistemology.

WEBER A. O., "Berkeley's Conception of Objectivity in the Physical World," The Philosophical Review 50 (September, 1941): 461-470. Read this in connection with Gelber's article. Where Gelber distinguishes "acquaintanceship" and "knowledge," Weber distinguishes empiricism and metaphysics, and finds that they are incompatible.

WILD, JOHN, "Berkeley's Theories of Perception: a Phenomenological Critique," Revue Internationale de Philosophie, 7 (1953): 134-151. The essay shows that although the principle of intentionality is altogether missing from Berkeley's early work, in Siris there are indications that he was aware of it.

_____, "The Concept of 'the Given' in Contemporary Philosophy: Its Origins and Limitations," Philosophy and Phenomenological Research 1 (1940-41): 70-82. Polemic against contemporary empiricists. Berkeley is one of the sources of all the confusion between that which is given in experience, and that by which it is given. Very important article for one wanting to understand the realist (intentional) theory of knowledge.

WILSON, CLYDE, "Calhoun & Community," Chronicles of Culture (Vol. 9, No. 7, July 1985: 17-20). An introduction to the political thought of John C. Calhoun, containing profound insights on the relation of community to government, specifically in U.S.A.

WILSON, FRED, "Acquaintance, Ontology, & Knowledge," New Scholasticism 44 (1970): 1-48. Apparently seeing no difference between classical and modern philosophy, a super-sophisticated effort to avoid skepticism, with Berkeley represented as a first user of Wilson's Principle of Acquaintance.

Index

logic (continued),
  as instrument of knowing,
    125-8, 168-9
logical empiricism, 150-1
loyalty, 19, 27
Luce, A.A., 5, 37, 162-5, 183,
  190, 201, 206

Mabbott, J.D., 206
MacIntyre, Alasdair, 2, 142,
  148, 201
Madison, James, 17
Magdalen College, 64
Malebranche, Nicolas, 111-2
Mandeville, Bernard, 43, 44,
  185
Marc-Wogau, Konrad, 206
Marx, Karl, 150
materialism,
  meaning of, 02
  Berkeley's attack on, 105ff
matter,
  Aristotle's meaning of,
    99-103
  Descartes' meaning of, 98-9
McArthur, Ronald, 64-5, 69
Meilaender, Gilbert C., 2,
  197,201
metaphor, 152-6
metaphysics,
  meaning of, 79
  Berkeley's, 95-122, 132-3
  Descartes', 82-5
  in classical realism, 99-
    103, 161-8
Mill, John Stuart, 147-8
minute philosophy, see free-
  thinking
Monroe, James, 17
Morgan, Richard E., 197

Newton, Isaac, 1, 6, 80, 178
Nietzsche, Friedrich W., 148-9,
  175

Olscamp, Paul J., 198, 202, 206

Parker, Francis, 190, 192,
  194, 202
Percival, Lord, 8
Petrella, Frank, 206
phenomenology, 151
Pitcher, George, 202
Plato, 2, 20, 22, 26, 38,
  41, 48, 52, 55, 63, 64,
  71-2, 74, 79, 103, 104,
  171, 172, 177, 178, 179,
  183, 184, 185
  his political theory, 26
  his psychology, 171
  on rewards and punish-
    ments, 48-9
polis (polity, body
  politic)
  origin and nature of,
    25-8
Pols, Edward, 92, 182, 189,
  194, 195, 198, 202
Pope, Alexander, 7
Popkin, Richard H., 207

Rand, Benjamin, 202
Reformation, 5, 13
religion,
  as source and support of
    politcal stability, 1-
    75 passim
  opposed by free-
    thinking, 13-15
  vs. science, 19
Renaissance, 5
representative perception,
  theory of, 89-93
  Descartes' version of,
    87-92
  Lockes' version of,
    92-3
Robertson, J.M., 52, 182
Rome, S.C., 207
Rorty, Richard, 151-2

Sartre, Jean-Paul, 148
Schmitz, Kenneth L., 197,
  207

About the Author

Theodore A. Young is a graduate of North Denver High School (1944), the University of Denver (B.A., 1949), and Indiana University (Ph.D., 1964). He has taught philosophy at the University of Connecticut, Indiana University Fort Wayne Campus, and since 1964, Grand Valley State College, Allendale, Michigan. He wishes to express his gratitude to his teachers, especially the late Tunis Prins, the late Newton P. Stallknecht, the late W. Harry Jellema, and most especially Henry B. Veatch, Professor Emeritus, Georgetown University.